BONFIRE OF HISTORY

ALSO BY CHRISTOPHER JOLL

Uniquely British: A Year in the Life of the Household Cavalry

The Speedicut Papers, vols 1–9

The Speedicut Memoirs, vols 1–6

WITH ANTHONY WELDON
The Drum Horse in the Fountain

WITH CORIE MAPP
Black Ice: The Memoir of Corie Mapp

WITH PENNY COBHAM
The Imperial Impresario

BONFIRE
of
HISTORY

*The lost treasures, trophies and trivia of
Madame Tussaud & Sons' Exhibition*

CHRISTOPHER JOLL
& PENNY COBHAM

NINE ELMS BOOKS

First published in 2023
by Nine Elms Publishing,
Unit 1G, Clapham North Arts Centre,
26–32 Voltaire Road, London SW4 6DH
www.nineelmsbooks.co.uk

Text © Christopher Joll 2023

ISBN 978-1-910533-69-7 HB

All rights reserved. This book must not
be circulated in any form of binding or cover
other than that in which it is published and without
similar condition of this being imposed on the
subsequent purchaser. No part of this publication
may be reproduced, stored on a retrieval system
or transmitted in any form, or by any means,
electronic, mechanical, photocopying, recording
or otherwise, without either prior permission in
writing from the publisher or a licence permitting
restricted copying. In the United Kingdom such
licences are issued by the Copyright Licensing Agency,
90 Tottenham Court Road, London, W1P 9HE.
The rights of Christopher Joll and Penny Cobham
to be identified as the authors of this work
have been asserted in accordance
with Copyright, Designs and
Patents Acts 1988.

The images, unless indicated otherwise
in the captions, are in the public domain. In all other
cases, every effort has been made to trace copyright
holders, but if any have been inadvertently overlooked,
the author will be pleased to make the
necessary arrangements at the
first opportunity.

Cover and text design, typesetting and layout
by Lyn Davies *www.lyndaviesdesign.com*
Text set in Rory Snow's *Barbou*
Printed and bound in India
by Imprint Press.

*This book
is dedicated to the memory of*
MADAME MARIE TUSSAUD
*and her lineal descendants who
carried on her business*

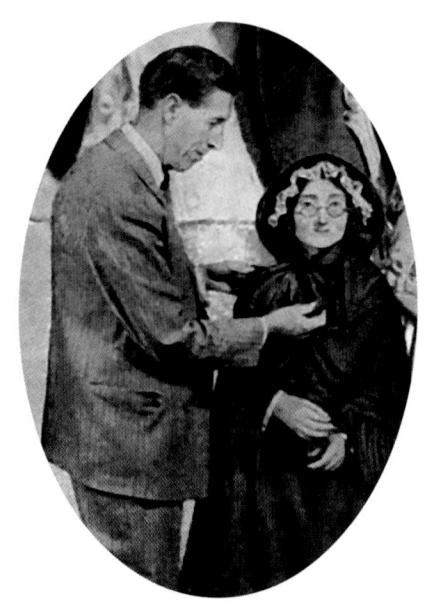

Bernard Tussaud (1896–1967)
tidies the figure of his great-great grandmother,
Madame Marie Tussaud (1761–1850) in 1952

CONTENTS

Foreword by Nick Varney — 9

Preface by James Tussaud — 11

Acknowledgements — 13

Authors' Note — 14

Introduction — 19

Prologue — 23

1. The Great Illusionist — 31
2. From Pharaohs to the Renaissance — 45
3. Stuart Sovereigns and French Fakes — 57
4. King George I to the French Consulate — 75
5. Napoléon and the Imperial Family — 95
6. Napoléonica — 115
7. The Paintings by Jacques-Louis David — 131
8. Elba, Waterloo and Wellington — 145
9. St Helena — 167

10.	The Bourbon Restoration & the Second French Empire	179
11.	King George IV to Queen Victoria	195
12.	A Cabinet of Curiosities	217

Epilogue 225

Index 227

About the Authors 239

FOREWORD

by Nick Varney
Founder & former CEO of Merlin Entertainments Ltd

TODAY MADAME TUSSAUD'S IS one of the most successful and well-known brands in the location-based entertainment industry with 23 attractions spanning four continents. At the time of writing over 9 million visitors every year experience the uncanny and thrilling sensation of coming face-to-face with celebrity and fame. But in many ways this is something of a miracle – for Madame Tussaud's is a great British survival story. The lady herself was caught up in the French Revolution, threatened with the guillotine, shipwrecked just outside Liverpool en route to Ireland in 1822 and mixed up in the Bristol riots of 1831. More recently, the building in the Marylebone Road was bombed in the Blitz during the Second World War. However, our most devastating set back was suffered on the night of 18th March 1925 when Madame Tussaud & Sons' Exhibition was destroyed by fire.

On that dreadful night not only did we lose original waxworks dating back to the eighteenth century, but we also lost a priceless collection of art, artefacts, relics and historical mementoes that had been acquired over the previous 150 years. In fact, prior to the fire, Madame Tussaud's was as much a museum of historical curiosities as a collection of waxworks.

The story of Madame Tussaud's has been told many times already and, doubtless, will be again, but in all previous accounts the 1925 fire has been treated just as one incident in our long history. When Penny Cobham and Christopher Joll asked me for permission to access our archives, so that they could write a book about the lost collection, I immediately agreed as I knew that it would fill a yawning void.

In the pages that follow, using our archives and historical research, Penny and Christopher have brought our lost collection back to life. In so doing, they have also filled in much of the missing historical background relating to the collection and have uncovered some uncomfortable truths about the authenticity of some of the items that were on display.

This is neither a surprise nor a matter of regret, for Madame Tussaud herself

FOREWORD

was both the original female entrepreneur and a highly skilled illusionist. The fact that our founder, and later generations of her family, innocently or deliberately used what we now know to be fakes, alongside genuine items, to illustrate the stories told in the exhibition is not unique to Madame Tussaud's. The only regret that we do have is that such an important collection of genuine historical artefacts – particularly the irreplaceable and fully-authenticated Napoléonica in our collection – was lost in the flames.

NICK VARNEY

PREFACE

by James Tussaud

WHEN, IN 1802, MY FOUR-TIMES great-grandmother, Marie Tussaud, left Paris for London, she took with her a 'Grand Cabinet of Curiosities'; this was a collection that she had assiduously built and safe-guarded for over two decades. Leaving not only the horrors of the French Revolution behind, but also her home and family, she set off for a new life in Britain with little money, her collection, skill and determination. By the time of Marie's death in 1850, Madame Tussaud & Sons' Exhibition had, against considerable odds, long-since become a household name and a London landmark.

Although my ancestor was a single-minded and often ruthless businesswoman, she would undoubtedly have been surprised to know that, in the first quarter of the twenty-first century, the business was still flourishing and expanding, currently with twenty-three sites around the globe. For Madame Tussaud's today still embodies Marie's entrepreneurial vision, embellished and built upon by successive generations of original and bold thinkers, formerly within our family and latterly by many others to whom she would owe a huge debt of gratitude.

But while Marie would undoubtedly be in huge admiration of today's business, she would no doubt also have been greatly saddened by the subject of this book: the fire of 1925, which saw the destruction of many of the treasured and priceless artifacts she had collected and transported to and around Britain in her lifetime, and those collected after her death in 1850. As is often the case, history played an ironic hand in that these treasures survived shipwrecks, highwaymen and the riots in Bristol, only to perish on a quiet night in central London. Nevertheless, Marie Tussaud's vision would, not for the only time, be reborn.

Although most people assume that Madame Tussaud's has always been a waxworks, Marie never intended that her eponymous exhibition should be solely a display of the good, the great and the notorious, modelled in wax. In fact, her vision was for a visitor attraction that illustrated history in three dimensions. This involved creating not just life-like and life-size models of famous historical and contemporary characters, but dressing them in authentic costumes, and

≈ PREFACE ≈

supporting the displays in which they featured with art and artefacts that had belonged to the people portrayed or were contemporary with them. For that reason, the exhibition included objects as diverse as the blood-stained shirt of the assassinated King Henri IV of France and one of Napoleon's teeth, alongside items of questionable provenance and authenticity such as Voltaire's chair, General Gordon's camel saddle and paintings alleged to be by Jacques-Louis David and François Boucher.

The story of the lost collection is part of my family's folklore and whilst every family has its tragedy, this one goes beyond the confines of narrow self-interest. When, in the wake of the fire, my great-great-grandfather, John Theodore Tussaud, was asked by *The Times* about the losses and whether or not they were insured, he said: 'you cannot put a price on the Napoléonic relics...' As this book forensically uncovers, that was, to say the least, a very considerable understatement in relation to a 'bonfire of history'.

JAMES TUSSAUD*

---

* James Tussaud is the only member of the Tussaud family, other than Marie herself, to have appeared in Madame Tussaud's as a figure in wax, having been cast in 1989 as William Brown, the eponymous hero of Richmal Crompton's *Just William* series.

ACKNOWLEDGEMENTS

THE AUTHORS WOULD LIKE to start by thanking Nick Varney, who until recently was the chief executive of Merlin Entertainments Ltd (the owners of Madame Tussaud's), for his permission to access the exhibition's archives and for us to use copyright material found there. We did this with the invaluable help of Angela Jobson and Julia Maynard of Madame Tussaud's. We would also like to thank James Tussaud, a direct lineal descendant of Madame Tussaud, for his support.

During the course of researching the royal material in the book, considerable help was given to us by Tim Knox, Director of the Royal Collection Trust, and his staff in the Royal Archives at Windsor Castle. Advice on values was provided by Philip Mould, the noted art dealer, and by John Hudson, the well-known collector of Napoléonic-era porcelain. The shelves of the National Art Library at the Victoria & Albert Museum held many of the answers to questions about the authenticity of Madame Tussaud's paintings attributed to Jacques-Louis David. We thank them all.

This book owes much to Samantha Wyndham, who provided hours of copy editing, historical advice, the retrieval of valuable information from Madame Tussaud's uncatalogued archives, and drafted the Epilogue; Lyn Davies of Lyn Davies Design, for his skill in designing the book; and Anthony Weldon, of Nine Elms Books, who once again put his faith in the authors. Finally, we would like to thank His Majesty The King for his Gracious Permission to use images in this book from the Royal Collection Trust.

AUTHORS' NOTE

Titles and spelling This is a very tricky subject on which there are no universal rules, the etiquette being different in each country. Accordingly, the authors have decided that in the interests of consistency, the titles and spelling of the names of the people included in this book are, for the most part, in their native language and as in use at the time they are mentioned. However, for ease of comprehension, their appointments and military ranks are expressed in English. The principal exceptions to this rule are the use of 'King' and 'Queen', rather than 'Roi' and 'Reine', and the English version of the titles of Napoléon and Joséphine. The practice on the continent of using the Christian name *after* the title is adopted here for non-British aristocrats.

The names of non-British regiments are those which would have been used in English at that time, thus the '1er Régiment de Grenadiers-à-Pied de la Garde Impériale' is written as '1st Regiment of Foot Grenadiers of the Imperial Guard'. However, the 'Chasseurs à Cheval de la Garde Impériale' were usually referred to as the 'Chasseurs à Cheval', so the French spelling has been retained.

Finally, Madame Tussaud & Sons' Exhibition was the name of the waxworks until relatively recently. Although, 'Madame Tussauds', without an apostrophe, is the brand today, for the purposes of this book and in the interest of simplicity, 'Madame Tussaud's' *with* an apostrophe is the grammatical style used throughout.

Dates With certain exceptions, which are explained, the dates used throughout are those of the Gregorian calendar rather than the Julian calendar, which was used in Russia and Eastern Orthodox countries until the 1920s, or the French Revolutionary calendar, which was in use in France from 1793 to 1805 and then again for nineteen days during the Paris Commune of 1871.

Currency valuations In 1800, one French Franc was worth £2.77 today. The difference between the value of the Pound at the time quoted and in 2022 has been computed using the Bank of England's inflation calculator.

Image attribution and copyright Unless otherwise stated, the artist is unknown, and the images are in the public domain.

Catalogue item numbers The item number references given in the text are from Madame Tussaud's *Catalogue of Napoléonic Relics and other Works of Art & Curiosities*, last published in 1925; some items in that catalogue were given the same number as they were grouped in a single display.

Typography This book has been set in 'Barbou', a twentieth-century revival of an eighteenth-century font by French typefounder Pierre Fournier. Many of the ornaments decorating the page are also copies of Fournier's work. Incidentally, this distinctive atmosphere was in mind when the authors decided (with the enthusiastic support of their publisher) to adopt the baroque practice of capitalising the first letter of titles, appointments and military formations.

Insurance Plan. Tu

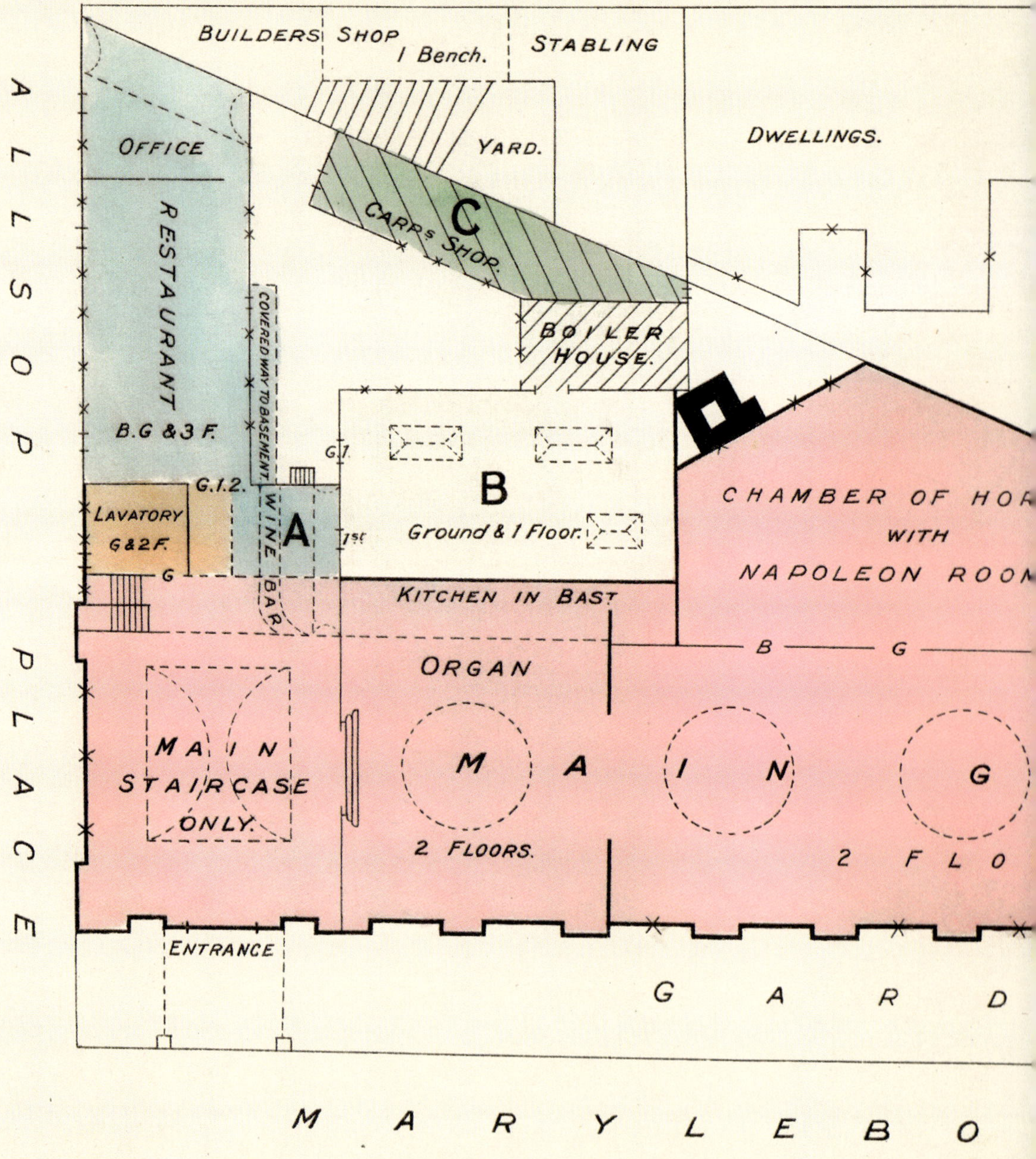

SAUD'S EXHIBITION.

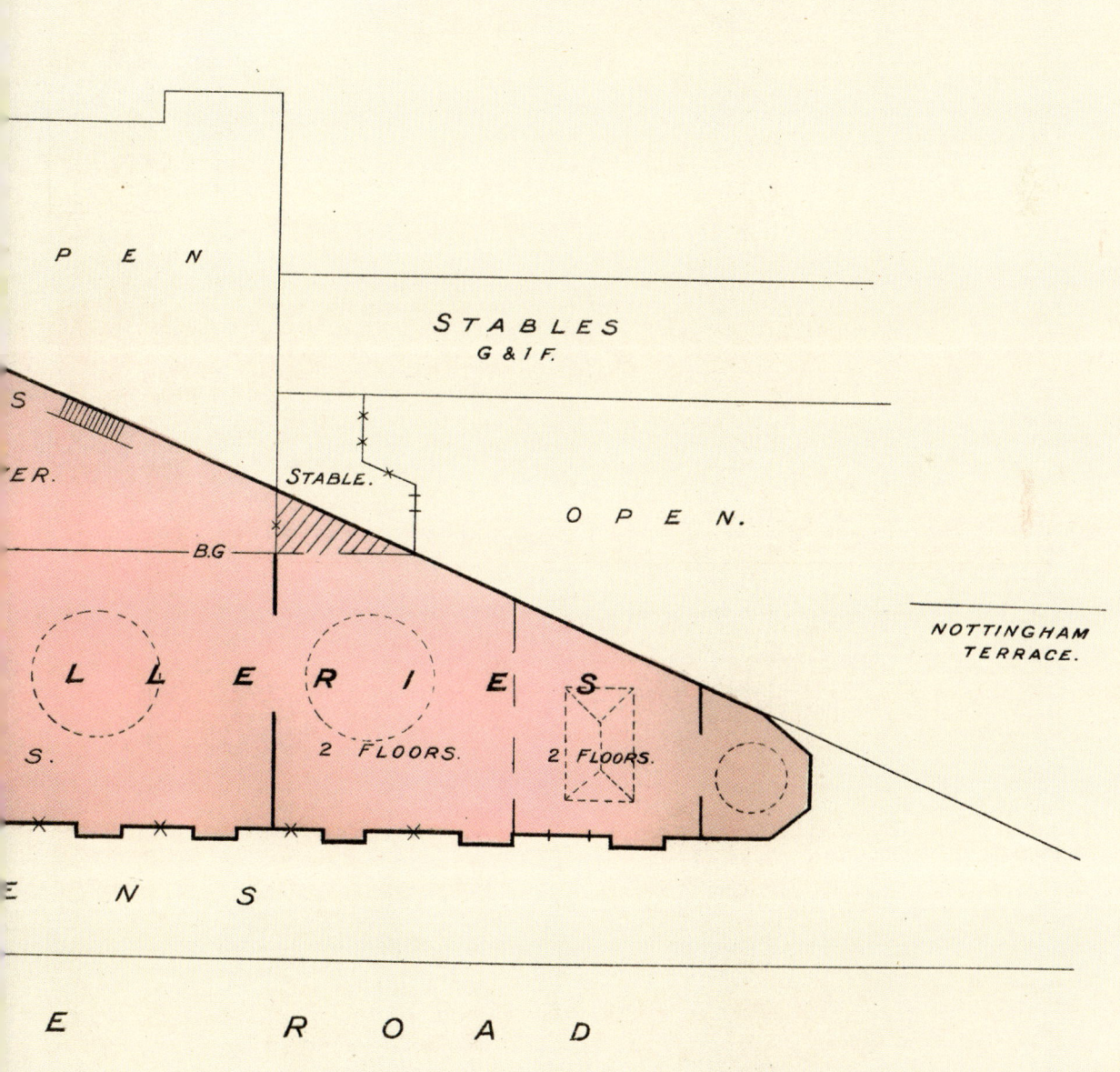

Exhibition de Mme TUSSAUD & FILS,
58, Baker Street, Portman Square,

Ouverte depuis 11 heures du Matin jusqu'à 10 heures de Soir.

MADAME TUSSAUD ET FILS ont l'honneur d'informer les Etrangers et le Public, qu'ils ont ajouté à leur MAGNIFIQUE EXHIBITION DE FIGURES DE CIRE, la plus curieuse Collection qui existe d'objets ayant appartenu à Napoléon, comme Général, Consul, et Empereur, et qui sont exposés dans deux nouvelles Salles décorées avec la plus grande richesse et ornées de tous les emblêmes de l'Empire. On pourra se faire une idée de leur magnificence par la somme énorme de 6,000 livres sterling qu'elles ont coûtée. Madame Tussaud et Fils ne voulant point que le public conçoive le moindre doute sur l'authenticité des objets qu'ils ont l'honneur de lui représenter, et dont la plus grande partie provient du Prince Lucien et du Docteur O'Meara, ont cru devoir mettre sous ses yeux, dans l'une des Salles, tous les titres, pièces et certificats qui attestent leur origine.

PARMI CES PRECIEUSE RELIQUES ON REMARQUE PRINCIPALEMENT.

Le Lit de Camp avec la Courtepointe, le Traversin et les Deux Matelats sur lesquels Napoléon est mort à Ste. Hélène. Les Matelats et le Courtepointe sont tachés de son sang par suite de l'autopsie faite par le Docteur Antomarchi. Le Manteau qu'il portait à la Bataille de Marengo, et qu'il a légué à son Fils. Un Costume complet porté par lui à Ste. Hélène ainsi que plusieurs Mouchoirs et paires de Bas. La Chemise, le Gilet de Flanelle et le Madras qu'il avait sur lui quand il est mort. Un Dent, et l'Instrument dont s'est servi le Docteur O'Meara pour la lui extraire. La Robe de son couronnement et celle de Josephine. Le Drapeau donné par lui à la Garde Nationale de l'île d'Elbe. Le Sabre qu'il portait à la Bataille des Pyramides. Le Sabre d'honneur qui lui a été offert par le Directoire à son retour de sa première campagne d'Italie. Le Service en Porcelaine, le couvert en vermeil et la tasse à café dont il se servait à Ste. Hélène. La Croix d'honneur qu'il a constamment portée à l'île d'Elbe, Sa Tabatière en or avec son chiffre, et Un Camée à son image monté en bague ; Ces trois objets ont été offerts par lui à son frère Lucien lors de leur réconciliation en 1815. Le Coffre de son nécessaire pris dans sa voiture à Waterloo, et dont la serrure a été brisée par les soldats. Le superbe Berceau du Roi de Rome ne fait par Jacob. La Voiture Militaire de Napoléon prise à Waterloo, et achetée par M. Bullock à S. M. George IV. pour la somme de 2,500 livres sterling. Le Portrait en Pied de l'Empereur peint par Robert Lefèvre. Ceux idem de Josephine, Marie Louise, Lucien, Caroline sa Sœur, Reine de Naples, Madame Mère, et le Duc de Reischtadt, peint par David, Gérard, Lethière, et Sales, (ce dernier, peintre de S. M. l'Empereur d'Autriche). Enfin, la magnifique Table des Maréchaux, chef d'œuvre de la manufacture de Sèvres, peinte par Isabey et donnée par Napoléon à la ville de Paris. Après avoir été exposée cinq ans dans la grande galerie du Louvre, ne précieux monument national fut vendu sous la restauration en 1815.

MADAME TUSSAUD prévient également le Public qu'elle a en sa possession, depuis plus de 50 ans, la Chemise que Henry IV. avait sur le corps quand il fut assassiné par Ravaillac ; elle est ensanglantée, et percée des deux coups de poignard dont il a été frappé. (Cette relique inappréciable fait partie de l'exhibition).

A l'extrémité de la grande Salle des figures, est située la Salle du trône ou est représentée la figure de S. M. George IV. revêtu de la veritable robe de son couronnement. Ce magnifique costume a coûté dans l'origine 18,000 livres sterling.

Au nombre des Anciennes Figures, dont le nombre dépasse 130, on remarque toujours le Groupe intéressant de Louis XVI. et Marie Antoinette, avec Madame la Duchesse d'Angoulême dans son enfance, et le Dauphin ; et parmi les nouvelles, on distingue particulièrement celles du Marquis de Wellesley, frère du Duc de Wellington, d'Espartero, et Père Mathew.

Prix d'Entrée :—1 Shilling pour la Grande Salle, et 6 pence de Supplément pour les Deux Salles des Reliques de Napoléon et la Chambre des Criminels.

⁎⁎⁎ La musique commence à 8 heures du Soir, heure à laquelle toutes les Salles sont brillamment illuminées.

G. COLE, Printer, Westminster.

INTRODUCTION

From the restoration of the British monarchy in 1660 to the present day – with the exception of German aerial bombing during the Second World War – the greatest single threat to England's cultural and historical heritage has not been bombs, iconoclasts or property developers, but fire.

Much of the City of London, including many of its churches, livery halls and the old St Paul's Cathedral, was destroyed by the Great Fire of London on 6th September 1666. The Palace of Whitehall (with the exception of the Banqueting House) was similarly destroyed on 4th January 1698. The old Palace of Westminster went up in smoke on 16th October 1834; and, in more recent times, parts of York Minster, Hampton Court Palace and Windsor Castle have been badly damaged by fire, although almost all their contents were saved from the flames and the water used to douse them. However, it is not just churches and royal palaces that

opposite Madame Tussaud's advertising poster, 1835.

St George's Hall, Windsor Castle, after the 20th November 1992, fire.
©Royal Collection Trust / His Majesty King Charles III 2023

⁂ INTRODUCTION ⁂

have perished, for the long list of lost buildings and contents includes many historic houses, unique museums and iconic municipal edifices.

In the course of researching *The Imperial Impresario: The Treasures, Trophies & Trivia of Napoléon's Theatre of Power*, which was published in 2021 by Nine Elms Books, we discovered that one of the most remarkable collections of Napoléonica ever assembled in England had also been lost in a long-forgotten fire. This occurred on the night of 18th March 1925 at the Marylebone Road premises of Madame Tussaud & Sons' Exhibition. We were able to identify the extent of the loss from various documents in Madame Tussaud's then uncatalogued archives, including receipts, correspondence and copies of the exhibition's catalogue, which was published at regular intervals between the opening of the permanent exhibition in 1835 and the year of the fire; the 1883 catalogue was particularly helpful, as it contained greater detail and explanatory footnotes.

In the archives we also discovered that not only was a priceless collection of Napoléonica lost in the wax-fuelled flames, but that Madame Tussaud, her uncle Philippe Curtius, and her lineal descendants had actually acquired and assembled a very broad collection of historical artefacts, including many paintings attributed to some of the greatest artists of their day. The collection ranged from an Egyptian mummy, via the blood-stained shirt worn by King Henri IV of France on the day of his murder in 1610, to a copy of King Edward VIII's cot. It was clear from the surviving archives that, prior to 1925, Madame Tussaud & Sons' Exhibition retained its original concept as a museum of curiosities, illustrated with lifelike representations of historical characters modelled in wax, rather than the exhibition of waxworks we know today.

Then, towards the end of 2022, our editor, Samantha Wyndham, was appointed by Madame Tussaud's to collate and catalogue their archive material. Shortly after the first draft of this book had been completed, and in the course of that cataloguing, Samantha discovered in an unmarked box a previously unknown insurance catalogue and valuation dated July 1911 (hereafter referred to as the 'insurance catalogue'), and the unpublished diary of Joseph Randall Tussaud (1830-1892), Marie Tussaud's grandson.

The first of these documents provided individual valuations for not only the entire contents of the exhibition as it was in 1911, including many items not listed in the 1925 exhibition catalogue, but also for all the fixtures and fittings in the building on the Marylebone Road. It also gave details of the alleged provenance of many of the items in the collection, some of which contradicted the entries in the exhibition catalogues. Joseph Randall Tussaud's diary, which covered the period 1870 to 1875, provided valuable insights into the provenance of certain items acquired at that time. Although these discoveries necessitated many changes to the text, which delayed publication, they have been an absolutely invaluable source of background information to which frequent reference is made in the pages that follow.

As no one now alive is old enough to remember Madame Tussaud & Sons' Exhibition as it was before the fire, this book seeks to describe, and where possible illustrate, the items in the collection. We have also set them in their historical context and given an account of their values over the years – and along the way we have debunked some myths and exposed a number of fakes. Although this last was not our original intention, it was an inevitable consequence of applying historical research and common sense to the items listed in the exhibition catalogues. This is turn begs the question: were fakes *deliberately* misrepresented as genuine by Madame Tussaud and her successors? As to this, readers must apply their own judgment based on the evidence we here present, while bearing in mind that, before 1925, artistic attribution was based on scholarship, provenance and trust, not carbon dating, x-rays and other scientific techniques such as pigment analysis.

PENNY COBHAM & CHRISTOPHER JOLL

PROLOGUE

A Wonderful Spectacle

WEDNESDAY 18TH MARCH was not particularly different to any other late-winter day in London in 1925. The deep snow that had fallen in mid-January had long since given way to the usual English cold and wet of the season, although the 18th was both a rain- and a smog-free day.

On the other side of the globe, and long before Londoners awoke, a large area of north-eastern Tokyo was destroyed by fire. That was an event that barely rated a paragraph in the following day's British newspapers: Japan was, after all, a very distant country about which most Englishmen knew nothing beyond the jolly tunes and lyrics of Gilbert and Sullivan's *Mikado*. Closer to home, and possibly of interest to the Japanese government, during the afternoon of the 18th questions were asked in the House of Commons about the establishment of new Royal Navy facilities in Singapore. The First Lord of the Admiralty replied that MPs would have to wait for a statement until the following day's debate on the subject.

Meanwhile, a 'most superior person' and one of the greatest statesmen of his age, George Nathaniel Curzon, 1st Marquess Curzon of Kedleston, lay dying in his London house. While an undergraduate at Balliol College, Oxford, the future Marquess was mercilessly lampooned with a verse of sardonic doggerel composed by Cecil (later Sir Cecil) Spring Rice and published as part of *The Balliol Masque* (1880):

My name is George Nathanial Curzon,
I am a most superior person.
My cheek is pink, my hair is sleek,
I dine at Blenheim once a week.

Curzon would later comment: 'Never has more harm been done to one single individual than that accursed doggerel has done to me'. Other than those historical facts, the day was unremarkable.

Soon after dark on 18th March 1925, Madame Tussaud & Sons' Exhibition,

opposite The London Fire Brigade at work during the Madame Tussaud's fire.

The Hall of Kings at Madame Tussaud's after the 1925 fire.

≈ PROLOGUE ≈

Madame Tussaud's building, before 18th March 1925.

Lieutenant Colonel Charles James Fox (1855–1930), Chief Officer of the London Salvage Corps.

housed in a large stone-and-red-brick building on the Marylebone Road, close to the Baker Street underground station, had closed its doors. The orchestra that played daily promenade concerts in the main hall had packed away its instruments, the building was locked, and the exhibition staff went home, leaving a Union flag fluttering above the entrance.

Meanwhile, the Chief Officer of London's Fire Brigade, Mr A. R. Dyer, was getting into evening dress, prior to attending a play in the West End. Lieutenant Colonel Charles James Fox, Chief Officer of the London Salvage Corps, was at home at 64 Watling Street in the City, with his long-term mistress, Miss Gertrude Elbourne. Mr Woods, in charge of the Regent's Park area of the London Water Board, was also at home; Superintendant Peel of the Metropolitan Police was on duty at the local police station; and a green parrot in a large, square cage with a domed roof was minding its own business in one of the side rooms of the exhibition.

At about 10.15 pm, men working for the Metropolitan Railway, at near-by Baker Street station, noticed that a section of the roof of Madame Tussaud's appeared to be on fire and they raised the alarm. Within forty-five minutes, twenty-five fire engines and three turntable ladders were at the scene, under the supervision of Mr Dyer, who was still in his dinner jacket. Mr Woods, summoned from his house, ordered his engineers to open a 21-inch mains water supply for the Fire Brigade's pumps; and Superintendant Peel's policemen had formed an exclusion area around the building, although a growing crowd of gawpers tried to get closer and some, reported *The Daily Telegraph*, even tried to interfere with the mile of pipes supplying the pumps

As *The Times* recorded the day after the fire:

> Thousands of people watched the scene from behind the police cordons drawn across Marylebone-road at either end of the burning building. It was a strange sight. In addition to the motor pumps, there were three water towers ranged along the front of the building, and on the top of each one stood a fireman, now dimly, now sharply, silhouetted against the sky, playing on what at times appeared to be a roaring furnace. Down in the road stood a small squad of firemen equipped with breathing apparatus, but up to 11.30 the inside of the building had been too hot for them to penetrate very far.

Sir Henry 'Chips' Channon (1897–1958).

Through one of the large entrances to the building there passed to and fro other firemen and men of the Salvage Corps, engaged in rescuing whatever they could reach. The property brought out through this doorway consisted chiefly of pictures, with some wax figures and busts, which were dumped across the road.

An eye-witness, the name-dropping snob *par excellence*, Henry (later Sir Henry) 'Chips' Channon, noted the event in his diary with his customary purple prose and a fair disregard for the truth, given where he alleges that he first saw the fire:

> Driving home [to Victoria from the Palace of Westminster] we saw the sky a blaze of pink-orange and I realised a gigantic fire was at Madame Tussaud's.* [Having driven to the Marylebone Road] I watched the battle between the vast sheets of copper flames and the men for two hours, the building was a den of flames completely wrecking the venerable old institution. Charred wax remains of Crippen and Queen Victoria and Gladstone were carried out. Firemen on top of gigantic ladders vomited water on the building in vain but prevented the fire from spreading. It might easily have lit all London. Madame Tussaud's burning as Lord Curzon lies dying – perhaps dead.

* Channon is surely lying as it is quite impossible to see a blaze in Marylebone from Westminster. The likelihood is that he either heard about the fire and drove over to see it, or simply invented his involvement in order to add some ironic sensationalism to the death of Lord Curzon.

By 12.30 am on 19th March the wax-fuelled fire was under control, although the roof and the top two floors had collapsed, and the glass had fallen from the famous dome. Beneath it, the large, gilded letters that spelled out the wax modeller's name were blackened by soot, and those areas not destroyed by the

☙ PROLOGUE ☙

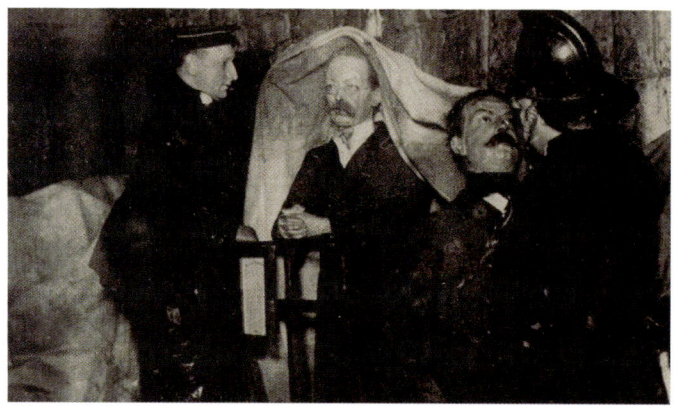

above Dr Crippen (1862–1910) in the Chamber of Horror.

above right The rescue of the parrot.

fire were badly damaged by smoke and water. Only the Chamber of Horrors in the basement was largely untouched, albeit knee-deep in water. 'The devil looks after his own', John Theodore Tussaud (1860-1943), great-grandson of Madame Tussaud, ruefully remarked to *The Times* the following day.

Nonetheless, as the men of the Salvage Corps fought their way into the smoke-filled building in an attempt to rescue what was left, the Union flag was still flying. Shortly thereafter, this reassuring sight was dampened for the (by-now) thousands of onlookers, with the emergence through the smoke of a parrot's cage, borne by a brace of Salvage Corps men. Lying on its floor was a green parrot, apparently dead. However, moments later the bird stirred into life, hopped back onto its perch and, as firemen placed pictures around the cage to protect it from the cold, in a surprisingly loud voice that was croaky from smoke inhalation, the parrot said: 'This is a rotten business'. The crowd cheered in response, but it was about the only thing they or anyone else had to cheer about. The cause of the fire, which was later thought to have started in the orchestra pit in the main hall, was never established. The damage, however, was all too apparent. As *The Times* stated in its 20th March edition:

> Of the famous galleries ranging from the Grand Hall nothing remains but charred wood and fantastically twisted iron. Priceless relics, gorgeously robed figures, ornate decorations – all have vanished. The floor is thickly covered by a mixture of ashes, wax and water. One noted the iron frame of a pianoforte, which was all that remained of a Bechstein concert grand. The great pipe-organ had completely gone. A few sheets of music appeared here and there among a pile of *debris* which M. Jacques Taube,* the musical director, said was the musical library that had been accumulated through years. His violin, a Nicholas Amati, had been destroyed, along with other valuable instruments [used in the daily promenade concerts that were a popular

* Jacques Taube (1874–1952), a noted Polish violinist.

PROLOGUE

All that was left of the 'sports group'.

feature of Madame Tussaud's]. Of the most treasured possessions of the exhibition, the Napoléonic relics, only scrap iron remains to suggest the coach in which the Emperor rode at Waterloo.

In the entrance hall water still trickled down the staircase. The walls were black with smoke, and the famous picture of George IV, painted by Sir Thomas Lawrence, and presented by the monarch to General Nicolay,* was blistered almost beyond recognition, and was shrouded in heavy curtains, which had been of a rich wine colour, but were now crêpe [i.e. black]. The clock at the head of the staircase, however, still ticked away, unaffected by the fire and the confusion…

It is too early yet to estimate the extent of the financial loss. Mr John [Theodore] Tussaud has mentioned a quarter of a million pounds (2022: £23.35 million), but he added, "You cannot put a price on the Napoléonic relics… which cannot be replaced. I consider many of the most valuable things in the collection have been destroyed." He explained that the losses were covered by insurance, so far as a price could be put on the collection.

In fact, as Madame Tussaud's archives reveal, the insurance claim for the lost items (as opposed to the damage to the building) appears to have been less than £3,000 (2022: £280,221). This was despite the fact that the 1911 insurance catalogue put a value of £20,655 (2022: £1,929,323) on the 'relics', £17,930 (2022: £1,674,788)

* Lieutenant General Sir William Nicolay (1771–1842).

~ PROLOGUE ~

above The execution of Charlie Peace (1832–1879) on 25th February 1879 at Armley Gaol – one of the tableaux in the Chamber of Horrors at Madame Tussaud's before the 1925 fire.

above right Some of the rescued waxworks.

on the 'works of art & pictures' and £45,046 (2022: £4,207,615) on everything else, from wax figures to tea spoons. Although the total of £83,631 (2022: £7,811,727) was rather less than John Tussaud's estimate to the media, there is no explanation in the archives for this discrepancy.

Further details of the damage were given by the *Manchester Guardian* which, along with virtually every other regional and national newspaper in the United Kingdom, reported the fire:

> It was stated that all the Napoléonic relics had been destroyed. The total amount of damage cannot yet be estimated ... When signs that the outbreak was becoming under control began to be evident, the men of the Salvage Corps entered the ground floor and basement of the building. Almost immediately they began to bring out some of the portable property. This at first consisted mainly of pictures of all descriptions ... The Salvage Corps, after an interval, were able to enter and rescue some of the [wax] figures.

The report also noted that members of the crowd inquired after the safety of the burglar and murderer, Charlie Peace, the wife murderer, Dr Crippen, and other notorious criminals in the Chamber of Horrors. The sight of the salvage men shouldering the wax models was apparently a strange one.

PROLOGUE

Warming to its theme, the *Manchester Guardian* then went on to describe how an eye-witness, who lived opposite Madame Tussaud's, said that the fire was 'a wonderful spectacle' and that 'strong red and golden flames leapt 50 feet from the roof of the building [and] the wax models could be distinctly heard sizzling'. The newspaper ended its report with a typically political sneer:

> It is strange to think of the number of eminent, and highly respectable people being burned in effigy in London. Madame Tussaud's famous waxworks spread its net far and wide, and at least forty people of the present Parliament and scores of notabilities outside were represented in wax in these burning galleries. Criminals represented in the Chamber of Horrors, however, will have no feelings in the matter, as they are all dead.

The fire at Madame Tussaud's resulted not only in the loss of a waxworks display but also the incineration of a substantial number of historical items, many of which would not have been out of place in a museum. But how and why had this collection of historical artefacts and paintings come together in the seemingly unlikely setting of Madame Tussaud & Sons' Exhibition? The answer lies in the origins of the business and the character of Madame Tussaud herself.

CHAPTER ONE

THE GREAT ILLUSIONIST

*I*N 1838, MADAME MARIE TUSSAUD published her *Memoirs & Reminiscences of France*. They are now generally acknowledged to be highly inaccurate, being designed by the author to bolster her legend rather than to provide posterity with a truthful record of her life. A slightly more accurate account was published in the opening pages of the *Catalogue of Pictures and Historical Relics*, compiled by W. Wheeler, illustrated with photographs by Benjamin Foulkes Winkes, and dedicated to Queen Victoria, which was on sale to visitors to Madame Tussaud's in the Marylebone Road from 1901. More recently, Kate Berridge has published *Madame Tussaud: A Life in Wax* (John Murray, 2006) in which the author, making extensive use of contemporary French records, corrects many of the myths and misconceptions created by Madame Tussaud and perpetuated by her successors.

The plain fact is that Marie Tussaud was an illusionist who deliberately sculpted a story of her life that would enhance both her business and her legacy. This explains much of what follows in this book – and this chapter, in particular, sets the known facts against the Marie-manufactured myths.

opposite A portrait study by John Theodore Tussaud, 1921.

According to the Tussaud legend, the future Madame Tussaud was born a few days before 7th December 1761 to Marie Krutz, the daughter of a French-Swiss clergyman who was resident in Berne, Switzerland, and the (conveniently) late Joseph Grosholtz, a German-Swiss officer whom Mademoiselle Krutz had supposedly married in 1760 in Berne. Grosholtz was an Aide-de-Camp to General Dogobert Sigmund von Wurmser and was killed during the Seven Years War two months or so before Marie's birth. However, Marie's nationality was for years uncertain. According to Wheeler, she was born in Berne where 'her parents had been married', which would make her Swiss. But in William E. Hurt's Preface to *The Romance of Madame Tussaud's* (1921) by her great-grandson, John Theodore Tussaud, he states

CHAPTER ONE

above Dr Philippe Curtius (1737–1794).

above right John Theodore Tussaud (1858–1943).

that Marie was born in Strasbourg, then the capital of French Alsace-Lorraine, thus establishing her nationality as French. This is confirmed by Kate Berridge who uncovered Marie's certificate of baptism that confirmed her place of birth as Strasbourg, and the date of her baptism at Old St Peter's Catholic Church in Strasbourg as 7th December 1761. The reason for the Grosholtz family being then resident in the French city is unknown, but was probably a result of the late Joseph's military service.

Either way, the Tussaud legend asserts that it wasn't long before the widowed Madame Grosholtz removed herself and her infant daughter from Strasbourg and returned to her family in Berne, thus creating the myth that Marie was Swiss-born as well as Swiss-bred. Mother and daughter remained in Berne until 1768 when they were invited to Paris by Madame Grosholtz's brother, Dr Philippe Guillaume Mathé Curtius, as he is called in all official French documents despite being known in the family as 'Christopher'. His family name, like that of his sister, was – so it was claimed by Marie – actually Krutz, but Philippe changed it to the more French-sounding Curtius in the early years of the French Revolution. It is as Philippe Curtius that he will be identified in the text hereafter.

Before moving on, it is worth noting that the current generation of the Tussaud family has cast doubt on the precise nature of the relationship between Philippe Curtius and Madame Tussaud's mother, Marie Grosholtz, questioning whether they were brother and sister or lovers. Additionally, Kate Berridge asserts that Curtius was, in fact, the future Madame Tussaud's father and had impregnated her mother while she worked for him as a maid. If this is correct, then the rest of the story of Marie's paternal antecedents looks like a Marie-created fiction designed to enhance her social standing. The authors have not been able to shed any further light on this, but accept its probable trut.h

Whatever his actual relationship with the Grosholtzs, it is a fact that Philippe Curtius was originally established in Berne as a doctor, but that as early as 1758 he was modelling human limbs and organs in order to demonstrate the results of his anatomical research. According to Madame Tussaud's great-grandson, John Theodore Tussaud in his 1921 book, Dr Curtius 'soon extended the scope of his labours to the execution of miniature [wax] portraits . . . and [thereby] gained the patronage of many of the leading members of the [Swiss] aristocracy'. By the early 1760s, he was practicing more as an artist than a family doctor, and

[32]

CHAPTER ONE

had established a studio in the medieval Swiss capital city where his wax portraits and anatomical models were on public display.

In 1762, the French Prince de Conti was taking an enforced tour of Europe, having fallen foul of Madame de Pompadour who was the then *maîtresse-en-titre* of his cousin, King Louis XV. Today, de Conti is best known for his *Grand Cru* vineyard, Romanée-Conti, but in the eighteenth century his reputation was based on his skills as a soldier, as a connoisseur and extensive collector of fine art, his unsuccessful candidacy for the Polish throne, and his political role as a royal dissident.

On his arrival in Berne, de Conti heard of Curtius's studio and paid it a visit. He was impressed by what he saw and told the doctor: 'If you will leave Berne and come to Paris, I will undertake to find you a suitable *atelier* in which to carry out your work, and hold myself responsible for your receiving as many commissions as you feel disposed to execute. Come! You will not regret it'. Before the end of 1762, Curtius had accepted the invitation and established himself in an apartment in the seventeenth-century Hôtel d'Aligre in the fashionable rue St Honoré, Paris. This *hôtel particulier*, although well-situated, was not as grand as it sounded, having long since been converted from a famous noble residence, used for meetings by King Louis XIV's *Conseil du Roi* (Royal Council, i.e. the French government), into a utilitarian block of flats. Nonetheless, it retained its *grand salon*, which had been repurposed from a government council chamber into a picture gallery by the Académie de Saint Luc, a guild of artists and sculptors established in 1391.

Louis François de Bourbon, Prince de Conti (1717–1776) aged 17, by Alexis Simon Belle.

Over the ensuing months, the Prince de Conti was as good as his word and important commissions flowed in, including a bust of King Louis XV's neglected wife, the Polish Princess, Marie Leszczyńska, and later the King's new *maîtresse-en-titre*, Madame du Barry who was depicted as the 'sleeping beauty' (a copy of the 1765 original, made in 1989, is still on display at Madame Tussaud's). Thanks to these and other orders, Curtius was invited by the Académie de Saint Luc to display his work in the Hôtel d'Aligre's *grand salon*. By 1776, the former doctor was so well-established in Paris that he felt able to fetch his only 'sister' and her daughter from Berne, and instal them in his apartment. This arrangement was an immediate success, as the young Marie quickly formed a loving relationship with her bachelor 'uncle' who,

Jeanne Bécu, Madame du Barry (1743–1793) as *The Sleeping Beauty* at Madame Tussaud's.

[33]

CHAPTER ONE

above Comte Honore Gabriel Riqueti de Mirabeau (1749–1791) by Joseph Boze.

middle François-Marie Arouet, known as Voltaire (1694–1778), modelled from life by Philippe Curtius.

above right Dr Benjamin Franklin (1706–1790) modelled from life by Philippe Curtius.

Joseph-François Foulon de Doué (1715–1789).

shortly thereafter, she insisted on calling *papa*. This is, perhaps, a telling fact.

Beyond the inaccurate *Memoirs*, there is hearsay but not much documented evidence as to precisely what happened to Madame Grosholtz and her daughter, from their arrival in Paris to the outbreak of the French Revolution twenty-one years later in 1789. What is known is that the young Marie became extremely adept at modelling in wax, and her 'uncle' was inducted into the Académie de Saint Luc in 1778.

Nor is there much hard evidence extant as to the output of Curtius's studio, as much of it was destroyed during the years of revolutionary turmoil, and most of what remained was lost in the fire of 1925. It is known, however, that the majority of the early work produced by Curtius was, according to John Theodore Tussaud, 'miniatures in coloured wax, modelled [from life] in fairly high relief and framed and glazed … as pictures'. Although no list of his sitters and patrons exists, it is clear that, thanks to his princely sponsor, Curtius's *atelier* quickly attracted the leading figures of the day. These ranged from royalty and aristocrats to philosophers and intellectuals, many of whose writings and actions would precipitate the Revolution including Mirabeau, Voltaire, Rousseau, and the American, Dr Benjamin Franklin.

At some point in the 1770s, the precise date in not known, Curtius started to create three-dimensional, life-size portrait models and busts in wax. Many of these were not intended for sale, but for a paying-visitor attraction which he opened as a *cabinet de cire* (wax exhibition) in the house of the former Finance Minister, Joseph-François Foulon, in the popular Boulevard du Temple.

Foulon would later be notorious for his remark that if there was insufficient bread the people should eat hay. In 1789, he had the distinction of being the first man in the French Revolution to be lynched, *à la lanterne*, following which he was decapitated. His head was then paraded through Paris on a pike, with a

CHAPTER ONE

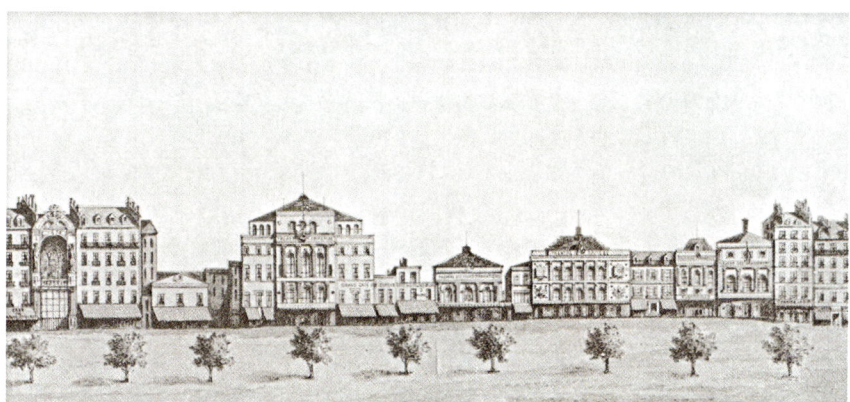

Boulevard du Temple.

whisp of hay protruding from his mouth. As to the Boulevard du Temple, it was at the time a wide Parisian street lined with cafés and theatres. It was in the basement of Foulon's former residence that, in the late 1770s, Curtius added a morbid attraction to pull in the crowds: the *Caverne des Grans Voleurs*, the precursor of Marie Tussaud's Chamber of Horrors.

The establishment of his *cabinet* did not end Curtius's commissioned portraiture business. This is evidenced by a bust (recently rediscovered in the Madame Tussaud's archives) and several miniatures of Voltaire, created in 1778, catalogued in the nineteenth century, but lost in the 1925 fire. It is also recorded that the American statesman, Benjamin Franklin, ordered his own likeness in 1783, along with a suite of portrait miniatures of 'many other notable characters of the day', which were displayed in Franklin's chambers in the French capital. In the 1780s, the exact date is not known, Curtius also established the *Salon Cire* in the arcade at the Palais Royal, Paris.

Quite when Marie started working with her 'uncle' is uncertain, but it is thought that she had a hand in the creation of Franklin's collection and was probably working in wax several years before that. So far, so good. But what is almost certainly untrue is the self-aggrandising story in Marie's *Memoirs & Reminiscences of France*, that her fortunes changed forever in 1780. Despite the very considerable doubts that now exist as to the veracity of what follows, Marie's account is repeated here as a classic example of her commercially-driven disregard for the *actualité*, in this case by fabricating a close association with France's *Ancien Régime*.

According to the *Memoirs*, at some point in 1780 Madame Élizabeth de France, the sixteen-year-old youngest sister of King Louis XVI (who had ascended the throne of France in 1774), paid the first of several visits to the Curtius *atelier*. Wax modelling had recently become a fashionable craze of the French leisured (and

top Madame Élizabeth de France (1764–1794) modelled by John T. Tussaud.

above King Louis XVI (1754–1793) modelled by Philippe Curtius.

[35]

CHAPTER ONE

perennially bored) upper classes, and Madame Élizabeth had reputedly caught the bug, albeit that her subjects tended to be religious in nature.

In Marie's account, the Princess, who spent most of her time at Versailles, asked Curtius if his 'niece' could move to the palace in order to give the royal devotee intensive one-on-one instruction in the art. Recognising the considerable social and commercial advantages that such a move would generate, Curtius (whose political sympathies were republican) immediately agreed, despite the loss of his talented assistant who – so she asserted – moved into the Princess' apartments at the end of the palace's south façade overlooking the Swiss Lake.

It wasn't long, so Marie's story alleged, before her role in Madame Élizabeth's household expanded into that of companion and secretary. She was, so she said, moved into the bedroom next to that of her patroness and, when the two of them weren't sculpting, Marie would carry out administrative tasks for the Princess. These included distributing charitable largesse to the Princess's royal pensioners, a role that continued for nine years.

However, in her research for *Madame Tussaud: A Life in Wax*, Kate Berridge examined the extensive surviving household accounts of Madame Élizabeth and could find no mention of Marie Grosholtz in any year. Indeed, among sixty-six named roles in the Princess' household – including that of Léonard, the coiffeur, who came in when required from Paris – there is not one mention of Marie. Nor is she mentioned in the *Almanac de Versailles*, which names 'every spit-mender and commode carrier' at the palace. It is Ms Berridge's evidenced-based opinion that the whole story of Marie working with Madame Élizabeth, as detailed in the *Memoirs*, is false and was plagiarised from the *Memoirs of the Private Life of Marie Antoinette*. This book was written by the executed Queen's First Woman of the Bedchamber, Madame Henriette Campan, and was published posthumously in 1823 – fifteen years before Marie's own *Memoirs*.

The ambassadors of Tipoo Sultan of Mysore (1751–1799) being received at Versailles by Louis XVI, 10th August 1788, by Jean Baptiste Morret.

Meanwhile, in the Boulevard du Temple, Philippe Curtius was developing his *cabinet du cire* by creating themed groups, a format that is still in use today at Madame Tussaud's. Three of these are recorded. In the first, Curtius depicted the Royal Family holding a *grand couvert* (dining in public) at Versailles, seated at a horseshoe-shaped table and surrounded by the Swiss Guard. The second tableau depicted the reception of Tipoo Sultan of Mysore's ambassadors in a tent pitched outside the Grand Trianon at Versailles.

CHAPTER ONE

The third group, initially installed in the Petit Trianon at Versailles, comprised a scene of King Louis XVI and Queen Marie Antoinette, seated and wearing full Court costume, with their two eldest children. These were the ill-fated Louis Joseph, Dauphin de France, who would die of neglect and tuberculosis in 1795 while imprisoned in the Temple; and Marie-Thérèse Charlotte de France, known as Madame Royale, who survived the Revolution and would later be known as the Duchesse d'Angoulême. This last group was moved to the *Théatre Curtius* in 1789 and was later exhibited at Madame Tussaud's until the fire of 1925. After the fire – as with many other 'originals' at Madame Tussaud's today – the figures in the third group were remade using the 1780s moulds. This was possible because the moulds had been stored in an outbuilding at the Marylebone Road premises, and so escaped the inferno.

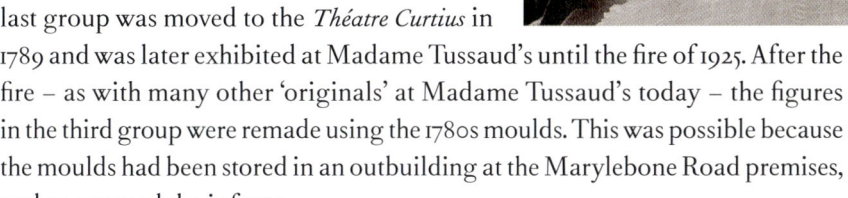

King Louis XVI and Queen Marie Antoinette (1755–1793) modelled from life by Philippe Curtius and/or Marie Grosholtz.

At some point between 1782 and 1789, Curtius closed his premises in the Palais Royal, moved the displays there to the theatre-lined Boulevard du Temple, and re-named the exhibition the *Théatre Curtius*. As the contemporary historian, Jacques-Antoine Dulaure, recorded in 1791: 'One may see [there] waxen coloured figures of celebrated characters in all stations in life'. However, those of the so-called 'friends of the people', the dissident Duc d'Orléans and the exiled, former Finance Minister, Jacques Necker, had been forcibly removed from the exhibition by the mob on 12th July 1789. These busts were paraded through the streets as heroes, as depicted in a contemporary cartoon reproduced here.

The bust of Necker was destroyed later in the day, when the rioters were routed by royalist troops in the Place Louis XV, but that of Orléans survived, albeit that a member of the Civil Guard was killed protecting it. This was the

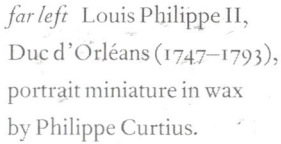

far left Louis Philippe II, Duc d'Orléans (1747–1793), portrait miniature in wax by Philippe Curtius.

left First scene of the French Revolution.
©Bridgeman Art Library

CHAPTER ONE

Storming of the Bastille prison, 14th July 1789, by Jean-Pierre Houël.

first blood of the French Revolution to be shed in Paris and occurred two days before the Storming of the Bastille on 14th July 1789, which now marks the Revolution's official start. It also marked a change in fortune for Philippe Curtius and his 'niece', Marie Grosholtz, who was still allegedly ensconced at Versailles with Madame Élizabeth.

According to Marie's *Memoirs*, realising that his 'niece' was in danger from direct association with the Royal Family, the republican-inclined Curtius ordered her return to Paris, where she arrived on the same day that the Bastille fell. What happened next is not entirely clear. What is verifiable is that Curtius joined the Army and left Paris, later becoming a member of the National Convention for which, by 1793, he was acting as an Envoy Extraordinary of the Republic, a job that took him away from the capital for months at a time.

Meanwhile, Marie and her mother were left to manage the business and, in due course, to satisfy the morbid demands of the revolutionaries. These included, during the Reign of Terror (5th September 1793 to 27th July 1794) and after, making *post-mortem* casts of many of the famous royal and other heads that had fallen into the basket of Charles-Henri Sanson's guillotine. Sanson was originally King Louis XVI's royal executioner, but he remained in office after 1789 becoming High Executioner of the First French Republic. The first public executioner to use the guillotine, during his forty-year career Sanson executed more than 3,000 people. He did not, however, have the task of decapitating Marie Thérèse Louise de Savoie, Princess de Lamballe, who was a close friend of Queen Marie Antoinette. Her head was hacked off by the mob during the September Massacre of 1792 and, along with some of her more intimate body parts, was paraded on a pike through the streets of Paris, before being sculpted in wax by Marie.

Following the Thermidorian Reaction (27th July 1794 to 2nd November 1795), which signalled the end of the Terror and the ascendancy of more moderate revolutionaries, Marie's subjects in wax included the toppled extremists Robespierre, Danton, Fouquier-Tinville, Hébert and Carrier. After Marie's death in 1850, all these casts would be exhibited in Tussaud's Chamber of Horrors in London, alongside the blade claimed to be from the very guillotine that had severed the original heads from their bodies (see Chapter 4). The royal casts were valued in 1911 at £400 (2022: £37,362) and those of the revolutionaries at £200 (2022: £18,681).

However, until the Thermidorian Reaction, Marie by her own account and despite (and, at times, because of) her 'uncle's' position in the revolutionary government, was in almost constant danger. When the Swiss Guard was massacred at the Tuileries Palace on 18th August 1792, among their number – so she claimed – were three of her half-brothers and two more of her uncles. Worse still, she

Charles-Henri Sanson (1739–1806) as imagined by Eugène Lampsonius.

CHAPTER ONE

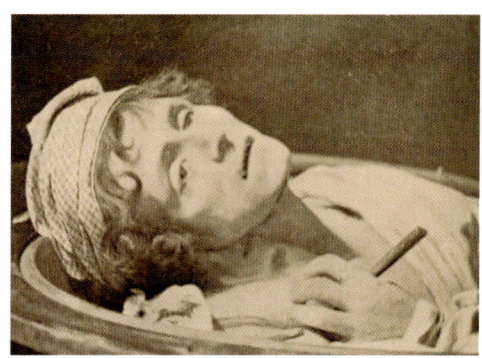

was constantly (and reluctantly) in the company of revolutionaries, whose fortunes could change overnight and whose associates would then find themselves on Sanson's list.

At the height of the Terror, and notwithstanding her works in wax for the revolutionaries, Marie's royalist past allegedly caught up with her. Although the precise dates are conveniently unrecorded, Marie asserted in her *Memoirs* that she, her mother and an unnamed aunt, were imprisoned for several months in the summer of 1794 in La Force prison, Paris, on the grounds that they were recidivist royalists. Apparently, despite her incarceration, Marie continued to model the decapitated heads of the enemies of the Revolution.

In her *Memoirs*, Marie also claimed that she shared her cell at La Force with Vicomtesse Joséphine de Beauharnais. Apparently, the future Empress 'did not give way to despondency' but 'on the contrary did all in her power to infuse life and spirit into her suffering companions, exhorting them to patience and endeavouring to cheer them up'. Joséphine was, in fact, incarcerated in Les Carmes prison. Apart from this obvious discrepancy, one of Madame de Beauharnais' fellow prisoners in Les Carmes wrote that 'far from being stoic in her captivity, she wept copiously and her emotional incontinence made her a total embarrassment'. Furthermore, as Anita Leslie & Pauline Chapman state in *Madame Tussaud, Waxworker Extraordinary* (Hutchinson, 1978), even if Marie was imprisoned it could not have exceeded more than a week as her then name, Grosholtz, does not appear on any prison records in France. If further proof of Marie's habit of playing fast and loose with the facts to suit her own ends were needed, she claimed in her *Memoirs* to have been an eye-witness to Jacques-Louis David's republican extravaganza on 8th June 1794, the Festival of the Supreme Being. Unfortunately, this conflicted with the dates of her alleged incarceration alongside Joséphine, who was not released until 28th July.

Assuming for a moment that Marie was imprisoned, and accepting her claim that she suffered the terrifying indignity of having her head shaved prior to a

above first Queen Marie Antoinette, modelled by Marie Grosholtz on 16th October 1793 immediately after the Queen's execution.

above second Maximilien Robespierre (1758–1794) a member of the Committee of Public Safety and a leading architect of the Reign of Terror. Cast by Marie Grosholtz an hour after Robespierre had been guillotined, 28th July 1794.

above third Jean-Baptiste Carrier (1756–1794), cast by Marie Grosholtz after Carrier had been guillotined, 16th December 1794;

above fourth Jean-Paul Marat (1743–1793), one of the more radical revolutionaries, was stabbed in his bath by Charlotte Corday (1768-1793). The model by Marie Grosholtz was made immediately after Marat's murder on 13th July 1793, and then put on display in the *Théatre Curtius*. Marie also made a cast of Corday's head following her execution on 17th July 1793.

CHAPTER ONE

meeting with Sanson and his machine on the Place de la Révolution (now the Place de la Concorde), at some point all three Grosholtzs were released. This, Marie asserted, was thanks to the change in revolutionary mood signalled by the Thermidorian Reaction and, so she claimed, the intervention either of the actor and revolutionary, Jean-Marie Collot d'Herbois or the revolutionary General Jean-Baptiste Kléber.

As with so much connected with Marie prior to her arrival in England in May 1802, verifiable details are (conveniently for *her* narrative) thin on the ground. However, it is known that in 1794 Philippe Curtius returned to Paris from his revolutionary-military duties and that he died on 26th September of that year at his second home at Ivry-sur-Seine. In his will, he bequeathed to his 'niece' the business of which she already had the full-time management. It is also a recorded fact that on 18th October 1795, Marie married François Tussaud, a French engineer who was her junior by seven years. The marriage was not a success and, despite producing two sons, Joseph and François, and a daughter who didn't survive infancy, the couple separated in 1800.

That, however, was not the end of François senior who, after Marie's move to England in 1802, continued to be responsible for her French properties and the residue of the collection. Although they never again met before his death in 1838, François corresponded regularly with his ex-wife, usually to demand money. When this failed to materialise, he sold off the residual Curtius collection in Paris in order to pay off his debts.

However, before any of that was to happen, at some point after 10th November 1799, when Napoléon Bonaparte was appointed First Consul and before Marie Tussaud left Paris for London, she claimed – probably incorrectly according to Kate Berridge – that she was summoned to the Tuileries Palace to sculpt the future Emperor's features in wax. The event was recorded for posterity in an interview given by Marie to the popular British women's magazine, *La Belle Assemblée or Bell's Court & Fashionable Magazine*, as quoted in John Theodore Tussaud's *The Romance of Madame Tussaud's*. Tussaud's 1921 book does not date the edition of *La Belle Assemblée* in which the article appeared, but it must have been between 1806, when the magazine was founded, and 1837 when it ceased publication. It was an interview in which Marie almost certainly deliberately included as many misleading facts as in her *Memoirs*.

However, whether or not Marie told the truth to *La Belle Assemblée*, there can be little doubt that Bonaparte knew of Madame Tussaud, or at least knew of the *Théatre Curtius*. That said, this commission – according to *La Belle Assemblée* – was placed not by Bonaparte but by Joséphine, formerly de Beauharnais, the First Consul's wife since 9th March 1796. If it was Joséphine who placed the

Vicomtesse Joséphine de Beauharnais (1763–1814) *c.*1809 by Baron Antoine Jean Gros.

[40]

CHAPTER ONE

commission, for which she would have expected a backhander, that may explain why Marie invented the fiction in her *Memoirs* of the two women being imprisoned together. In any event, arriving at 6 o'clock in the morning (Napoléon was invariably an early riser, and usually started work at 4 o'clock), Marie was, so she claimed to *La Belle Assemblée*, 'greeted with kindness [by Joséphine who] conversed much and most affably'. By contrast, the future Master of Europe 'spoke in sharp sentences and rather abruptly.'

Despite the claimed accolade of a Consular commission, and probably because of the breakdown of her marriage and her experiences in Paris since 1789, it seems that Madame Tussaud had no intention of remaining in France. For no sooner was the Treaty of Amiens signed on 27th March 1802, than she took the opportunity of peace with England to accept a business offer to exhibit some of her best pieces from the *Théatre Curtius* in Paul de Philipsthal's show at the English Opera House (now the Lyceum Theatre) in Covent Garden.

De Philipsthal, whose name appears in several different versions and whose origins are uncertain, was a pioneer of phantasmagoria or magic lantern horror shows, which purported to bring back the dead. With successful performances around Europe before the turn of the eighteenth century, particularly in Paris in the period December 1792 to July 1793, de Philipstahl achieved instant commercial success when he opened in London in October 1801, with a show that he patented the following year. Marie Tussaud's pieces, particularly her casts of decapitated revolutionaries' heads and the contents of the *Caverne des Grans Voleurs*, made a natural fit with de Philipstahl's schlock-horror presentations. She readily agreed to pay him half of her profits from ticket sales, closed the theatre in the Boulevard du Temple and, after some problems extracting exit visas from the Paris Prefect of Police – allegedly solved by an appeal to the First Consul – removed the best

Napoléon Bonaparte (1769–1821) as First Consul by Baron Antoine-Jean Gros.

Late-eighteenth century illustration of a phantasmagoria show performed by Paul de Philipstahl (*d*.1829).

CHAPTER ONE

Poster for Curtius's Grand Cabinet of Curiosities.

pieces and her four-year-old son, Joseph, to London. Once there, she adapted the name of the exhibition from *Théatre Curtius* to 'Curtius's Grand Cabinet of Curiosities'.

An examination of a British advertising poster (opposite) for the exhibition, published in the years following 1802, shows that it was an eclectic assembly of items, linked only by their curiosity value. First on the list to be described were 'Paintings, Sculptures, Engravings, [and] Drawings in Black Ink', followed by items in ivory and glass. It was only half-way down the poster that there was list of figures of the famous, and only several lines below was there any mention that they were in wax. This is not the current perception of Madame Tussaud's exhibits, but it was, in fact, the case until 1925.

Although the partnership was weighted very much in de Philipstahl's favour, Marie remained at the English Opera House until it was closed in 1803 for the installation of gas lighting. Liberated from her contract with de Philipstahl, Marie then took her show on the road. Starting in Edinburgh, over the next thirty years Curtius's Grand Cabinet of Curiosities was temporarily established in every important city or town in the United Kingdom outside London. During that time, it was apparently shipwrecked *en route* to Ireland in 1822, and nearly destroyed in the Bristol Riots of 1831; Joseph (and later his brother, François) joined the business, and the name over the door was changed from Curtius's Grand Cabinet of Curiosities to Madame Tussaud & Sons' Exhibition. Meanwhile, the collection was continuously expanded through acquisition to include many items of historical interest. It is worth noting that, during their very extended round-Britain tour, Marie and her sons were also busy with portrait commissions from the great and the good including King George III (1809), Tsar Alexander I of Russia (1814), Princess Charlotte of Wales (1816), King Leopold I of the Belgians (1817), and many others. In 1828, Marie modelled from life the serial killers, Burke and Hare, to add to her Chamber of Horrors.

CHAPTER ONE

At last, in late-1833, Madame Tussaud & Sons' Exhibition returned to London, where Marie opened its doors on 26th December in the Assembly Rooms adjoining the Royal London Bazaar in Gray's Inn Road. There the exhibition remained for fifteen months until, on 21st March 1835, it re-located to the Baker Street Bazaar (later the site of the Portman Rooms) between Blandford Street and Dorset Street. Then, in July 1884, the exhibition moved to the current site on the Marylebone Road where it has remained ever since.

The great illusionist herself died on 15th April 1850, active and myth-making almost to the end. Following her death, the business, which continued to acquire historical art and artefacts as well as creating portraits in wax of the famous and notorious, remained in the ownership of her descendants until 1889. Despite the sale of the business, the Tussaud family's direct involvement with it continued until the death of Bernard Tussaud in 1967.

William Burke (1792–1829).

William Hare (dates unknown).

Marie Tussaud in 1845, engraving after a portrait by Paul Fischer. The original was valued in 1911 at £75 (2022: £7,005), survived the 1925 fire and was valued by Sotheby's in 1983 at £500 – £700 (2022: £1,585 – £2,220).

CHAPTER TWO

FROM PHARAOHS TO THE RENAISSANCE

THE OLDEST ITEM (Item 185: Chamber of Horrors*) in the pre-fire exhibition was first recorded in a poster announcing the arrival of Madame Tussaud & Sons' Exhibition at the Royal London Bazaar in 1833:

opposite Pharaoh Senusret II (1897–1839 BC) of the Dynasty XII (1991–1802 BC).

AN EGYPTIAN MUMMY
Proved by the Hieroglyphics to be the body of the Princess of Memphis, who lived in the time of Sesostris, King of Egypt, a.m. 2528 [*sic*], 1491 years before Christ, being actually 3328 years old.

There is no explanation in any of the surviving archives as to how or when the mummified remains of an Egyptian Princess, and the sarcophagus or 'case' containing them, were acquired by Madame Tussaud's and displayed in the Chamber of Horrors, although such an acquisition would be entirely in keeping with the collection of a cabinet of curiosities.

The Mummy and Sarcophagus in the Madame Tussaud's stores at Wookey Hole in the 1980s.

Despite the evidence advanced by the hieroglyphs on the case, the legend of King Sesostris is largely the creation of the Greek historian, Herodotus, who lived and wrote some 450–425 years before the birth of Christ. According to Herodotus, who caveated the account in his *Histories* with a warning that the evidence was based on Egyptian priestly hearsay, Sesostris was a successful warrior-Pharaoh of the Twelfth Dynasty (1991–1802 BC) who conquered not only most of Asia Minor, but also made incursions into eastern Europe. However, modern research has cast doubt on the existence of Sesostris, and other assertions relating to him, and re-identifies him as a composite pharaonic figure, principally based on the life of Pharaoh Senusret III, who had three wives and several daughters including Princess Sithathor. Her empty tomb, and some jewellery that had been overlooked by the tomb robbers, was discovered in 1894.

* The various items described in the pages that follow are cross-referenced with their catalogue number and location to the last catalogue published before the 1925 fire.

The probability that Sesostris was a myth, means that the case containing

◈ CHAPTER TWO ◈

and identifying the mummy was almost certainly not genuine. The faking of Egyptian artefacts was by no means unknown in the early-nineteenth century and was the direct result of the enormous demand for pharaonic relics that followed the discoveries made by the scientists, engineers, artists and scholars who accompanied Napoléon to Egypt in 1798. Although, thanks to their location in the Chamber of Horrors, the case and its contents survived the 1925 fire and were still in Madame Tussaud's stores at Wookey Hole, Somerset, during the 1980s, their present whereabouts is currently unknown. While their authenticity remains in doubt, it is worth noting that the 1911 valuers were similarly suspicious of the 'Egyptian mummy in a case', for they were valued at only £50 (2022: £4,670).

With a more certain history was a three-quarter length 'Wax Statuette of Cleopatra Dying' (Item 131: Napoléon Room), depicted offering a naked breast to the fangs of an asp. Following the defeat of Cleopatra and her lover Mark Anthony, by the Roman General Octavian at the battle of Actium in 31 BC, and the subsequent suicide of Mark Anthony, Cleopatra took her own life on 10th August 30 BC. This was to avoid the humiliation of being paraded through the streets of Rome in a triumphal procession. That much is agreed by historians. The facts of her suicide, as recorded by contemporary chroniclers, were more prosaic than the now commonly accepted narrative. Puncture wounds were indeed found on her arm, but they could have been made by a needle or other instrument which Cleopatra used to introduce poison into her blood stream. However, the snake bite with its phallic symbology makes a better story, and one that is in keeping with the Egyptian Queen's louche reputation.

right Cleopatra VII Philopator (69–30 BC), Queen of the Ptolemaic Kingdom of Egypt. Photograph in the 1925 catalogue of the 'Wax Statuette of Cleopatra Dying'.

far right Dame Elizabeth Taylor (1932–2011), depicted as Queen Cleopatra at Madame Tussaud's in the 1960s.

CHAPTER TWO

Somewhat curiously, given the subject matter and the title 'Cleopatra Dying', this mildly erotic effigy at Madame Tussaud's was not displayed alongside the Egyptian mummy in the Chamber of Horrors, but instead was placed in the Napoléon Room in the Marylebone Street premises. This was possibly as an allusion to his scientific and archaeological activities in the land of sand in the late-1790s. But, for whatever reason it was in the Napoléon Room, the statuette of Cleopatra was actually sited next to the 'Wax Statuette of Voltaire Dying' (Items 130). As this – and its companion piece, a 'Wax Statuette of Voltaire' (Item 123) – are thought to have been sculpted by Philippe Curtius from life, it is possible that he was also the artist of the statuette of Cleopatra. That said, the 1911 insurance catalogue stated that all three were modelled by Madame Tussaud herself, and ascribed a value of £15 (2022: £1,401) to each of them.

The later wax model of Cleopatra at Madame Tussaud's was that of Elizabeth Taylor playing the eponymous role in the 1963 film, which was directed by Joseph L. Mankiewicz. Although the movie was the highest grossing epic of the decade, it was notorious for its massively over-budget production costs, the life-threatening illness of Miss Taylor during early filming, and her scandalous extra-marital affair with her co-star, Richard Burton, whom she would later marry – twice.

Even more notorious, at least historically, was the alleged murder of King Edward V and his brother, Prince Richard, Duke of York, on the order of their uncle the Lord Protector, the Duke of Gloucester, who reigned as King Richard III. Known as the Princes in the Tower, the two boys disappeared from the Tower of London where they had been imprisoned in the late summer of 1483. Their fate has never been definitively established, although in late-2021 compelling evidence was advanced that Edward V was not murdered but sent to a remote Devon village, where he lived under the pseudonym, John Evans.* Whatever the truth of their fate, since William Shakespeare's late-sixteenth-century play about the hunchbacked King Richard III, the romanticised story of the Princes' incarceration, murder and burial in the Tower of London has been the subject of innumerable interpretations on canvas, in print, on the stage and on the screen.

Not least amongst the artists who have captured the alleged events was James Northcote. His painting, *The Murder of the Princes in the Tower*, was exhibited at the Royal Academy in 1786, the year in which it was painted, and now hangs at Petworth House, West Sussex. A companion piece, *The Burial of the Princes in the Tower*, (Item 191: Chamber of Horrors) also by Northcote†, hung at Madame Tussaud's until 1925, although it was listed in the 1911 insurance catalogue as 'Murder of the Princes in the Tower', and assigned a value of £50 (2022: £4,670).

Northcote is known to have painted several versions of both paintings, which were part of a set of nine, designed to illustrate scenes from Shakespeare's plays

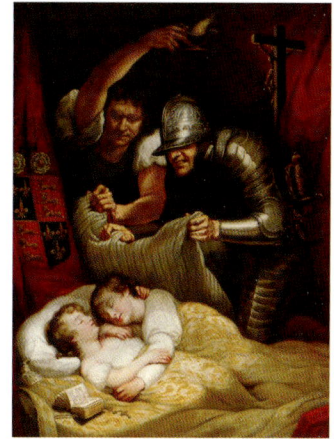

The Murder of the Princes in the Tower, King Edward V (1470–148?) and his Brother Prince Richard Duke of York (1473–148?) (from William Shakespeare's Richard III, Act IV, Scene iii) by James Northcote RA.

* Bill Gardner, 'Richard III may not have killed young Princes in the Tower of London', *Daily Telegraph*, 28th December 2021.

† Item 191 survived the 1925 fire and was valued by Sotheby's in 1983 at £1,000 – £2,000 (2022: £3,171 – £6,343).

[47]

CHAPTER TWO

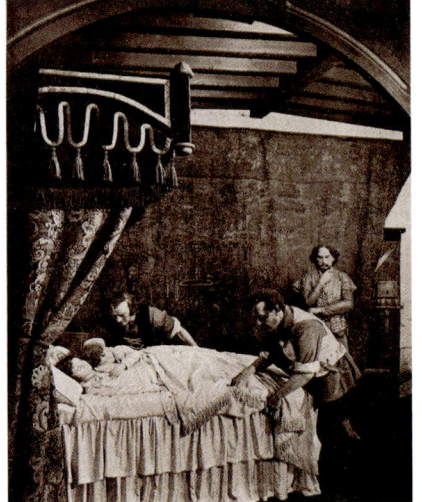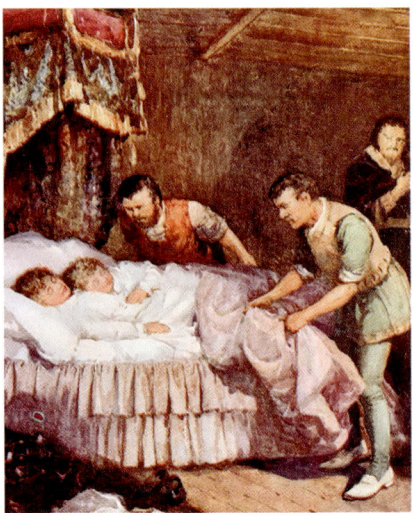

left Murder of the Princes in the Tower tableau at Madame Tussaud's, and *right*, illustration by Howard Davie from *The Palace of Enchantment*.

and destined for the short-lived Shakespeare Gallery, a project masterminded by the engraver and publisher, John Boydell. Interestingly, it is the murder rather than the burial of the Princes that was illustrated by Howard Davie in Captain Edric Vredenburgh's 1920 guidebook to Madame Tussaud's, *The Palace of Enchantment*, which was obviously based on the tableau of figures then on display.

To muddy further the water, the title of Item 191 in the exhibition catalogue was 'The Burial of the Princes in the Tower', but the catalogue description of the painting referred to the 'brutal murder' not the burial. As there was no photograph or illustration in the catalogue, and the painting was lost, sold or more probably destroyed in the 1925 fire, it is impossible to be sure now which painting hung at Madame Tussaud's.

When it comes to antiques, antiquities and other works of art, provenance – particularly a royal provenance – is a key ingredient in valuation. This is true even where the provenance derives from a relatively minor member of the Royal Family, such as the sixth son of King George III, Prince Augustus Frederick, Duke of Sussex. The only one of his brothers not to pursue a military or naval career, in later life Sussex had the distinction of being Queen Victoria's favourite uncle. This was despite having twice married a non-royal bride, on both occasions without the consent of the sovereign and so in contravention of the Royal Marriages Act 1772. Sussex's other principal distinction was his liberal political outlook, which included being a vociferous supporter of Napoléon (particularly during the former Emperor's exile on St Helena), and arguing for the reform of parliament, the abolition of the slave trade, Catholic Emancipation and the ending of civil restrictions on Jews and Dissenters.

A dedicated Freemason and Grand Master of the United Grand Lodge of

HRH Prince Frederick Augustus, Duke of Sussex (1773–1843), dated 1798, by Guy Head.

CHAPTER TWO

England, despite being relatively poor Sussex was also an avid collector, particularly of Napoléonica; he had acquired 50,000 theological manuscripts by the time of his death. With little cash to leave to his surviving wife, and the children from his first marriage, his extensive collection of historical ephemera, paintings, miniatures, furniture, clocks, watches, and gold and silver plate, was sold at six auctions in 1843 by Messrs Christie & Manson; the Prince's vast library was auctioned the following year by Messrs Evans of Pall Mall. Buyers at the Christie's sales included Madame Tussaud's sons, who acquired – amongst many items of royal and other interest, to be described later – a piece of the 'Cloth of Gold', which was somewhat incongruously displayed in the Napoléon Ante-Room as Item 165.

Eleven years into his reign, and still married to Catherine of Aragon, King Henry VIII commanded his Chancellor, Cardinal Wolsey, to organise what today would be called a summit with King Francis I of France. Its advertised purpose, as so often before and since, was to strengthen the 'bonds of friendship' between the two perennially rival nations. The seventeen-day event was staged, with considerable magnificence, at Balinghem, near Calais, which was sited conveniently between the crown lands in France of Henry and Francis.

In addition to regal negotiations, the programme included French- and English-hosted feasts, music, jousts and games, which competed with each other for extravagance. These events were set in and around a temporary camp, comprising a French complex featuring a vast royal tent made from cloth of gold, and a British enclave that included a *faux* castle made of wood and painted to look like brick-and-stone. To enhance the spectacle, the principals and their courtiers wore elaborate silk and damask costumes, heavily embroidered with

King Henry VIII (1491–1547) *c.* 1530 by Joos van Cleve.

King Francis I of France (1494–1547) *c.* 1530 by Jean Clouet.

left The Field of the Cloth of Gold, 1520.

CHAPTER TWO

The Court for the Trial of Queen Katharine by George Henry Harlow, John Philip Kemble (1757–1823) as Cardinal Wolsey is on the left of the picture.

gold and silver thread. The combination of all this bling led to the summit ever after being labelled 'The Field of the Cloth of Gold'.

From the Christie & Manson sale catalogue, Lot 925 of the sale on Monday 3rd July 1843, it is clear that the item acquired by the Tussauds at the auction of the Sussex Collection was a fragment of tentage, being described in the 1925 exhibition catalogue as 'Piece of the "Cloth of Gold"' (Item 165: Napoléon Ante-Room). Valued in 1911 at £50 (2022: £4,670), the fragment went up in smoke in 1925, as did a ring, listed under 'Miscellaneous Relics' (Item 155: Napoléon Ante-Room), and in the same case the 'Cross and Shoes' worn by the actor, John Philip Kemble, in his portrayal of Cardinal Wolsey in Shakespeare's *Henry VIII*, as depicted by George Henry Harlow in *The Court for the Trial of Queen Katherine*, painted in 1817. The ring was given a rather elevated value of £15 (2022: £1,401) in the 1911 insurance catalogue, but the 'Cross and Shoes' were assessed at only £10 (2022: £934). Kemble was also celebrated for playing the lead in Shakespeare's *Richard III*, giving him – if not the ring, cross and shoes – another connection to Madame Tussaud's.

Displayed with the ring, as part of Item 155 in the Napoléon Ante-Room was a chemise or undershirt worn by Henry VIII's second daughter, Queen Elizabeth I. None of the published catalogues or books about the exhibition, nor the Madame Tussaud archives, provide any further information about this item of clothing or its provenance. Nor was it in any of the Sussex Collection auctions, although the Queen's prayer book was the last lot in the sale on 3rd July 1843.

During her lifetime, Elizabeth was known to give away her clothes as gifts, or *in lieu* of payment for services rendered; she also used her extensive wardrobe to advertise her status. When she died in 1603 there were more than 2,000 gowns in the royal closet. Despite this, only one fragment of a dress has survived, now incorporated into the Bacton Altar Cloth, although several of her fashion accessories, such as gloves and shoes but *not* a chemise, are in British royal, national and private collections. If the chemise was genuine, and had survived the fire, it would today be of enormous interest and worth. For some reason, this unique garment only attracted a value of £10 (2022: £934) in the 1911 insurance catalogue.

Queen Elizabeth I (1533–1603) c.1600, wearing a dress very similar to the one later made into the Bacton Altar Cloth, formerly attributed to Marcus Gheeraerts the Younger and/or Isaac Oliver.

Elizabeth I's greatest political rival was her first-cousin-once-removed, Mary, Queen of Scots, whose botched execution was the subject of one of Madame Tussaud's more dramatic tableaux in the Chamber of Horrors. For Mary was not beheaded cleanly with a single stroke; instead, the first blow struck the back of her head, and the second only part-severed her neck. The inept executioner then had to cut through the remaining sinew, using the axe as a knife. Once the head was detached, he picked up the grisly trophy by the hair and held it aloft with the words: 'God Save the Queen.' At that moment, Mary's red locks (of

CHAPTER TWO

far left Mary I of Scotland, aka Mary Queen of Scots (1542–1587) by François Clouet, painted c.1558–60. Mary's great uncle was Elizabeth's father, King Henry VIII.

left Madame Tussaud's tableau of the Execution of Mary Queen of Scots at Fotheringhay Castle, 8th February 1587.

which the bald Queen Elizabeth was reputed to be inordinately jealous) turned out to be a wig, and the decapitated head fell with a thud onto the wooden scaffold, revealing that the late Scottish Queen was as folically challenged as her English rival. To add to the macabre situation, an eyewitness reported that Mary's lips moved for a quarter of an hour after her head was cut off, and that her dog emerged from hiding under her skirt.

Items supposedly worn or carried by Mary at her execution are of doubtful provenance, as contemporary accounts state that all her clothing, the block, and everything touched by her blood was burnt in the fireplace of the Great Hall at Fotheringhay Castle. This was done to prevent them becoming icons of her martyrdom. Nonetheless, Madame Tussaud's claimed to have both the rosary Mary carried to the scaffold in the Great Hall (Item 23: Grand Saloon), and an earlier piece of embroidery worked by her and described as a 'toilette cover', part of the 'Miscellaneous Relics' numbered Item 155 in the Napoléon Ante-Room. In 1911 they were valued together at £100 (2022: £9,340); they were exhibited in the Scots Group in the Grand Saloon up until 1925, although whether or not the rosary was genuine will now never be known.

The Scots Group tableau at Madame Tussaud's in 1925, including Mary Queen of Scots' rosary (in her left hand) and her embroidery (under the glass dome).

In 1558 the Catholic Mary Queen of Scots married the Dauphin of France, who briefly reigned as King Francis II from 1559 until his death in 1560. She was thus related by marriage to the Protestant King Henri IV of France, who in 1589 inherited the French throne from his cousin, King Henri III, who was himself a younger brother of the Scots Queen's short-lived husband. Although this may sound like a tenuous royal family connection, it was of real political significance at the time, given the struggle for religious supremacy between Catholics and Protestants that was being waged on both sides of the Channel.

In order to end the French Wars of Religion, Henri IV converted to Catholicism in 1589, four years into his reign, cynically remarking that 'Paris is well worth a

King Henri IV (1553–1610) by Frans Pourbus the Younger.

[51]

CHAPTER TWO

above François Ravaillac (1578–1610), brandishing the dagger with which he killed King Henri IV, engraving by Crispin de Passe.

above middle Assassination of Henri IV, engraving by Gaspar Bouttats.

above right Execution of a regicide in the Place de Grève (an engraving of the execution on 28th March 1757 of Robert-François Damiens, who had attempted to assassinate King Louis XV).

* D'Epernon wasn't privy to the plot, and he wasn't in the coach either.

Mass'. Then in 1598 he promulgated the Edict of Nantes, which granted freedom of conscience to individuals, thereby giving civil and religious liberty to the French Protestants, known as Huguenots. This religious tolerance, combined with accusations of apostasy (by the Protestants) and usurpation of the crown (by the Catholics), gave both sides of the religious divide in France reasons to plot his death. In total, there were at least twelve assassination attempts, the last of which succeeded on 14th May 1610.

There are differing accounts of his murder but, as Henri's pierced and bloodstained shirt was a prized Tussaud exhibit, and listed as 'Shirt of Henri IV. of France' (Item 137: Napoléon Room), the occasionally inaccurate account in the catalogue will be used in an abbreviated form here:

Following the Coronation of Henri's second wife, Marie de Medici, on 13th May [*sic*] 1610, Henri announced his intention of driving to the Tuileries [Palace] and [despite very crowded streets] sallied forth accompanied by the Duc d'Epernon, who is suspected of having been privy to [the assassination plot]*…the carriage was brought to a standstill by a block in a narrow street [rue de la Ferronnerie]…the assassin, [François] Ravaillac by name, a crazy fanatic, sprang upon the wheel and drove his dagger into the King's body. Henri threw up his arms, exclaiming 'I am wounded! It is nothing!' But as he spoke, the murderer struck a second and then a third blow, and with a groan his victim fell back in his carriage and ceased to breathe.

Saved from lynching by the mob, Ravaillac was taken first to the Hôtel de Retz in the rue Charlot, then transferred to the Conciergerie prison, where he was interrogated in an attempt to find out if he had any accomplices. Despite the infliction of brutal but unspecified tortures, Ravaillac resolutely maintained that he had acted alone. The Tussaud catalogue, which includes a photograph of a framed shirt, then stated that he was found guilty of regicide and 'condemned to death with the most dreadful tortures'. On 27th May, stripped naked and brandishing a lighted candle, Ravaillac was taken in a tumbril from the Conciergerie prison to his public execution on a scaffold in the Place de Grève (now the Place

[52]

CHAPTER TWO

de l'Hôtel de Ville). There, the hand with which he had committed the crime was successively scalded with burning sulphur, molten lead, boiling oil, and boiling resin, presumably in an act of ritual cleaning of the offending limb. Gobbets of his flesh were then torn off him with pincers, before he was briefly hanged, swiftly emasculated, painfully eviscerated and finally pulled apart (after several attempts) by four horses. From start to finish it took two-and-a-half hours for Ravaillac to die. Once dead, his component parts were burned to a cinder and the ashes scattered.

This, readers will be relieved to learn, was a punishment reserved for regicides until 1791, when it was replaced by simple decapitation with the guillotine. Nonetheless, capital punishment remained a public spectacle in France until 1939, and the last execution by guillotine took place in 1977. In England such spectacles ended in 1868. *Vive la différence.*

Fortunately, while drawing a veil over the details of Ravaillac's end, the catalogue recorded that this royal *memento mori* was purchased by Madame Tussaud's 'uncle', Philippe Curtius, 'at the sale of the collection of the great Cardinal Mazarin'. When he died on 9th March 1661, Cardinal Mazarin's vast collection of fine art included 858 paintings, 128 statues, 185 portrait busts, 150 carpets, 514 pieces of jewellery and silver, 317 precious stones, and a number of historical 'curiosities', including the blood-stained shirt of King Henri IV. This enormous collection, with the exception of the famous Mazarin diamonds bequeathed to King Louis XIV, was left to two of the Cardinal's seven nieces, known collectively as the *Mazarinettes*. One of these was Hortense Mancini, the bi-sexual mistress of 'the Merrie Monarch', King Charles II, who was later created Duchesse Mazarin in her own right.

In the eighteenth century, much of Mazarin's collection was sold at eighteen separate auctions. The first such sale comprised pictures, drawings and bronzes belonging, through inheritance, to the Duc de Valentinois; these were auctioned in London on 26th-28th February 1765. The second was a sale of gems, porcelain, sculptures and furniture belonging to the sartorially-extravagant and impoverished-by-gambling Louise d'Aumont, Duchesse Mazarin; they were sold in Paris on 10th-15th December 1781. The last sale, also of Mazarin collection items belonging to the spendthrift Duchess, comprised porcelain, furniture and 'curiosities', which were auctioned in Paris on 27th-28th July 1784. This auction was held only a year after Curtius had opened the *Caverne des Grands Voleurs* at his museum in the Boulevard du Temple, and the shirt would certainly have been a major attraction in his nascent Chamber of Horrors.

What remains unclear, however, is how the shirt of the murdered King Henri IV came into Mazarin's collection in the first place. What follows is a possible,

Cardinal Jules Mazarin (1602–1661) by Simon Vouet.

Louise d'Aumont, Duchesse Mazarin (1759–1826) by Antoine Vestier.

[53]

CHAPTER TWO

above Laura Mancini, Duchesse de Mercoeur (1636–1657), circle of Louis Ferdinand Elle the Elder.

above right Louis de Bourbon, Duc de Mercoeur (1612–1669) by Daniel Dumonstier, 1630.

King Charles X (1757–1836) by François Gérard, 1825.

but unverifiable explanation. One of the Cardinal's aforementioned seven nieces was Laura Mancini, who was married to Louis de Bourbon, a grandson of King Henri IV. Although Laura pre-deceased her uncle, Mazarin could have bought the blood-stained shirt from her husband. However it was acquired, the Tussaud Catalogue goes on to state:

> When Madame Tussaud was visiting Edinburgh during the early years of her sojourn in this country, the French Prince who afterwards became Charles X of France showed much anxiety to possess himself of the venerable relic, and made many offers to its owner to induce her to sell it, but she resolutely refused to part with it, and it has remained the property of her and her descendants ever since.

From his arrival in the United Kingdom in 1792, until his move to London in 1805, the exiled Charles (then known as the Comte d'Artois) lived at the Palace of Holyrood in Edinburgh – and Madame Tussaud was in Edinburgh in 1803. Charles was already in possession of other items of clothing worn by Henri IV on the fateful day, and it seems unlikely that the exiled Frenchman would have made 'many offers' to buy a fake. Elaborately framed, what was almost certainly a genuine relic of the ill-fated seventeenth-century French King hung in the equally ill-fated Napoléon Room at Madame Tussaud's. The price paid by Curtius for the bloody shirt is not recorded, but in 1911 it was valued at £1,000 (2022: £93,407). Had it survived, its present-day value is incalculable.

On the face of it, Item 40 in the Grand Saloon, which was listed as 'Picture by Rubens', would also have been extremely valuable had it survived. As evidence of this, *Lot & His Daughters* by Rubens sold at Sotheby's in 2016 for US$58 million (2022: £47 million), and a small drawing from the artist's notebook was valued in 2020 at a price in excess of £600,000. However, although there was a brief biography of the Flemish artist in the catalogue, there was neither an image nor a description of the listed work. This lacuna was filled by the 1911 insurance catalogue, which stated that Item 40 was 'a large painting' and that the subject was *The Coming Storm*. Rubens painted several storm scenes, but none of them has that title; the nearest subject is *A Storm*, which now hangs in the Ashmolean Museum in Oxford. Sadly, although the exhibition catalogue gave the impression that the painting was a valuable work by the seventeenth-century master, the

CHAPTER TWO

A Storm c.1620 by Sir Peter Paul Rubens.

insurance catalogue unequivocally stated that the picture was a 'studio copy' worth only £50 (2022: £4,670). Despite this disappointment, the Rubens copy provides a link with the next chapter, for the artist was commissioned in 1629 by King Charles I to commemorate his father, King James I, the first Stuart to sit on the English throne. The completed commission included an apotheosis of the deceased monarch that formed the central ceiling panel of the newly-constructed Banqueting House at the Palace of Whitehall.

CHAPTER THREE

STUART SOVEREIGNS & FRENCH FAKES

WHEN THE UNMARRIED and childless Queen Elizabeth I died on 24th March 1603, she left no direct heir to the English and Irish thrones. The most obvious, but by no means the only claimant, was King James VI of Scotland, the son of Mary, Queen of Scots, and her second husband, Henry Stuart, Lord Danley. Both Mary and Henry were grand-children of Margaret Tudor, King James IV of Scotland's consort and sister of King Henry VIII.

Whatever the merits of King James VI of Scotland's claim to the crown of England, he doesn't seem to have appealed to Marie Tussaud for there were no relics of England's first Stuart monarch in the collection. There are two possible explanations for this. Either no relics were available, or Madame Tussaud was not attracted to the bi-sexual King, who – on account of his over-large tongue – had the unfortunate habit of slobbering when he spoke. However, the more romantic figures of James's son, King Charles I, and grandsons, Kings Charles II and James II, were represented, while – not unsurprisingly for an unreconstructed monarchist like Marie Tussaud – relics of Charles I's nemesis, Oliver Cromwell were absent.

That said, Cromwell merited an extensive entry in the 1925 catalogue in connection with 'The Duchess of Braganza, by Sir Peter Lely' (Item 9: Hall of Kings). Having stated, correctly, the Dutch-born artist's popularity with both Royalists and Parliamentarians, following his arrival in England in the 1640s, including a commission to paint a portrait of King Charles I, the catalogue asserts that:

> ... after the execution of that monarch he was commissioned to paint one of Oliver Cromwell, who addressed him with the exhortation which has so often been quoted. 'Mr Lely,' said the Lord Protector, 'I desire you will use all your skill to paint my picture truly like me, and not flatter me at all; but remark all those roughnesses,

opposite King James VI of Scotland and I of England (1566–1625) by John de Critz.

Oliver Cromwell (1599–1658) by Sir Peter Lely.

CHAPTER THREE

King Charles II (1630–1685) by Sir Peter Lely.

Queen Anne (1665–1714) by Sir Peter Lely, painted *c.*1667–8 when Anne was 3 years old and still a Princess.

pimples, warts, and everything as you see me, otherwise I will never pay you a farthing for it.'

Following the Restoration of the monarchy in 1660, King Charles II appointed Lely as his Principal Painter-in-Ordinary and later knighted him in 1679. According to the 1925 catalogue, Item 9, which was included for its 'artistic' rather than its historical merit, represented a little-known wife of 'a member of the royal house of Portugal – Constantine, Duke of Braganza, for some time Viceroy of the Indies'. Constantine was indeed Viceroy of Portuguese India from 1558 to 1561, and died in 1575. However, if the picture really was by Lely, and the sitter's identity was as listed, it is much more likely that it depicted not the wife of Viceroy Constantine but Luisa de Guzmán, Duchess of Braganza. She was the Queen Consort of King John IV (the first Braganza monarch of Portugal), and mother of Catherine of Braganza, who married King Charles II in 1662. To further complicate matters, the 1911 insurance catalogue, while confirming the attribution of Item 9 to Lely and valuing it at a modest £200 (2022: £18,681), asserted that it was of Queen Anne rather than 'the Duchess of Braganza', as listed in the exhibition catalogue.

Queen Anne was painted at least twice by Lely as a young Princess, but he had been dead for twenty-two years when she ascended the thrones of England, Scotland and Ireland in 1702. Given the foregoing, the 1911 insurance catalogue's identification of the sitter must be questionable – unless 'Queen Anne' was depicted in Item 9 as a young Princess – and the value given to the picture would seem to indicate some doubt on the valuer's part as to the artist. Despite all of this, the exhibition catalogue stated that 'competent judges' had appraised Item 9 'to be one of [Lely's] happiest efforts'. As it no longer exists, there is no way of judging this somewhat implausible encomium, nor of verifying either the artist or the sitter.

Returning to Charles I. In the wake of his defeat by the Parliamentarians he was put on trial for his life. The proceedings at the High Court of Justice, sitting in Westminster Hall, London, lasted from 20th to 27th January 1649, at the end of which the Court found the King guilty of attempting to 'uphold in himself an unlimited and tyrannical power to rule according to his will, and to overthrow the rights and liberties of the people'. He was then sentenced to death. The legitimacy of the trial, which Charles refused to acknowledge and at which he declined to plea, has been debated ever since. Whatever the trial's merits, or otherwise, on the 28th January the King was moved from the Palace of Whitehall to St James's Palace, while a scaffold was built outside the Banqueting House on Whitehall.

CHAPTER THREE

Early on the morning of 30th, the day scheduled for his execution, Charles rose early and dressed in a black doublet, waistcoat, breeches, stockings, shoes, gloves, cloak and hat, with the Lesser George of the Order of the Garter hanging around his neck from a blue ribband. Although not recorded by eyewitnesses, all the pictures of the King's dress on that day (and at other times) depict him wearing a large white lace collar over his doublet. Thus dressed, at 10 am he walked under armed guard to the Palace of Whitehall. There, having experienced the bitter cold of the day as he crossed St James's Park and so as not to shiver on the scaffold and be thought a coward, he added to his outfit a knitted silk overshirt or waistcoat. Some accounts say it was an undershirt or second shirt but, under the circumstances, this seems unlikely.

A last-minute problem with finding an executioner meant that the execution itself was delayed to 2 pm, but eventually the King stepped out onto the scaffold where – according to an eyewitness account – he took off his cloak and doublet, and encased his long hair in a night cap, leaving the back of his neck bare to the blade of the axe. Neither this, nor any other account, states that he also took off his lace collar, but this would seem likely, given the need to bare his neck from the nape to the shoulder. After making a short speech, and instructing the executioner to wait for his signal, he lay down almost prone on the scaffold, with his neck resting on the abnormally low block. Shortly after, he gave the pre-agreed sign and was decapitated with a single blow.

Immediately after his execution, Charles's body was placed in a coffin and taken to a room in Whitehall Palace. There it was embalmed, during which the head was sewn back on and the clothing he had worn on the scaffold was distributed to some of the people present. The knitted silk waistcoat was given to the King's Physician-in-Waiting, Dr Hobbs; his gloves to the former Bishop of London,

King Charles I (1600–1649) by Sir Anthony van Dyck, painted c.1635–37.

The Execution of King Charles I.

[59]

CHAPTER THREE

The overshirt or waistcoat worn by Charles I at his execution, now in the Museum of London.

William Juxon, who had by royal request given his sovereign the last rites; and the cloak was handed to the monarch's valet, Mr Herbert. The waistcoat and the cloak are now in the Museum of London and the gloves are in the Lambeth Palace Library. A bloodstained handkerchief bearing King Charles I's monogram was sold to a private buyer at auction in 2008 for £3,700.

However, the existence of items whose provenance is unquestioned is no proof that a 'Piece of Cravat worn by Charles I on the morning of his execution' (Item 22: Grand Saloon) was genuine. For a start, cravats were not in fashion at the time of the King's execution, and ruffs had fallen out of use to be replaced with wide lace collars known as bands. Describing the relic as a 'cravat' may, of course, have been a cataloguing error rather than a mis-attribution, but was it the genuine article? Probably not. This is because, within months of the execution, there were numerous 'relics' of the scaffold and the King's clothing circulating, and the cult status of the martyred monarch in subsequent decades only increased their proliferation. Rather like fragments of the 'true Cross', the number of such items greatly exceeded the originals. Failing an account of how and when it came into the collection at Madame Tussaud's, it is reasonable to assume that the 'cravat' was a fake. Despite this, the 1911 insurance catalogue that gave it a rather low value of £2 (2022: £2,335).

Less doubtful was 'a piece of the curtain from [the King's] State bed', listed under 'Stuart Relics' (Item 65: Napoléon Room), although which of his beds was not stated. It was not uncommon during this period for State beds and other furniture to be given to, or acquired by, courtiers as perquisites. This was the custom, which lasted well into the nineteenth century, by which certain Officers of the Royal Household had the right to claim old or unwanted furniture from the palaces. Knole in Kent, the ancestral home of the Sackville family, has three State beds from the Stuart period.

Following the execution of the King Charles I in 1649, most of his possessions, including his priceless collection of paintings, were sold, looted, or given away. However, according to Dr Olivia Fryman, much of the furniture from the Palace of Whitehall was returned to his son, King Charles II, at the Restoration, presumably by those wanting to curry favour with the restored monarch. It is possible that this scrap of curtain was part of a perquisite or a State bed that was not returned at the Restoration,

King James II's State bed at Knole.

CHAPTER THREE

but without the provenance or the piece, it is impossible to know. The valuers in 1911 were more sceptical, valuing the scrap at a mere £5 (2022: £467).

After the embalming, the late-King's coffin was transferred by boat to Windsor where a private funeral service in St George's Chapel was held on 9th February 1649. The casket was then placed in a small vault beneath the chapel, alongside the coffins of King Henry VIII and his third wife, Jane Seymour. The vault was then bricked up and, over the years, its location was forgotten. The King's final resting place remained lost until April 1813, when workmen engaged in creating a new royal vault under the chapel, accidentally made an opening in a passage wall. Behind the fallen bricks they saw three coffins, one of which was covered with a black velvet pall.

The vault beneath St George's Chapel with King Charles I's coffin on the left. Illustration made after the tomb was opened.

The Prince Regent (later King George IV) was told of the discovery and assembled a group to make an examination of the contents of the vault. This party included the Duke of Cumberland, the Dean of Windsor, and Sir William Halford Bt (the Prince Regent's Physician-in-Ordinary). Once they were inside the vault, the velvet pall was removed to reveal a plain lead coffin inscribed with the name of King Charles I and the year of his death. A hole was then cut in the lid to reveal a further piece of fabric, beneath which was the perfectly preserved, long oval-shaped face with a pointed beard of the martyred King. To make sure of the identification, the Prince Regent commanded that the preserved head be removed from the coffin, to prove that it had been separated 'by a heavy blow, inflicted with a very sharp instrument'. Once this had been established, it was then replaced and the coffin was soldered up, but not before Sir Henry Halford had retained the severed fourth cervical vertebra, a tooth and some hair from Charles I's beard.

In 1888, these relics were returned by Sir Henry's grandson to the Royal Family and re-interred with the coffin. For those interested in a full account of this – at times – bizarre saga, it is worth reading C E Newman's article, *The Fourth Cervical Vertebra of Charles I* (PubMed, October 1979). In his piece, Newman dismisses the story that Sir Henry would show the relic to his dinner guests, without adding that other sources allege that the royal physician had, for that purpose, had the severed vertebra set in the base of a gold-mounted crystal salt cellar. Although most of these stories are almost certainly apocryphal, they may account for the existence of another piece of what is believed to be Charles I's neck bone.

Salt Cellar at Fort Paull Museum, Hull.

[61]

CHAPTER THREE

King Charles II (1630–1685), as an infant in 1630, attributed to Justus van Egmont.

As can be seen in the image here, this vertebra had been used as a salt cellar and was on display in the Fort Paull Museum, Hull, until it closed, and the Fort's contents were auctioned in 2020. The royal relic sold for £1,000 to an unknown buyer, which may indicate that its provenance was doubtful for two reasons: first, as can be seen clearly in the image, Fort Paull's relic is an intact vertebra; second, that there is no evidence that Sir Henry parted with either piece of Charles I's severed neck bone prior to their return to the Royal Family, along with the King's tooth and beard hair.

Charles II was slightly better represented in the Napoléon Room than his father, albeit that the description in the 1925 catalogue of his personal effects amounted to just a line stating that Item 65 included (unspecified) clothing worn during the King's infancy, and a 'horn book'. The 1911 insurance catalogue was more informative and stated that there were 'seven items of baby clothing worn by King Charles II', which were given a value of £75 (2022: £7,005); the horn book – 'in a case' but without any further description – was valued at £15 (2022: £1,401).

Mementos of the Merry Monarch's mistress, the orange-seller-turned-actress, Nell Gwynne, merited their own catalogue entry under 'Nell Gwynne Statuettes' (Item 64: Napoléon Room), and a somewhat longer and rather inaccurate entry:

> One of these curious little wax models is said to show Nell Gwynne, the light-hearted, good-natured mistress of Charles II, singing in opera, and the other, a little to the right, to represent her at an earlier stage of her strange career, when she hawked fruit and flowers, and even fish, in the streets. It is difficult, however, to believe that an artist capable of such admirable work as this could have done so little justice to the charms of 'pretty, witty Nell'.

This last comment would seem to indicate that the statuettes were not the work of a Tussaud wax-modeller. The quote was a reference to Samuel Pepys' opinion of the actress, as noted in his diary entry for Monday 3rd April 1665, made after seeing her on the stage. Nell, who had been brought up in a brothel, started selling oranges to the audience at the King's House (later the Theatre Royal, Drury Lane, London) at the age of twelve. Two years later she was treading the boards there as a bit-part player. Within a year she was taking leading roles, while sharing her off-stage favours with a series of men, including the actor Charles Hart and Charles Sackville, Lord Buckhurst, a Court wit and gentleman of the Bedchamber to the King. By 1668, she was in what would prove to be a long-term relationship with the King himself, referring to him jokingly as her 'Charles the Third'.

Alone among his mistresses, Nell never sought either to influence Charles politically or to acquire great rank for herself, but she did achieve a title for her

CHAPTER THREE

eldest son, Charles Beauclerk. He was created Earl of Burford in 1676 and later Duke of St Albans in 1684. There are differing accounts of his ennoblement. One asserts that one day at Court the King asked to see their eldest son, who was playing in a corner. 'Come hither, you little bastard!' Nell cried. When the King protested, she replied: 'But Your Majesty has given me no other name to call him by.' In response, Charles created him Earl of Burford. Another less likely tale states that Nell held her six-year-old son out of a window of her house, as the King approached, and threatened to drop him unless he was given a peerage. Charles supposedly cried out: 'God save the Earl of Burford!' and thereby created that peerage.

Always popular with the public, in contrast to Charles's mistress and Louis XIV's secret agent, Louise de Kérouaille, Duchess of Portsmouth (who the English King called 'Fubbs' on account of her *embonpoint*), Nell was famed for her wit. Many examples of this were recorded by her contemporaries, including an incident in Oxford in 1681, which appears in the *Mémoires* of Comte Philibert de Gramont. According to him, as Nell's carriage trundled through the city, it was jeered by the mob, who thought it contained the hated Louise. 'Pray, good people,' Nell said smiling, as she put her head out of the window, 'you are mistaken; I am the *Protestant* whore!'

King Charles II died in 1685, followed two years later by Nell, who died on 14th November 1687 after suffering two syphilitic strokes. She was just thirty-seven years old. In the interim, King James II, obeying his brother's dying wish to 'let not poor Nelly starve', helped to discharge her debts and granted Nell an annual pension of £1,500 (2022: £317,000). This was generous, given that James undoubtedly knew that she referred to him as 'dismal Jimmie'.

According to the 1925 catalogue, only one item associated with or belonging to the last and dismal Stuart King of England was on display at Madame Tussaud's. This was a snuff box (Item 88: Napoléon Room) that was part of the Sussex Collection already referred to in Chapter 2. Although there is no description in the 1925 catalogue, it was listed by Christie & Manson (Lot 924 of the sale on Monday 3rd July 1843) as 'of silver and mother-o'-pearl, with a letter stating the history and authenticity of the box'. The 1911 insurance catalogue assigned to it a value of £20 (2022: £1,868), which seems modest; it also listed, 'at the foot of the stairs to the Bazaar'

King James II (1618–1701), school of Sir Peter Lely.

[63]

Nell Gwynne (1650–1687) as Venus, by Sir Peter Lely.

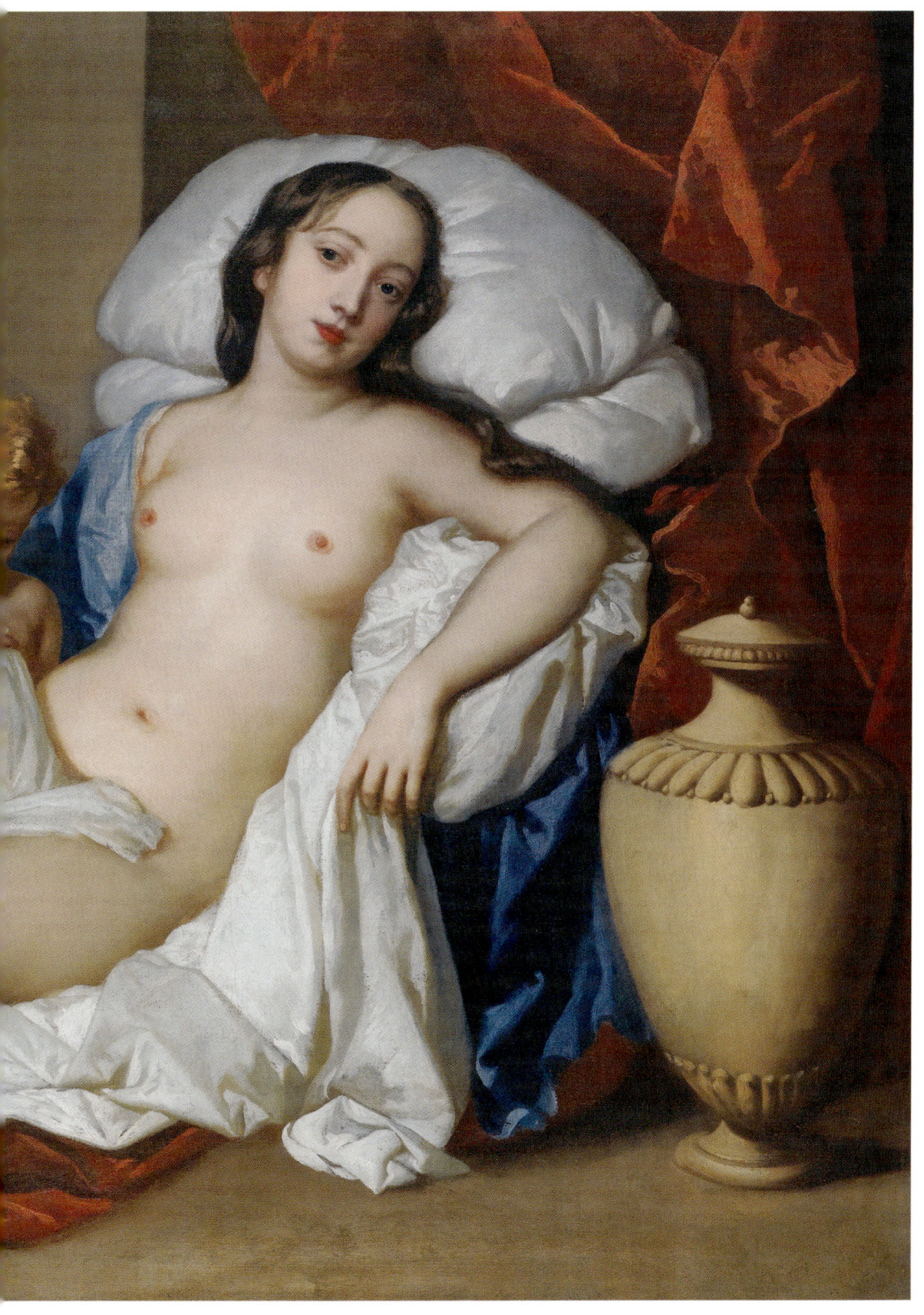

CHAPTER THREE

above Equestrian portrait of King Louis XIV of France (1638–1715) by Charles Le Brun.

above right Equestrian portrait of Queen Christina of Sweden (1626–1689) by Sébastien Bourdon.

a 'Full-length Portrait of James II by Sir G Kneller', with a value of £200 (2022: £18,681). Why it was not included in the 1925 catalogue, if it was indeed by Kneller, is just another Madame Tussaud mystery.

Even less is known about the large equestrian portrait of Charles II's brother-in-law and Louise de Kérouaille's paymaster, King Louis XIV of France, also known as the 'Sun King'. It was listed in the exhibition catalogue as 'Louis XIV of France' (Item 10: Hall of Kings), valued without an artistic attribution in 1911 at £200 (2022: £18,681), and hung beneath three ceiling panels. These were allegedly by the Baroque artist and muralist, Sir James Thornhill, who had decorated the dome of St Paul's Cathedral, the Painted Hall at the Royal Hospital, Greenwich, and the ceiling of the Great Hall at Blenheim Palace, Oxfordshire. Described in the exhibition catalogue as *Venus in a Wood*, *The Death of a Warrior* and *The Feast of Bacchus*, in the 1911 insurance catalogue they were identified as six (not three) 'mythological and bacchanalian subjects' with a value of £250 (2022: £23,351).

Meanwhile, the exhibition catalogue described the painting of Louis XIV as 'a striking equestrian portrait' and attributed it to Sébastien Bourdon, a painter without his own recognisable style who was, until recently, regarded by art historians as a *pasticheur* or imitator. Despite this, Bourdon was a founding member the French Royal Academy of Painting & Sculpture in 1648 and is

[66]

CHAPTER THREE

credited with the magnificent 1643 *Crucifixion of St Peter* that was commissioned in 1643 for the chapel of Sainte Geneviève within Notre-Dame Cathedral in Paris. Despite these attributes, no record exists of Bourdon having painted King Louis XIV on or off a horse. In 1652, as a Protestant, Bourdon fled to Sweden where Queen Christina appointed him as her first Court Painter, an appointment that he held until 1654. While there, he painted the equestrian portrait of the Queen now in the Prado, Madrid.

Although Bourdon returned to France in the mid-1650s, and perhaps due to his religion, the only royal commission he received – the decoration of the ceiling of the King's bedroom in the Tuileries palace – was barely started when he died in 1671. Given Bourdon's reputation for copying other artists' styles, the Tussaud catalogue attribution may have been correct, or the painting might have been a later copy of a work by a well-known artist, such as Charles Le Brun. Whoever was the artist of the portrait of the Sun King, it was valued in 1911, without an artistic attribution, exhibition at £300 (2022: £28,022).

Slightly less problematic, as to attribution and authenticity, were three paintings asserted by the 1925 catalogue to be by François Boucher and dating from the reign of King Louis XV, who inherited the throne of France from his great-grandfather the Sun King in 1715 at the age of five and died in 1774. Boucher was born in Paris in 1703, the son of a minor artist. Renowned in his lifetime and thereafter for the iconic paintings of his patroness, Madame de Pompadour, portraiture was by no means his main preoccupation as an artist. Boucher's considerable *oeuvre* included many paintings – some on a very large scale – depicting classical, allegorical and pastoral themes, all executed in the Rococo style.

The Four Seasons: Spring by François Boucher.

Two of the three Boucher paintings in the Tussaud collection, titled 'Allegorical Picture by Boucher' (Items 24 & 25: Grand Saloon), were described as 'belonging to a series [of four pictures] emblematic of the Seasons', although which of the Seasons was not specified. According to the *catalogue raisonnée* of Boucher's work, published in 1980, the artist created only one set of the Four Seasons. Painted in 1755 for Madame de Pompadour, King Louis XV's mistress, they are now in the Frick Museum, New York, which acquired the paintings in 1916 as part of the Henry Clay Frick Bequest. As the Frick's Bouchers have an impeccable provenance from the Marquise de Pompadour, it is safe to assume that those listed in the 1925 Tussaud catalogue were not the originals. Adding to the uncertainty, the 1911 insurance catalogue described the pair as 'Mythological Subjects by Boucher', rather than images of the seasons, and gave them a value of £400 (2022: £37,362).

[67]

CHAPTER THREE

This would seem to indicate that in the view of the valuer the attribution to Boucher was possible but far from certain.

The question then arises as to whether or not the same doubts can be applied to 'The Birth of Venus by Boucher' (Item 31: Grand Saloon), which was illustrated and described as:

The Birth of Venus by Boucher, photograph in the 1925 catalogue.

The Birth of Venus, compositional study, by François Boucher, Crocker Art Museum.

The Birth of Venus by Boucher. The principal figure in this fine painting has been thought by some to represent Mme. de Pompadour ... but there is little doubt that it really stands for the lovely Comtesse du Barry, another of the mistresses of the King, at whose death [in 1774] she was banished from the Court. At the beginning of the Revolution she took refuge in England, in order to place in security her diamonds and as much as possible of her ill-gotten wealth, but after the lapse of a few months she returned to France in the belief that she would not come under the ban of the law proscribing Royalists. But she had a cruel awakening. She was arrested in July, 1793, and in the following November sent to the guillotine.

Although not mentioned in this part of the exhibition catalogue, the blade that severed du Barry's head may have been 'Knife [and Lunette] of the Original Guillotine (Item 190: Chamber of Horrors). It survived the 1925 fire, albeit badly charred, and its authenticity will be discussed in the next chapter. As to the 1925 catalogue's attribution of Madame du Barry as the figure of Venus, the dates are important. Madame du Barry did not rise to any sort of wealth or prominence until 1763, when she clawed her way from the ranks of a common prostitute working in a brothel, to the considerably more elevated status of a courtesan. Initially kept by Comte Jean-Baptiste du Barry, in 1768 she was married to his brother, thereby allowing her to become the mistress of King Louis XV. Given the dates, it seems unlikely that she was painted by Boucher, who died in 1770. That Madame du Barry was not Venus in Madame Tussaud's Boucher is further confirmed by the history of the painting itself.

Until relatively recently, there were thought to be only four extant versions in oils of Boucher's *The Birth of Venus*. The first, dated 1740, hangs in the Nationalmuseum in Stockholm, Sweden. The second, dated 1743, is held in a private collection in New York, although a 'contemporary adaptation' of it 'after Boucher' and dated 1750 to 1770, hangs in the cloakroom at the Wallace Collection. The third painting, dated c. 1765, is in the collection of the Detroit Institute of

CHAPTER THREE

Arts, USA; and the last, dated c. 1743, belongs to the J Paul Getty Museum in California, USA. None of these canvasses bears any resemblance to the 'masterpiece by Boucher' that hung in Madame Tussaud's Grand Saloon.

Fortunately, a compositional study for the painting, in chalks and charcoal on beige laid paper and dated 1731, can be found in the collection of the Crocker Art Museum, Sacremento, USA. As can be seen in the adjacent image, it is *self-evidently* the working drawing for Item 31. According to the Crocker Museum, in 1731 François Derbais, a rich lawyer and member of the Parliament of Paris, commissioned a suite of five large paintings from Boucher to decorate the walls of the billiard room at his *hôtel particulier* in the rue Poissonière, Paris. The commission took three years to complete and included *The Birth of Venus*, of which the Crocker Museum has the working sketch. By the late-nineteenth century, the full-size version of *The Birth of Venus* was owned by a rich collector, Martine-Marie-Pol de Béhague, Comtesse de Béarn. In a neat piece of historical symmetry, her husband, Comte René-Marie-Hector de Galard de Brassac de Béarn, was a descendant of Angélique-Gabrielle de Sufferte-Joumard des Achards, Comtesse de Béarn, who had reluctantly sponsored Madame du Barry at Versailles in return for her considerable gambling debts being discharged by the King.

In 1893, Madame de Béhague hung the painting in the dining room of her mansion, the Hôtel de Béhague, at 123 rue Saint Dominique, Paris, which she largely rebuilt between 1890 and 1904. Following the death of the Comtesse in 1939, the hôtel was sold, along with all its immovable fixtures and fittings to King Carol II of Romania. Following his forced abdication in 1940, in favour of his son King Michael I, the Romanian government repurposed the *hôtel* as the country's embassy in Paris.

When, in 1945, the Iron Curtain came down across Europe (with Romania on the wrong side of it), the Boucher disappeared from sight. Following the Romanian Revolution in 1989, the Boucher was re-discovered in the early-1990s, still hanging in the dining room at 123 rue Saint Dominique. When this history is added to the mis-match of dates between the authenticated study (1731-1733) and the rise of Madame du Barry from 1763, it would seem certain that Item 31 was a copy. This is a conclusion that was confirmed by the 1911 insurance catalogue, which stated unequivocally that 'Boucher's Masterpiece' was a 'copy' with a value of just £75 (2022: £7,005), although why Madame Tussaud's exhibition catalogue continued to imply that it was the original is just one more question for which there is no easy answer.

The authenticity of 'Allegorical Painting by Jeaurat' (Item 30: Grand Saloon) may be less suspect. As the catalogue entry correctly stated, Étienne Jeaurat was one of the illustrators of the *Fables* by Jean de la Fontaine, published between

The Mountain in Labour (Fables V.10) by Étienne Jeaurat, engraved in 1736 by Edmé Jeaurat, in the collection of the British Museum.

[69]

≈ CHAPTER THREE ≈

1688 and 1694, with illustrations by François Chauveau. In 1732 that Jeaurat created a set of nine paintings, each illustrating one of the many fables by Fontaine, which were subsequently engraved by his older brother, Edmé. Some of these engravings are in the British Museum, including that for the fable, *La Montagne qui accouche (The Mountain in labour)* illustrated here. The whereabouts of the original paintings by Étienne are unknown, so it is possible that Item 30 was genuine. Unfortunately, the 1911 insurance catalogue muddied the water in this regard: it listed not one but 'Four Large Mythological Pictures' by Jeaurat and gave them a value of £600 (2022: £56,044).

Whether or not the paintings by Boucher and Jeaurat were authentic, their presence on the walls of Madame Tussaud's yet again underlines the true nature of the 1925 institution: that it was an art gallery and a cabinet of curiosities, designed to illustrate history in three dimensions, not merely a wax-works museum. However, why Madame Tussaud or any of her successors, knowingly or unwittingly, acquired fakes, copies or reproductions, *then claimed them as originals in the catalogue*, is uncertain. What is known, given the attributions, is that the alleged Boucher and

below François-Marie Arouet (1694–1778), known as Voltaire, painted *c.*1724, workshop of Nicolas de Largillière.

above middle Voltaire's Library Chair, photograph in the 1925 catalogue.

above right Copy of an Irish reading or library chair, made recently by Brights of Nettlebed.

Jeaurat paintings were shown for their artistic and historical interest, not just as a backdrop to the figures in wax of the same period.

Considerably less problematic, as regards authenticity and provenance, were Curtius's 'Wax Statuette of Voltaire' and 'Wax Statuette of Voltaire Dying' (Items 123 & 130: Napoléon Room), which have already been mentioned and illustrated in the Prologue. 'Voltaire's Library Chair' (Item 60: Napoléon Room) is, however, another matter altogether. Given the political and commercial connections

CHAPTER THREE

between Philippe Curtius and Voltaire it is, on the face of it, no surprise that one of the latter's chairs should have been in Madame Tussaud's collection. Her great-grandson, writing in *The Romance of Madame Tussaud's*, described it as: 'one of our most treasured relics … made to Voltaire's own design, and [is] unlike any other chair we have ever seen'.

There are, however, several issues with this attribution, starting with the fact that the chair was by no means unique, and as can be seen here was clearly Irish and not French in design. This would not be a problem, given that Voltaire resided in England for two-and-a-half years from May 1726, except that the chair was of a late-18th-century design, as evidenced by its straight front legs – and Voltaire died aged eighty-three in 1778, at which time such furniture designs were only just coming into fashion. Of course, in his final years the elderly Voltaire could have bought the chair in Paris, or ordered it from a Dublin cabinetmaker, and the chair could then have been acquired, *post-mortem*, by Philippe Curtius. This is a reasonable hypothesis, were it not for the following entry in the 1925 exhibition catalogue: 'This relic of one of the most illustrious men of letters of modern times was purchased at the sale [in 1859] of the collection of Lady Morgan, well known in her day as a novelist and miscellaneous writer.' The 1911 insurance catalogue was less definitive about this provenance, stating only that the chair was 'in the Collection of Lady Morgan'. It was, however, more specific in asserting that the chair had been 'used [by Voltaire] in 1770 in Paris'.

Sydney Owenson, later Lady Morgan, was a diminutive (barely 4ft tall) Anglo-Irish radical-feminist writer, best known as the author of *The Wild Irish Girl*, a political-treatise-in-novel-form that was published in 1806. Born and educated in Ireland, in 1812 Sydney entered into an arranged marriage with Sir Thomas Morgan, an English surgeon-philosopher, who at the time was physician to John Hamilton, 1st Marquess of Abercorn, in whose household Sydney was a governess. Their childless alliance did not stop the new Lady Morgan's literary output, although it did release her from her duties as a governess to the Abercorn family.

Following a six-month stay in France in 1816, Lady Morgan, whose political views were in sympathy with Voltaire and the other pre-Revolutionary *philosophes*, wrote a controversial and highly critical study of France under the Bourbon Restoration. Published the following year under the title, *France*, the book so angered the French authorities that they issued an injunction preventing Lady Morgan from ever returning to France. Fortunately, the election of a more liberal French parliament in 1818 allowed her to return to Paris in August of that year. While there, Lady Morgan mixed with Parisian high society, had her portrait painted by René Berthon, and was invited by the Marquise de Villette (*née* Reine Philiberte de Varicourt and known in society as *Belle et Bonne*) to join the radical

top Sydney, Lady Morgan, née Owenson, (1781–1859) by René Théodore Berthon.

above Sir Thomas Morgan (1783–843).

[71]

CHAPTER THREE

Madame Marie-Louise Denis (1712–1790) by Joseph-Siffred Duplessis.

Les Neuf Soeurs Masonic Lodge. This was an institution of which Voltaire and Benjamin Franklin had been members, and the Marquise was at that time a *Grande Maîtresse*.

Significantly, for the purpose of establishing the authenticity of Voltaire's library chair, in Lady Morgan's own memoirs she stated that the Marquise de Villette was 'Voltaire's niece'. If that is correct, then it is perfectly possible that Lady Morgan, as a noted Irish radical author, was given the famous French radical writer's chair by his niece. Except that there is a further problem: Voltaire's niece was *not* the Marquise de Villette, but another member of Les Neuf Soeurs called Marie-Louise Denis (*née* Mignot), who had died in 1790.

This fact, however, is not necessarily evidence of a misattribution, for the Marquise de Villette was taken under the wing of Voltaire when her marriage to his homosexual protégé, Marquis Charles de Villette, failed, and on Voltaire's death she was informally adopted by Madame Denis. The library chair may, therefore, have been inherited on Voltaire's demise by his niece, and then bequeathed on her death in 1790 to the Marquise. Given that *Belle et Bonne* died in 1822, it is also perfectly possible that – although not Voltaire's niece – she gave or bequeathed the chair to Lady Morgan. This would be a compelling argument in favour of the attribution, were it not for the probability that the Irish-made chair never belonged to Voltaire or his extended family, nor to Lady Morgan, but to her surgeon-philosopher husband, Sir Thomas.

There are several reasons for making this assertion. First, the chair was clearly designed to be used by a man; no lady of the period who valued her reputation would have dared to be seen sitting astride a chair, even if her hooped skirts had permitted such an indignity. Second, Sir Thomas died in 1843 and his effects were sold at auction later that year. From the evidence that follows in the paragraph below, 'Voltaire's chair' must have been in that sale and not, as was stated in the 1925 catalogue, 'purchased at the sale of the collection of Lady Morgan' after her death in 1859. Lastly, Lady Morgan had a novelist's tendency to play fast-and-loose with the truth: amongst other things, she falsified her date of birth by four years. It is highly likely, therefore, that the auctioneers of Sir Thomas's effects in 1843 did not question Lady Morgan's value-enhancing assertion of the chair's Voltairean provenance. This false attribution, with its powerful links to Philippe Curtius, was then accepted as fact by Joseph Tussaud when he bought the chair at the 1843 sale, and was perpetuated thereafter as the truth by Madame Tussaud's and the 1911 valuers. The latter accepted the false provenance and put a value on the chair of £250 (2022: £23,351), which is at least ten times what would have to be paid for a nineteenth-century Irish library chair today.

CHAPTER THREE

The (in part) date-based conclusion above is re-enforced by a passage in John Theodore Tussaud's *The Romance of Madame Tussaud's*:

> [In 1844], Tsar Nicholas I of Russia [visited London and] during his stay was conducted over the Exhibition by Madame Tussaud's son, Joseph.
>
> In the course of his tour round the galleries the Tsar's attention was arrested by the great Frenchman's wonderful chair. Being struck by its ingenious construction, he examined it very closely, and then … gave himself the pleasure of occupying the seat …
>
> So keen an interest did the Tsar take in the chair that we decided to make a replica and send it to him as a pleasant surprise. This was done, but no direct acknowledgement … was ever received.
>
> Months afterwards, however, two cases – one containing a splendid gallery portrait of Nicholas [by Georg von Bothmann, Item 39: Grand Saloon*] and the other a beautiful statuette of the same monarch – arrived at the Exhibition. These presents were accepted as a recognition, in practical form, of the chair.

If the chair had been acquired from Lady Morgan's collection in 1859, it could *not* have been viewed at Madame Tussaud's by Tsar Nicholas I in 1844. The Tsar's visit is not in doubt, nor the events that followed it, so the library chair *must* have been acquired at the sale of Sir Thomas Morgan's effects.

In closing this chapter, it is worth speculating whether Madame Tussaud & Sons would have received the studio copy of the painting of the Tsar, valued in 1911 at £100 (2022: £9,340), if Nicholas had known that the 'treasured relic' was not Voltaire's chair, but a piece of Irish domestic furniture, formerly in the ownership of an English surgeon, who had been married to an Anglo-Irish governess-turned-radical-feminist? Probably not.

Tsar Nicholas I of Russia (1796–1855) by Georg von Bothmann.

* Item 39 survived the 1925 fire and was valued by Sotheby's in 1983 at £6,000 - £8,000 (2022: £19,031 - £25,375).

CHAPTER FOUR

KING GEORGE I TO THE FRENCH CONSULATE

As THE STORY OF Madame Tussaud & Sons' collection moves forward into the Georgian era, in the middle of which Marie Tussaud herself stepped centre stage, the question of authenticity becomes less problematic. Nonetheless, some of the attributions in the exhibition catalogue remain questionable. A good example of this is 'Portrait of George I by Sir Godfrey Kneller' (Item 196: Hall of Tableaux). Described in the 1925 catalogue as a, and valued in 1911 at £200 (2022: £18,681), the catalogue entry provided brief biographies of both the King and the artist, but omitted any description of the picture itself. However, recent research in the archives has unearthed a black-and-white photograph of the painting in the Madame Tussaud's stores at Wookey Hole in Somerset in the 1980s. This photograph, shown here, indicates not only that it survived the fire, albeit in a damaged condition, but that it was probably a studio copy of the original hanging today at Houghton Hall in Norfolk. Further studio copies are in the Royal Collection, and at the Royal Hospital Chelsea in London. The painting's present whereabouts is unknown.

Two portraits of King George II, one catalogued in 1925 as by Thomas Hudson, (see page 76) were also listed (Item 11: Hall of Kings and Item 197: Hall of Tableaux), again without any description, other than biographical details of Hudson. Only the first of these was listed in the 1911 insurance catalogue, with a value of £200 (2022: £18,681). It may have been in the style of the Hudson portrait of George II hanging in London's National Portrait Gallery, but there can be no certainty about that. Nor can there be any certainty about the hand which crafted the wax statuettes of Kings George II & III (Item 124: Napoléon Room), neither of which are listed in the 1911 insurance catalogue.

Less problematic are the 'Relics of George III' (Item 154: Napoléon Room) which were described as his 'sword, uniform, etc'. None of these items appear

opposite King George I (1660–1727), studio of Sir Godfrey Kneller.

below Photograph of the portrait of King George I by Kneller in the stores at Madame Tussaud's Wookey Hole, c.1980.

CHAPTER FOUR

above King George II (1683–1760) by Thomas Hudson at the National Portrait Gallery.

above middle King George III (1738–1820), aka 'Captain King', by Peter Edward Stroehling.

above right Queen Caroline (1683–1737) with her son Prince William Augustus, Duke of Cumberland (1721–1765) by Charles Jervas.

to have been in the collection in 1911, so they must have been acquired after that date. As the exhibition catalogue provided no further details, George III's uniform and accoutrements, if genuine, were probably either those of a General or of his favourite regiment, the Royal Horse Guards (The Blues), in which the King had appointed himself a mere Captain. *À propos* of which, apparently when The Blues' regal enthusiast arrived on parade for the first time, the Commanding Officer called the regiment to attention and ordered a Royal Salute. 'No, no, Colonel!' exclaimed the monarch, 'Here, I am merely *Captain* King.' So fond of The Blues was George III that he adapted their uniform – a blue coat with red facings – for civilian wear, and commanded that it be worn by all male members of the Royal Family (and certain members of the Royal Household) when in residence at Windsor Castle. Known as the Windsor Uniform, it is still – in a modified form – worn today.

Item 37 in the Grand Saloon made up for the paucity of information about the portraits of the early Georges, as follows:

> *Allegorical Picture of the Duke of Cumberland* by Sir James Thornhill – 'The Hero of Culloden' [HRH Prince William Augustus] here represented in his childhood, with his mother, Queen Caroline, *née* Princess Caroline of Brandenburg-Anspach [*sic*], was the second son of George II. A fearless soldier, he was not a successful General, and there was in him a strain of brutality which prevented him from becoming a popular favourite. The weapons which the artist has introduced into the picture are, of course, emblematic of the Duke's career as a warrior.

CHAPTER FOUR

This work may have been the large gallery painting, listed and described in the 1911 insurance catalogue as the 'Apotheosis of the Duke of Cumberland'. Despite not having an artistic attribution, it was relatively highly appraised at £500 (2022: £46,703). The ceiling panels in Tussaud's Hall of Kings were copies of the work of Sir James Thornhill, so it is reasonable to assume that Item 37 above was also a copy of the Baroque artist's work. However, although there are at least three portraits in national collections of Queen Caroline with the young Prince William, including the one illustrated her in the Royal Collection, none of them are painted in an allegorical style, so it is possible that Tussaud's was an original. Somewhat unusually, there was no mention of this work in the 1911 insurance catalogue, although a large gallery painting was listed and described as 'The Apotheosis of the Duke of Cumberland'. Despite not having an artistic attribution it was relatively highly appraised at £500 (2022: £46,703).

What is certain is that there existed before the fire an unlisted and posthumous wax figure of the Duke, sculpted by Marie Tussaud's eldest son, Joseph. This was created in 1835, as the result of a remark made by the 1st Duke of Wellington during a visit to the new premises in Baker Street. Somewhat typically, the Iron Duke thought that soldiers, even bad ones, were under-represented in the exhibition.

Uncontentious as to authenticity, was 'Specimen of Art Needlework' (Item 28: Grand Saloon), which was described as a 'beautiful piece of work ... by the dextrous needle of the famous Miss Linwood'. Now almost entirely forgotten, except by antiquarians with a penchant for Georgian tatting, Mary Linwood was, indeed, very famous in her day. Born in 1755 and by profession a schoolteacher, her copies of Old Master paintings in crewel wool achieved over-night fame following her first London exhibition in 1787. So well regarded was her work thereafter, that her copy of a landscape painting by the seventeenth-century artist, Salvator Rosa was sold for more than the original; and she is believed to have refused an offer of 2,000 guineas (2022: £145,845) for her version of *Salvator Mundi* by Carlo Dolci. Instead, she bequeathed it to Queen Victoria; it remains in the Royal Collection (RCIN 11902).

That, however, was not Mary Linwood's only association with fine art. The first commissioned work of the landscape artist, John Constable, was to paint the background details in one of her works; and in 1800 she was able to commission John Hoppner, the principal painter to the Prince of Wales (later George IV), to execute her portrait. In this painting, illustrated here, the artist referenced both Linwood's tatting and its subject matter. It is now in the Victoria & Albert Museum, along with

Mary Linwood (1755–1845) by John Hoppner RA.

༄ CHAPTER FOUR ༄

King George III, studio of Sir Joshua Reynolds, painted c.1799.

Queen Adelaide (1792–1849) by Sir William Beechy, painted in the year of her Coronation, 1831.

her portrait of Napoléon, said to have been done from life, and the needlework copy of the Salvator Rosa landscape.

By the age of thirty-one, in 1786, Linwood had been invited to Windsor Castle by Queen Charlotte, and she later received a medal from the Society of Arts. After her death, she was mentioned in *A Plated Article* by Charles Dickens, not a fan, who described visiting 'that awful storehouse … a gloomy sepulchre of needlework dropping to pieces with dust and age'. If genuine, Item 28, which was not listed in the 1911 insurance catalogue, was probably a copy in wool of an Old Master.

Greater certainty, at least as to provenance, is associated with two gallery portraits of King George III and Queen Charlotte, listed as Item 44 in Hall No 4. The catalogue stated that they came from the collection of the Dowager Queen Adelaide, widow of King William IV. It is almost certain that she inherited them from her husband: portraits of royal parents, no matter how disliked, were a pre-requisite of nineteenth-century royal establishments. Annoyingly – and despite an attribution of both portraits to Sir Joshua Reynolds in the 1911 insurance catalogue – the 1925 exhibition catalogue was unspecific about the artist of the Queen's portrait, and merely stated that the picture of the King was 'attributed by some authorities to Sir Joshua Reynolds'; it was probably similar to the one illustrated here. In any event, the likelihood is that they were both studio copies; they were valued in 1911 at £300 (2022: £28,022) each.

While it is difficult to draw any further conclusions about these lost portraits, and jumping ahead of this chapter's chronology, the Queen Adelaide provenance is entirely credible, given that her effects – like those of her brother-in-law, The Duke of Sussex – were sold after her death in 1849. By then, Madame Tussaud was in her late-eighties, but her sons may have bought these portraits then or at a later sale.

There is a coda to this story that highlights Queen Adelaide's generosity with her personal property, as told to one of the authors by Miss (Elizabeth) Moyra Goff, a direct descendant of the Queen's husband, King William IV. Although Queen Adelaide had five pregnancies, none of her children survived infancy, so she directed her maternal affections onto the FitzClarences, her husband's ten illegitimate children by the beautiful actress, Mrs Dorothea Jordan.

Her particular favourite was the youngest boy, Lord Augustus FitzClarence. In 1829, he was given the living of the parish of Mapledurham in Oxfordshire. The following year, he built himself a modest stuccoed vicarage, with three bays facing the garden. However, like all the FitzClarence children, Lord Augustus had little money and – after building the vicarage – none to furnish his new home in the manner befitting his paternal antecedents. Fortunately, shortly after

CHAPTER FOUR

far left Dorothy Jordan (1761–1816) by John Hoppner.

left The Rev Lord Augustus FitzClarence (1805–1854), unknown engraver.

his father became King in 1830, Queen Adelaide used her position as the chatelaine of Windsor Castle to send a large collection of items from the castle to Mapledurham. The resulting haul included Louis XVI-period furniture (acquired by King George IV when Prince Regent and stamped 'Windsor Castle'), Meissen china, English pictures, and a dinner service of porcelain and silver made for her husband while he was serving in the Royal Navy in the 1780s. The collection remained intact in the ownership of Lord Augustus's descendants until the death of his great-great-grand daughter, Moyra Goff, in 1990.

This section closes with Item 67 in the Napoléon Room, listed in the 1925 exhibition catalogue as a 'Case of Miscellaneous Relics'. These included the christening robe of Princess Amelia, described as 'the favourite daughter of King George III'. Also included were a lock of hair and a pair of slippers, purported to have belonged respectively to George IV's daughter, Princess Charlotte, and Queen Victoria's eldest daughter, Victoria, Princess Royal. Rather incongruously, the fourth of these miscellaneous relics was a watch, said to have belonged to the nineteenth-century Italian conductor and composer, Sir Michael Costa (see Chapter 12). The christening robe was valued in 1911 at £10 (2022: £932), the lock of hair at £1 (2022: £93), and the slippers at £2 (2022: £186).

The focus on items in Madame Tussaud & Sons' collection now moves to the continental side of the Channel, and in particular to France, where Marie learned her wax-modelling and acquisitive skills from her 'uncle', and would later be caught up in the French Revolution.

In spite of her personal experiences in revolutionary Paris, many doubts arise concerning the authenticity and provenance of the associated items on display

The Three Youngest Daughters of George III, 1785, by John Singleton Copley. HRH Princess Amelia (1783–1810) is the baby in the centre.

CHAPTER FOUR

above Queen Marie Antoinette and her children, 1787 by Élizabeth Louise Vigée Le Brun.

above right Portrait of Queen Marie Antoinette, as illustrated in the 1925 catalogue.

at the exhibition in Marylebone Road. The catalogued portraits of 'Marie Antoinette' (Item 35: Grand Saloon), which was illustrated in the catalogue, and 'Portrait of Louis XVI' (Item 194: Hall of Tableaux), which was not, pose more questions than they answer. Beyond stating that the Queen's picture was painted 'some time prior to the Revolution', the exhibition catalogue was silent on all other details, and the extant photograph of the Queen's portrait in its rococo frame offers up no clues as to the artist or the painting's authenticity. It was not listed in the 1911 insurance catalogue, which did list the unillustrated portrait of King Louis XVI with a value of £125 (2022: £11,719), albeit without an artistic attribution. The only information provided was that the portrait was 'a Large Painting – in the Lobby next to the Cinema'.

There was no such paucity of information when it came to 'Keys of the Bastille' (Item 186: Chamber of Horrors). The exhibition catalogue stated that one of these keys was bought 'at the sale of a great historical collection at Messrs Chinnock & Galsworthy's Rooms'. The sale referred to was the contents of the Napoléon Museum, formerly owned by the Napoléon fan and collector, John Davis Sainsbury. Born in 1793, Sainsbury started his working life as a Smithfield coal merchant, but from 1823 he worked in Covent Garden as a literary, clerical and scholastic agent. Sainsbury acquired his Napoléonica at various auctions from 1820 onwards, although it was only in 1835 – having failed to sell his collection to the architect and collector, Sir John Soane, for £6,000 (2022: £603,343) – that

Sketch of John Davis Sainsbury at the Napoléon Museum.

[80]

he put it on display as the Napoléon Museum, initially in rented space at the Egyptian Hall in Piccadilly. Sainsbury charged a shilling to view his collection (2022: £4.65).

By 1845, the ex-coal-merchant's mania for buying Napoléonica had got him into such serious financial difficulties that he was forced to sell much of his collection at a Christie's auction. The Tussauds acquired several items, to appear in later chapters. Relieved of pressure from his creditors, Sainsbury carried on collecting and was eventually able to reopen his museum. History, however, was to repeat itself in 1860, when he was successfully sued by the auctioneers, Chinnock & Galsworthy, for the recovery of monies due on a large number of unpaid lots. Once again, Sainsbury was obliged to sell the contents of his museum, this time in an auction held by his creditors over six days in June 1860.

The front page of the Chinnock & Galsworthy auction catalogue described the Tussauds' first key as 'The Key of the Front Gate Entrance, certified by J S Bailly, Mayor of Paris, and dated September 4, 1790, to M. Palloy.' Madame Tussaud's catalogue was, however, silent as to how, where or from whom the second key was acquired. Nonetheless, it assigned to the *second* key an expanded version, with photograph, of the provenance of the *first* key as written by Chinnock & Galsworthy:

Front page of the Chinnock & Galsworthy auction catalogue for the sale of the contents of the Napoléon Museum, 1860.

> This key is fastened to small wooden plugs, let into the centre stone of the late prison's gateway, which is 24-in. by 18-in., with the inscription, deeply cut, as follows:- '*Cette pierre vient des cachots de la Bastille donne A. M. Moreau St Mery, President des Electeurs, 1789, par le patriotte Pallow, L.A.N Ae*'. It is a heavily carved frame, and looks to be, as it is, an ancient, invaluable, and important historical memento of the Bastille.

By way of comparison, the Tussaud exhibition catalogue entry for the second key, which was remarkably similar to the Chinnock & Galsworthy description of the first, read:

[81]

CHAPTER FOUR

Keys of the Bastille, photograph in the 1925 catalogue.

The other, the key of the principal gate, is affixed by iron hoops to a stone, 24 inches by 16 inches, which formed part of the main entrance. There is also a ground plan of the building, and a representation of the Monument of President St Méry, with the autograph certificate of M. Palloy, framed and glazed, with the inscription, in French, 'This stone comes from the dungeons of the Bastille; given to M. Moreau St. Méry, President of the Electors, 1789, by the patriot Palloy, Year 4'. There are, further, the original letters to M. Palloy, from the mayor of Paris, J S Bailly, thanking him for the stone and inviting him to dinner. The key was affixed to the stone subsequently.

This was either a Tussaud cataloguing error or a falsification of the facts. According to the Chinnock & Galsworthy catalogue there *was* a second Front Gate key, but it was 'taken from Paris to America by General Lafayette, who presented it to General Washington', and he deposited it in his house at Mount Vernon in Virginia, USA, where it remains there to the present day (see: www.mountvernon.org). The second key at Madame Tussaud's cannot, therefore, have been that one. However, by splitting the acquisition and the provenance of Sainsbury's Bastille key, as listed by Chinnock & Galsworthy, to the two keys listed under Item 186, the exhibition catalogue entry seemed to imply as much. That there was only one key of the Bastille was confirmed by the 1911 insurance catalogue, which stated, under Relics and Mementos of the Revolution Period: 'Key of the Bastille mounted in stone taken from the Bastille'. It gave it a value of £150 (2022: £14,011). Nonetheless, two keys were in the Chamber of Horrors on the night of 18th March 1925, escaped the fire and are still on display at Madame Tussaud's. However, they are no longer 'affixed by iron hoops to a stone...which formed part of the main entrance' – but the assertion that they were from the Bastille remains unaltered.

One further relic acquired by the Tussauds at the sale of the Sainsbury collection in 1860 was also listed under Item 186. It was catalogued as 'twenty lines written by the Man with the Iron Mask, on the leaf of his book, and had apparently been found by M. Palloy under the floor of the mysterious prisoner's cell'. There is little historical doubt that the Man in the Iron Mask existed, although his face was hidden behind a mask of black velvet not iron. His identity, however, remains a mystery that has excited the attention of amongst others, Voltaire, the nineteenth-century writer, Alexandre Dumas, and numerous TV and film producers, all of whom have allowed their imaginations to run riot on the subject. Historians have, however, established that a prisoner, later known as the Man in the Iron Mask, spent the last of his thirty-four years imprisonment in the Bastille, where he died in the third chamber of the Bertaudière tower on 19th November 1703. Although the cell at the Bastille in which the relic was allegedly discovered was not identified

CHAPTER FOUR

by Chinnock & Galsworthy, or by Madame Tussaud's, the scrap of paper may have been genuine. It was not listed in the 1911 insurance catalogue and its current whereabouts is unknown.

Also in the Chamber of Horrors were Items 188 and 189, described respectively as 'Instruments of Torture and Door of a Cell from the Bastille' and a 'Model of the Bastille'. Neither of the catalogue entries gave any descriptions of these items, and merely referred back to the entry for Bastille keys. The model was illustrated, and given a value in 1911 of £45 (2022: £4,203). The 'instruments of torture' were valued in 1911 at £100 (2022: £9,340), but the inventory failed to mention the door. There was no further information, in any of the catalogues or inventories, as to where or how these items were acquired, although there was the following anecdote in the text of the 1925 exhibition catalogue:

> Madame Tussaud, in her Memoirs, says that all Paris flocked to see the gloomy cells in which so many innocent persons had spent years of hopeless captivity. She herself was prevailed upon to accompany her uncle and some friends on a visit to the place, and while she was descending the narrow stairs leading to the dungeons, her foot slipped, and she was only saved from falling by Robespierre, who remarked that it would have been a pity had so young and pretty a patriot broken her neck in such a horrid place.

This story needs to be treated with some scepticism, given Madame Tussaud's now recognised disregard for the *actualité*, added to the fact that the Bastille's cells were not below ground in the dungeons. Nonetheless, her great-grandson, John Theodore Tussaud, writing in his book *The Romance of Madame Tussaud's*, asserted in some detail that, although a royalist, Marie socialised with Robespierre and that she noted he was 'an agreeable conversationalist with good manners', albeit his 'verbal enunciation was poor'. As already noted, Marie alleged in her

above left Model of the fortress of the Bastille, Paris, at Madame Tussaud's, photograph in the 1925 catalogue.

above Man in the Iron Mask, anon print *c.*1789.

CHAPTER FOUR

above fire damaged guillotine knife recently rediscovered in the archives

above right Knife, lunette and axe 'of the original guillotine', photograph in the 1925 catalogue.

Memoirs that her friendship with the revolutionary leader did not prevent her from being arrested and imprisoned as a royalist recidivist by Robespierre's Committee of Public Safety, a fate that could potentially have left her facing execution.

This assertion brings this account neatly to Item 190 in the Chamber of Horrors, which was 'the knife, lunette and axe of the original guillotine'. Although not listed in the 1925 exhibition catalogue, the 1911 insurance catalogue stated that the collection also included in the Chamber of Horrors a facsimile guillotine as 'used during the French Revolution' and a model of the instrument of death. In 1911, these last two items were valued at £180 (2022: £16,813) and £25 (2022: £2,335) respectively.

As decapitation by the guillotine became the principal method for French executions in 1792 (and the only one after the Revolution), there were numerous such machines in use in France from that date. The Tussaud's insurance and exhibition catalogue entries were therefore speculative, when they claimed that the knife in the Chamber of Horrors was the 'original', and certainly incorrect to claim that it was used to execute more than 20,000 people. There is, nonetheless, some evidence that the grisly relic, which survived the 1925 fire in a damaged condition, may have been the one employed by Charles-Henri Sanson (1739–1806), the royal executioner during the reign of Louis XVI, and later High Executioner of the French Republic.

Known as Monsieur de Paris, Sanson was the first French executioner to use a guillotine, with which he claimed to have dispatched 2,918 (not 20,000) people, including Louis XVI and Robespierre. For the record, Marie Antoinette was executed in 1793 by Sanson's younger son, Henri. Sanson's elder son and official

CHAPTER FOUR

assistant, Gabriel, had the previous year slipped on the blood of a victim, whose head he was displaying, and had fallen to his death from the scaffold.

As to how Item 190 came into the Tussaud collection, according to John Theodore Tussaud's account, written in 1921:

> …the Reign of Terror gave way to the Directorate. Then easier times came, though still far from tranquil. Nevertheless, heads had ceased to fall, and Sanson, the executioner, finding his occupation gone, pawned his guillotine, and got into woeful trouble for allegedly trafficking in municipal property.

This is an odd claim, because guillotines belonged to the executioner and not the State, and guillotining for capital offences continued under the Directory, the Consulate, the Empire and beyond, albeit on a much-reduced scale. It is also recorded that Sanson actually retired in 1795, the year after the end of the Terror, when he handed on his job as High Executioner to his surviving younger son and assistant. Henri Sanson retained the post until his death in 1842, when the job passed to his nephew and Charles-Henri's grandson, Henry-Clément Sanson, who served as an executioner until 1847. Putting that to one side for the moment, John Theodore Tussaud's account continued:

> Years after Madame came to this country, she sent her son [unspecified] to Paris to search out this terrible instrument of death, and, with the help of the executioner, who was still living, and who solemnly vouched for its authenticity, she secured the knife, the lunette, and also the chopper that was used as a standby, lest the great knife should fail.
>
> It was only after much negotiation and the payment of a very considerable sum of money that her object was attained. And now the dread knife harmlessly reposes by the side of the impressions of those heads it so ruthlessly struck off…

In fact, John Theodore Tussaud's account – perhaps in an attempt to establish Item 190's authenticity – condensed names, dates and facts. It was, in fact, Henry-Clément Sanson who in 1847, deeply in debt as the result of a profligate lifestyle, pawned his guillotine for Francs 3,000 (2022: £12,915) and then attempted to conduct his next official execution using an axe. The French government was outraged by this action, redeemed the guillotine from the pawnbroker so that Henry-Clément could complete executions properly, but then dismissed him and appointed Charles-André Féry in his place. So, the 'woeful trouble for allegedly trafficking in municipal property' was no such thing: Henry-Clément was dismissed for trying to use an axe, not for pawning his own property. Nor

Queen Marie Antoinette being led to the guillotine by Henri Sanson (1769–1840), 16th October 1793.

CHAPTER FOUR

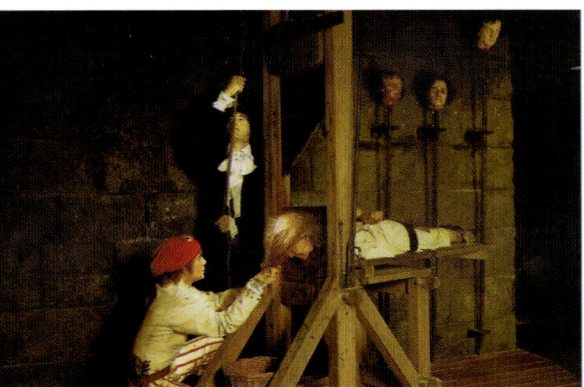

The guillotine tableau at Madame Tussaud's, 1971.

Naser al-Din Shah Qajar (1831–1896).

did Madame Tussaud's son buy the items from Charles-Henri Sanson, but from his grandson, Henry-Clément Sanson in the 1840s.

At this distance in time, and given all of the above, it is difficult to establish the full provenance of Item 190. However, as guillotines had a finite operational life and anyway evolved technologically, it seems likely that the one pawned by Henry-Clément Sanson was not the same as the one used by his grandfather fifty years earlier during the Revolution, although Henry-Clément may have inherited bits of that original machine. Without carbon-dating of the wood in which the blade is mounted, it remains unclear whether the knife, lunette and axe, which he sold the Tussauds came from the guillotine recently returned from the pawnshop, or from the machine belonging to his grandfather.

Whatever the truth of the matter, the exhibition catalogue did not exaggerate when it stated that the knife, lunette and axe, whether or not they had assisted in the royal and revolutionary executions, were 'the most memorable of all the relics in the Exhibition'. The 1911 valuers clearly thought that they were the originals and valued them accordingly at £1,500 (2022: £140,110). Whatever their authenticity, these items spawned a number of stories, some of which were apocryphal, but at least one of which was based on recorded fact.

The most bloodthirsty of the latter was recorded by John Theodore Tussaud in *The Romance of Madame Tussaud's* and related to the State Visit of the Shah of Persia, Naser al-Din, to London in 1873. During his time in England, the Shah was hosted by the Prince of Wales (the future King Edward VII), Queen Victoria believing that the Persian autocrat was altogether too 'brusque and rough' for her sensibilities. Desperate to keep the oriental potentate entertained, the Prince took the Shah on a visit to Madame Tussaud's on 2nd July. Included on the 'King of Kings' tour was the Chamber of Horrors, where he examined 'with unaffected delight the guillotine which cut off so many heads during the French Revolution.' Tussaud recalled that the Shah's interest in the machine was such he proposed that:

> a condemned prisoner should be brought from one of the English gaols to be decapitated on the spot for the edification of himself and his attendants. It was pointed out, as an evasive measure, that no condemned man was available at that moment, whereupon His Majesty turned to the members of his suite and called for volunteers... the Shah's retainers looked genuinely relieved when they gathered that their royal master was not to have his way.

CHAPTER FOUR

Naser al-Din may have had Item 190 in his mind when he later remarked to the Prince of Wales, shortly after a stay at the fabulously wealthy Duke of Sutherland's palatial country house, Trentham Hall in Staffordshire: 'Too grand for a subject. You'll have to have his head off when you come to the throne.' There is a postscript to this story. On 19th August 1902, Naser al-Din's son and successor as Shah, Mozaffar ad-Din, also paid a visit to Madame Tussaud's while attending the Coronation of King Edward VII. However, unlike his father he refused to visit the Chamber of Horrors, to the evident relief of both his suite-in-waiting and the Tussauds.

Back above ground, in the Napoléon Ante-Room, the Madame Tussaud & Son's 1925 catalogue listed under Item 171: Memorials of Marie Antoinette and Louis XVI, with a description that read:

> The piece of paper is from the wall of the Temple prison, in which the beautiful Queen of France was for some months imprisoned. The memorial rings are those of her amiable but vacillating husband, who preceded her to the guillotine.

No further descriptions were given, nor did John Theodore Tussaud's book provide any information. Had the Queen written on the piece of paper? Or was it merely a piece of otherwise undefaced wallpaper? If the former, its value today would be considerable, but in 1911 it was valued at a mere £5 (2022: £467). As for the memorial rings, the text seemed to imply that these belonged to the King, but that was probably a grammatical error. It is far more likely – and not inconsistent with the grammar used – that they were a collection of rings made *in memoriam* after his execution. Some, like the one in the Royal Collection Trust illustrated here, were engraved with the facts of the regicide; others bore the image of the King. The 1911 insurance catalogue stated that there were four such rings and gave them a value of £40 (2022: £3,736). It also added that the collection included a 'Portrait and Hair of Louis XVI, presented by George IV', a 'Piece of Shirt worn by Louis XVI', and a 'Piece of Hair of Marie Antoinette, in box'. Together these were valued in 1911 respectively at £75, £10 and £50, which today equates to a total of £12,609.

Louis XVI memorial ring.
©Royal Collection Trust/His Majesty King Charles III 2023

As for the 'Gun belonging to M. Curtius' (Item 58: Napoléon Room), it was described as 'an exceptionally interesting souvenir of the French Revolution', presented to Madame Tussaud's republican-inclined 'uncle' by the National

Gun presented to Philippe Curtius by the National Assembly of France, photograph in the 1925 catalogue.

[87]

CHAPTER FOUR

The young Napoléon Bonaparte by Francesco Cossia.

Assembly of France. This was the legislative body that existed from 17th June 1789 to 30th September 1791, so the presentation was not for Curtius's work as a roving ambassador, which started in 1793, but for an earlier service to the Revolution. What that amounted to was explained by an inscription on the barrel, which stated that the gun was given to Curtius in recognition for 'bravery shown in the capture of the Bastille'. No further details of his involvement in the fall of the notorious prison were recorded. The 1911 insurance catalogue gave the gun a value of £100 (2022: £9,340).

Similarly, although John Theodore Tussaud's book covers Maximilien Robespierre's relationship with Marie Tussaud, particularly details of her socialising with him before his death and then the grisly task of modelling his head after it had fallen to Sanson's blade on 28th July 1794, there was no explanation either by Tussaud or in the exhibition catalogue as to how she came to acquire the 'Robespierre Relics' (Item 79: Napoléon Room), comprising his pistols and rapier. However, in her *Memoirs*, although not the most reliable of sources, she did record that Robespierre's decapitated head was not the first likeness she had made of him. Apparently, he had requested that his portrait in wax should be displayed alongside her figure of Marat in Paris, and she stated that he and several other revolutionary heroes 'should send her their own clothes, in which the figures might be dressed, to afford additional accuracy to the resemblances'. Perhaps the pistols and rapier were donated in this way; in any event, they were valued at £100 in 1911 (2022: £9,340).

This chapter closes with three items from Napoléon's pre-imperial life, which started with his birth into a family of minor Italian nobility on 15th August 1769 at Casa Buonaparte, Ajaccio, Corsica. Nine years later, the young Napoléone di Buonaparte gained a scholarship to the Military School at Brienne-le-Château, from where, in 1784, he was admitted to the École Militaire, Paris, emerging in 1785 as a Second Lieutenant in the royal artillery. By the age of twenty-three, Buonaparte was a republican revolutionary and a Captain, who in 1792 was given command, as a local Lieutenant Colonel, of a Battalion of Corsican republican volunteers. The following year he changed his name to the more French-sounding Napoléon Bonaparte, allied himself with Augustin Robespierre, younger brother of Maximilien, and was appointed commander of the artillery in the Siege of Toulon (29th August – 19th December 1793), during which he was wounded and promoted to Brigadier General. Contrary to contemporary British black propaganda, at no point was Napoléon ever a 'Corporal' – but he was, of course, a Corsican

In 1794, Brigadier General Bonaparte devised a plan for the capture of the Kingdom of Sardinia but, following the French coup d'état of 9th Thermidor

CHAPTER FOUR

Year 2 (27th July 1794) and the fall of Robespierre, he was put under house arrest for two weeks. Worse was to follow when he was removed from the list of Generals in 1795 for refusing an infantry command (effectively a demotion) with the Army of the West. However, on 13th Vendémiaire Year 3 (5th October 1795) he was appointed by Vicomte Paul de Barras to defend the Convention, then sitting in the Tuileries Palace, from a royalist insurrection. Bonaparte famously achieved this with a 'whiff of grapeshot'.

The 'whiff of grapeshot' that ended the royalist revolt of 13th Vendémiaire, Year 4 – St Roch church, rue Saint-Honoré.

Under the Directory, established by de Barras, Bonaparte was promoted to General and given command of the Army of Italy. At about the same time, he met Vicomtesse Joséphine de Beauharnais, a former mistress of de Barras. Following a rather peremptory romance, they were married on 9th March 1796, and two days later, Bonaparte took command of the Army of Italy. During the first Italian Campaign, he established his reputation as a brilliant commander in the field, with victories at the Battles of Castiglione, Bassano, Arcole and Rivoli. Bonaparte's successes in that first Italian Campaign were marked at Madame Tussaud's in London with an engraving of the Battle of Arcole (14th-17th November 1796), displayed in the Napoléon Ante-Room as Item 169. This picture was neither illustrated nor described in the exhibition catalogue, although it was listed in the 1911 insurance catalogue with a value of £10 (2022: £937). Without any further information in either catalogue, it is impossible to know from which of the many paintings of the battle it was engraved.

By January 1797, Bonaparte had defeated the armies of Piedmont and Austria, and thereby secured French control of northern Italy. He then moved to invade southern Austria. In March the Austrians sued for peace, and ceded control of northern Italy and the Austrian provinces in the Low Countries. Although a secret clause in the peace treaty gave Austria a free rein over the Republic of Venice, Bonaparte advanced and forced its surrender on 12th May, and then comprehensively looted the city.

Once again in military support of de Barras, on 18th Fructidor (4th September) 1797 Bonaparte enabled another coup against the royalists in France, following which he started to plan an invasion of Britain. However, faced by the fact of the British Royal Navy's control of the Channel, Bonaparte abandoned this idea and in 1798 switched his attention to Egypt. The plan, agreed by the Directory, was to seize the Ottoman province

General Bonaparte leads his troops over the bridge at Arcole by Horace Vernet.

≈ CHAPTER FOUR ≈

above Rear Admiral Sir Horatio Nelson (1758–1805) *c.*1798 by Lemuel Francis Abbott.

above right Vice Admiral Viscount Nelson of the Nile, Duke of Brontë, *c.*1800 by Lemuel Francis Abbott.

along the Nile, use it as a staging post to India, take command of the lucrative British trade route with the East, forge an alliance with Tipoo Sultan of Mysore, and so both end British rule in India and strike a major blow at the British economy.

In June, *en route* to Egypt, Bonaparte's Army of the East seized the strategically important island of Malta. Following this, he landed his troops in Egypt at Aboukir Bay, seized Alexandria and then marched south to capture Cairo. In July, at the Battle of the Pyramids, he defeated the ruling Mamelukes. However, in August a Squadron of the British Mediterranean fleet, under the command of Rear Admiral Sir Horatio Nelson, destroyed the French fleet at the Battle of Aboukir Bay (also known as the Battle of the Nile), thereby cutting off Bonaparte's lines of supply and reinforcement with France.

The second relic at Madame Tussaud's from this period was Item 56 in the Napoléon Room. It was catalogued as Nelson's uniform coat that he wore at the Battle of the Nile on 1st-3rd August 1798 and was described as 'embroidered with silver Stars'; it was valued in 1911 at £100 (2022: £9,340). At this stage in his career, Horatio Nelson, the Norfolk-born son of a parson, was a Rear Admiral and a Knight of the Bath. It would have been the Star of that Order only that Nelson would have worn on his coat, as illustrated here. The decorations that were to follow, as shown in the companion portrait by Abbott, and which would

CHAPTER FOUR

be so ill-advisedly worn by the one-eyed, one-armed Vice Admiral at the Battle of Trafalgar, were yet to be awarded. If the 1925 exhibition catalogue and the 1911 insurance catalogue description of 'four Stars', in the plural were correct then the coat either dated from a later period in Nelson's career or was a costume made for a Tussaud waxwork. Probably the latter, given that the actual Undress uniform coat worn by Nelson at the Battle of the Nile is now in the National Maritime Museum at Greenwich (ID: UNI0022). Although not listed in the 1925 catalogue, the 1911 insurance catalogue included two more hats 'worn by Nelson', another complete Full Dress uniform, four more Stars, a letter written by Nelson (addressee not mentioned) and his Letters Patent conferring an unspecified 'Title on Nelson'. Together they were valued at £185 (2022: £17,280), although the likelihood is that the items of clothing listed were all copies.

Following the Battle of the Nile, in 1799 Bonaparte led the French Army of the East against the Ottoman province of Damascus. After initial successes, he failed to take the fortress at Acre and withdrew his plague-stricken troops to Egypt where, on 25th July, he defeated an Ottoman counter-invasion. In August, with political affairs in Paris once more in flux, he returned to France without the Directory's permission, leaving his Army behind. Back in France, on 18th Brumaire (9th November), Bonaparte led a coup d'état that toppled the Directory. He replaced it with a three-man Consulate, with himself as First Consul for a period of ten years, taking the Tuileries Palace as his residence.

In 1925, Item 174, located in the Napoléon Ante-Room at Madame Tussaud & Sons' Exhibition, was catalogued as the 'Coat worn by Napoléon as First Consul'. Fortunately, for the purpose of establishing its authenticity, it was also illustrated with a black-and-white photograph. During his rule as First Consul, Bonaparte has been depicted wearing two different versions of the consular uniform coat. The first version, worn by all three Consuls, was double-breasted, with an open, turned-down collar. The edges, tail and collar of the coat, and the front of the waistcoat, were embroidered with Egyptian-style palmettes in gold thread.

Once in power, it did not take long for Bonaparte to assert his superiority over the Second Consul, Jean Jacques-Régis de Cambacérès, and the Third Consul, Charles-François Lebrun, who almost immediately faded into the obscurity of titled but powerless

below left Bonaparte in the First Consul's original uniform by Jean Auguste Dominique Ingres.

below First Consul Bonaparte's second consular uniform, 1800.

[91]

CHAPTER FOUR

right The First Consul's uniform coat, photograph in the 1925 catalogue.

far right General Bonaparte c.1800, circle of Andrea Appiani the Elder.

General Bonaparte views the body of General Desaix at the Battle of Marengo (14th June 1800) by Jean Broc.

positions. Perhaps in order to underline the concentration of the consular power in his hands, in late June 1800 Bonaparte acquired a new consular uniform that was unique to him. The received wisdom is that this coat was given to him by the town council of Lyons, the centre of silk-weaving in France, where he stopped off on 28th-29th June 1800 on his way back to Paris, after his crushing victory over the Austrians at Marengo in northern Italy. However, far from being an unsolicited gift, it is far more likely that the silk-velvet coat was ordered by the First Consul to a specific design that was intended not only to differentiate him from the other Consuls, but also to send a subliminal message to his colleagues. Far more richly embroidered with gold and silver thread than the earlier uniform, this new coat's embroidery featured an olive-leaf motif, the classical symbol for a victor. It was also single rather than double-breasted, with a stand up, open-necked collar. Unlike the first iteration of the consular uniform, none of which appear to have survived, the First Consul's 1800 coat is now in the Napoléonic National Museum at the Château de Malmaison, albeit faded to the colour of rust.

This then begs the question: was the coat catalogued by Madame Tussaud's as Bonaparte's consular uniform the first version of the uniform, or a previously unknown copy of the second? The 1911 insurance valuers certainly thought that it was one or the other, and gave it a value of £500 (2022: £46,703). However, the gold embroidery on this coat, as can be seen in the photograph, was of a scrolling oak-leaf pattern, which was not used on either of the consular coats. Further, the cut of the jacket and the use of the embroidery appears to be that of a French General of the period. Although the coat may have been mis-catalogued, it could nonetheless have belonged to Bonaparte, and perhaps was worn by him during the Italian Campaign of 1800, in his role as a soldier, as opposed to that of his simultaneous role as First Consul. Evidence of the First Consul dressed as a General is provided by several contemporary paintings of the Battle of Marengo. These make an important point: during the Consulate, Bonaparte dressed as a soldier for battle, but in his role as a political leader he dressed as a civilian.

CHAPTER FIVE

NAPOLÉON & THE IMPERIAL FAMILY

*I*N 1802, FOLLOWING A rigged plebiscite, Napoléon Bonaparte was declared Consul for life, making him in effect the dictator of France. Eager to consolidate his rule and to prevent a Bourbon restoration, two years later he used a series of royalist and revolutionary assassination plots as the excuse to establish his imperial rule, again via a rigged referendum. This new republic, ruled by an Emperor, was based on the model of Ancient Rome, and included in the new constitution were provisions for the imperial succession to pass to his family. This necessitated the overnight creation not only of a whole new imperial iconography, but also the metamorphosis of the extended Bonaparte clan into the Imperial Family.

The matriarch of family was Napoléon's mother, the widowed Letizia Bonaparte, known henceforth as Madame Mère. She never fully approved of her son's imperial dynasty, refused to live at Court, and declined to attend her son's Coronation, although she was depicted as being present in Jacques-Louis David's painting of the event. Napoléon's wife, the former Viscomtesse de Beauharnais, of course became the Empress Joséphine. The Emperor's seven siblings were also absorbed into the new Imperial Family and often given important posts. Of the four brothers, Joseph was made King of Naples and then Spain; Lucien, being an ardent republican, never ruled a kingdom, but received the title of Prince of Canino from the Pope; Louis was appointed King of Holland; and Jérôme became King of Westphalia. Napoléon's three sisters also thrived during his ascendancy: Elisa became Duchess of Tuscany; Pauline married Prince Camillo Borghese and was created the first sovereign Duchess of Guastalla in Italy; and Caroline married Marshal Joachim Murat, Napoléon's principal cavalry commander and later King of Naples.

Napoléon's two step-children from Joséphine's first marriage were also absorbed into the imperial dynasty: Eugène de Beauharnais was appointed as Viceroy of the Kingdom of Italy; and Hortense married Napoléon's brother Louis, thus

opposite Coronation of Napoléon and Joséphine in the Cathedral of Notre-Dame de Paris, 2nd December 1804, by Jacques-Louis David and Georges Rouget.

CHAPTER FIVE

The Imperial Family

Madame Mère (1750–1836) by Robert Lefèvre.

Empress Joséphine (1763–1814) by François Gérard.

Joseph, King of Spain (1768–1844) by François Gérard.

Lucien Bonaparte (1775–1840) by François-Xavier Fabre.

Elisa Bonaparte (1777–1820) by Joseph Franque.

Louis, King of Holland (1778–1846) by François Gérard.

CHAPTER FIVE

Hortense de Beauharnais, Queen of Holland (1783–1837), with her son, Louis-Napoléon, the future Emperor Napoléon III (1808–1873), by François Gérard.

Pauline Borghese (1780–1825) by Marie-Guillemine Benoist.

Caroline Murat (1782–1839) by François Gérard.

Joachim Murat, King of Naples (1767–1815) by François Gérard.

Jérôme, robed as King of Westphalia (1784–1860) by François Gérard.

Eugène de Beauharnais, as Viceroy of Italy (1781–1824) by Andrea Appiani.

Empress Marie Louise (1791–1847) by François Gérard.

Duke of Reichstadt (1811–1832) by Leopold Bucher.

[97]

CHAPTER FIVE

becoming Queen of Holland and the mother of the future Emperor Napoléon III. Later additions to the Imperial Family included Napoléon's second wife, Marie-Louise of Austria, and their son, Napoléon II, later known as the Duke of Reichstadt.

For the most part, all went relatively well until 1812, when Napoléon took the disastrous decision to invade Russia. His defeat there, and the subsequent destruction of the *Grande Armée*, led inexorably to his first abdication and exile to Elba in 1814. This was followed in 1815 by the Hundred Days, during which he returned to France, was defeated at the Battle of Waterloo on 18th June, and forced into his second abdication and permanent exile to St Helena in the South Atlantic.

In the aftermath of Waterloo, items connected to Napoléon had a considerable notoriety value and attracted much public attention. However, as curiosity waned, the various displays were dispersed at auction. This gave Madame Tussaud and her sons the opportunity to acquire a wide range of art, artefacts and relics relating to Napoléon, his family, and his rule.

Napoléon following his first Abdication, 11th April 1814, by Paul Delaroche

It is appropriate, therefore, to start the examination of Madame Tussaud's imperial-era Napoléonica with 'Coronation Robes of Napoléon's and the Empress Joséphine' (Item 52: Napoléon Room). From 1804 until the Restoration of King Louis XVIII in 1814, these had been on display in the Cathedral of Notre-Dame de Paris, after which there are conflicting accounts of their fate. One states that they were sold at the Restoration of Louis XVIII by the Abbé Canolini, a prelate at Notre-Dame, although to whom is not recorded. Another account alleges that, although Napoléon bequeathed all his robes and uniforms to his son, they were not passed to him in Vienna in 1821 but, instead, given to Madame Mère, then living in Rome. She in turn distributed the collection on her death in 1836 to her surviving children.

Whatever the fate of the Coronation mantles after 1814, according to Madame Tussaud's 1842 inventory, they were apparently acquired for her exhibition on 16th January of that year for £105 (2022: £9,807). Although twice as much as a London housemaid earned for a year's work in 1842, this was a fraction of their original cost, which was given in the *Livre du Sacre* (the handbook of the Coronation) as Francs 74,118 (2022: £205,306). The mantles acquired by Madame Tussaud were used to dress the waxwork figures of the imperial couple, in a tableau copied from the David painting of their Coronation, an engraving of which

CHAPTER FIVE

was listed as Item 179 in the Napoléon Ante-Room. Also in this room was an engraving of 'Napoléon in his Imperial Robes' (Item 142) and an engraving of an unspecified 'Half-length Portrait of Napoléon' (Item 143). In 1911 these engravings were valued at £10 (2022: £937) and £3 (2022: £281) respectively.

At some point prior to 1925, the mantles were moved into a display case in the Napoléon Room, along with 'Imperial eagles [sic] from Malmaison'. As there was no further description, it is uncertain whether the 'eagles' were gilded-brass finials of the regimental variety or simply models of the imperial symbol. If the former, which is very doubtful, their present-day value would be well in excess of £100,000 each. So, were the Coronation mantles genuine?

In the 1925 catalogue they were described as 'the actual robes worn by Napoléon the Great and by his first wife at their coronations'. Given many of the other attributions in the exhibition catalogue, this cannot be taken as definitive, even though they were given a high insurance value in 1911 of £500 (2022: £46,703). Somewhat unhelpfully, the description in John Theodore Tussaud's *The Romance of Madame Tussaud's* is even less reassuring, stating only that the Emperor's robe was 'as worn by him at his Coronation'. The 16th January 1842 entry in the Madame Tussaud's inventory does not give their provenance either, so it is impossible to say with any certainty where they came from.

There is then a surprise: the mantles may not have been destroyed in the 1925 fire. In October 2005, Christie's offered for sale at auction on behalf of Madame Tussaud's 'a purple silk embroidered velvet robe train' (Lot 106), illustrated here. According to Christie's entry for this lot, which gave the vague provenance described above, the mantle had been 'stored in a loft' and had – it can be assumed – survived the fire. Nonetheless, Christie's were careful not to state unequivocally that the 'robe' was Napoléon's Coronation mantle, pointing out that there were differences between the garment at Madame Tussaud's and the one painted by Jacques-Louis David, including the colour of the velvet, the design of the gold-thread embroidery, and the absence of an ermine lining. These differences are also apparent in the *Livre du Sacre*, which illustrated and specified precisely the design of all the Coronation robes; these match closely the depiction of the mantle by David, but not the robe sold at Christie's.

Whether or not it was the original, Lot 106 sold in 2005 for £30,000, which indicates that the buyer thought that it probably was genuine. It seems more likely that, given the mantles were listed in the pre-fire exhibition catalogue as being on display in a cabinet, Lot 106 in the Christie's sale was a mid-nineteenth-century copy made for the Napoléonic Coronation tableau, the originals being too valuable to use for that purpose. This copy was then put into storage, and the genuine article put in a display cabinet (as Item 52), when the Coronation

Napoléon's *grand habillement* as illustrated in the *Livre du Sacré*.

Madame Tussaud's Napoléonic coronation mantle, sold at Christie's in 2005.

CHAPTER FIVE

right Empress Joséphine, photograph in the 1925 catalogue.

far right 1806 portrait of Empress Joséphine by Henri-François Riesener.

tableau was replaced in the 1860s by a Second Empire group, in which Napoléon I was placed off to one side. The whereabout of Josephine's mantle, whether a replica or the original, which had presumably been stored with the Emperor's, is currently unknown. If it still exists, modern fabric testing may be able to settle the question of the mantles' authenticity once and for all.

While on the subject of the first Empress, there was only one portrait of Joséphine at Madame Tussaud's (Item 109: Napoléon Room), which was illustrated in the 1925 catalogue, along with a lengthy biography of the Emperor's first wife and the claim that the portrait had 'long adorned the walls at Malmaison', but had been sold at the restoration of the monarchy in 1815. However, the artist was not identified, and the archives only reveal that it was bought in 1842 for £13.11.0 (2022: £1,400), as part of a lot acquired at the 'Customs House clearance sale', and valued in 1911 at £1,000 (2022: £93,407). The image in the catalogue was similar to, but not an exact copy of, a portrait of the Empress by Henri-François Riesener. This hangs in the collection at the Napoléonic National Museum at the Château de Malmaison and depicts Joséphine in the same dress and wearing the same jewels, albeit that the pose is very slightly different. Given the lack of an attribution in the exhibition and insurance catalogues, and the known location of the only similar portrait, it is probable that Item 109 was a studio copy, hence its inflated value.

Unlisted in 1925, but present in the 1911 insurance catalogue was a 'Bust of Empress Joséphine' valued at £50 (2022: £4,670), about which nothing else in known.

On the face of it, the authenticity of Item 68 in the Napoléon Room is beyond dispute. It was catalogued and illustrated as 'Gallery Picture of Napoléon the Great by Lefêvre [*sic*]', along with the following lengthy description:

> This magnificent work of art was painted by command of Napoléon himself for the palace of Fontainebleau. Napoléon is being crowned with the Wreath of Victory, and by means of the globe the painter suggests his lordship over Europe. It is unfortunate for his allegory that he should have made Moscow so prominent, and it is possible that the picture was executed when the expedition to the Russian capital was in progress, and before it had issued in irretrievable disaster.

Napoléon the Great by Robert Lefèvre (1755–1830), photograph in the 1925 catalogue.

Despite this unequivocal statement, there are a number of problems with the catalogue entry and its attribution to Robert Lefèvre, an artist who painted in the classical style and was heavily influenced by David. For a start, Item 68 depicted the Emperor in his pre-consular days, as a young man, gaunt of face and with long hair. Of itself, that does not invalidate the picture's authenticity. More compellingly, of the known forty-one portraits of Napoléon painted by Lefèvre, none has ever been described as allegorical or pre-dated the Consulate. The first, commissioned in 1803 by Dominique Vivant, Baron Denon, for the Town Hall in Dunkirk, depicted Napoléon as First Consul; it was deliberately incinerated on 3rd June 1817 by order of the Sub-Prefect of Dunkirk. Two contemporary copies of this portrait still exist, one in Bruges town hall by Marie-Joseph Vien, son of King Louis XVI's last Court Painter, Joseph-Marie Vien. The other, by Laurent Dabos, is in the Hôtel de Ville, Paris.

The remaining forty known portraits were produced after 1806, again to the order of Baron Denon (not Napoléon, although he liked Lefèvre's portrayals of himself). By this time, Denon was the Administrator of the Imperial Manufacturies and responsible for curating the imperial image as Director of the Musée Napoléon. Consequently, and unsurprisingly given Lefèvre's semi-official role as Napoléon's iconographer, his post-1806 portraits were all standard depictions of the mature Emperor in one or other of his customary uniforms. Besides which, and to judge from the image in the catalogue, the style of the painting at Madame Tussaud's bore little resemblance to any of Lefèvre's images of Napoléon or to the artist's wider *oeuvre*. Nonetheless, the attribution and the description were repeated in the 1911 insurance catalogue, with a value of £250 (2022: £23,351).

Two other pictures in the collection were attributed to Lefèvre. The first, valued in 1911 at £300 (2022: £28,022) was a full-length portrait of Jérôme Bonaparte (Item 89: Napoléon Room), wearing the *petit habillement* (Court dress) of a First Empire Senator, which he was not – although he was appointed President of the Senate in 1852 during the Second Empire. Jérôme's early career

CHAPTER FIVE

was naval not political, until he fell out with his eldest brother over his first marriage to an American, Elizabeth Patterson, in 1803. On their rapprochement in 1805, following Jérôme's agreement to divorce Elizabeth, Napoléon created him an Admiral, a General, and finally King of Westphalia in 1807.

A remarkably similar portrait to Item 89, showing Jérôme in the *petit habillement* of the King of Westphalia, was painted in 1811 by François Gérard, the imperial, royal and society portraitist, created Baron Gérard in 1809. Madame Tussaud's version may have been a later, and unintentionally inaccurate, adaptation of the Gérard canvas.

As for Item 102 in the Napoléon Room, this was simply described as 'Another Portrait of Jérôme' with an unhelpful cross-reference back to the one attributed to Lefèvre. The painting was, however, listed in the 1911 insurance catalogue with a value of £300 (2022: £28,022), but it was attributed to someone called 'Legras'. No one of that name was working as an artist in France during the First Empire, although in the second-half of the nineteenth century August, Auguste and François-Théodore Legras were established names in the field of fine art.

Jérôme Bonaparte by Robert Lefèvre, photograph in the 1925 catalogue.

Item 87 in the Napoléon Room was a portrait of Jérôme's second wife, Princess Catherine of Württemberg. Her dynastic union with the Emperor's youngest brother in 1807 had been arranged by Napoléon as part of his creation of the Confederation of the Rhine, a group of client states subordinated to France. Despite this unpromising start, and her husband's serial infidelity, the marriage was a success, producing two sons and a daughter and lasting until Catherine's death in 1835. Her portrait at Madame Tussaud's was not illustrated nor described in the 1925 catalogue, but it was attributed to Lefèvre and valued at £300 (2022: £28,022) in the 1911 insurance catalogue. Despite this attribution and value, and the existence of many portraits of Catherine by other artists, there exists no record of Lefèvre ever having painted her. However, like her husband, there is a full-length portrait of her by Gérard, now at Versailles. So, perhaps the Madame Tussaud's picture was a copy of that one.

Queen Catherine of Westphalia (1783–1835) by François Gérard.

Returning to images of the Emperor, and excepting the paintings by David which are the subject of Chapter 7, there were three busts of Napoléon and a curious picture called 'The Napoléon Ladder' (Item 61: Napoléon Room) in the 1925 catalogue. This last item was described in the exhibition catalogue as illustrating:

> Napoleon's rise and descent. The column on the left records his ascent, and should be read upwards; the other column shows the stages of his downward progress, beginning with that expedition to Moscow which formed the turning-point of his portentous career.

It was given a value of £10 (2022: £934) in 1911.

CHAPTER FIVE

far left Napoléon by Raimondo Trentanove (1792–1832) after Antonio Canova.

left Napoléon by Antonio Canova.

Turning to the busts, in addition to the three listed in the 1925 catalogue, there was also one by Henry Robinson, which was unlisted both in the 1911 insurance catalogue and in the 1925 catalogue, but which appeared in the 1842 inventory, with the information that it had been acquired in that year for £6.6.0 (2022: £600). The first of the listed busts was Item 8 in the Entrance Hall, which was attributed to the Italian sculptor, Raimondo Trentanove, and stated to have been exhibited 'in the London Museum, now the Egyptian Hall, by Mr Sainsbury'. As already noted in Chapter 4, Sainsbury's collection was sold at auction in 1845, at which time Madame Tussaud's sons acquired a number of pieces. Although not illustrated, the bust was almost certainly Trentanove's neo-Classical image of Napoléon, a copy of which is shown here. Given Trentanove's dates, the bust must have been based on the iconic, sculpted-from-life herms of the Emperor by Antonio Canova and Antoine Chaudet. Although not attributed to Trentanove, the bust was included in the 1911 insurance catalogue with a value of £35 (2022: £3,269)

The second bust, Item 77 in the Napoléon Room, was simply catalogued as 'by Franzoni'. He was Francesco Antonio Franzoni, an Italian sculptor and restorer based in Rome at the turn of the eighteenth century, who was best known for his animal sculptures. Without any further clues, and with no images in the public domain of a Napoléonic bust by Franzoni, it may have been one of those ranged behind the figures in the 1860s tableau illustrated earlier. In any event, it was valued in 1911 at £30 (2022: £2,802).

CHAPTER FIVE

above *Apotheosis of Napoléon* by Bertel Thorvaldsen (1770–1844), photograph in the 1925 catalogue.

above right Bertel Thorvaldsen by Horace Vernet.

Even more problematic is the 'Bust of Napoléon the Great by Thorwaldsen' [*sic*], catalogued as Item 95 in the same room. This was included, with the artistic attribution, in the 1911 insurance catalogue at £250 (2022: £23,351) and was illustrated in the 1925 catalogue. It is also clearly visible in the photograph of the 1860s Napoléonic tableau, sited between the waxworks of the Empress Eugénie and Napoléon III. The 1925 catalogue entry described the bust as: 'this magnificent work of art, considered one of the masterpieces of the sculptor...', which implied that it was the marble original, an assertion (as to the material) confirmed in the 1911 insurance catalogue.

Danish by birth, Bertel Thorvaldsen spent most of his working life in Italy, where he gained an international reputation and clientele for his robustly neo-Classical portrait sculptures and figurative groups in marble. Often compared to Canova, whose position as the leading sculptor-of-the-day he took on the Italian's death in 1822, Thorvaldsen's works are now less well-regarded than those of his predecessor.

The Dane's original bust of the Emperor, which he based on contemporary drawings and the subject's death mask, is better known as the *Apotheosis of Napoléon*. It was commissioned from Thorvaldsen in 1829 by a Scottish collector, Alexander Murray, and on completion it was sent to Murray's house in Kirkcudbrightshire, Scotland. There it remained until 20th January 1846, when it was purchased at auction by the enthusiastic collector of Napoléonica, Alexander Hamilton, 10th Duke of Hamilton & 7th Duke of Brandon, who installed it in the Tribune at Hamilton Palace, his ducal pile in South Lanarkshire. Then, in 1882, it was again sold at auction to help pay-down the accumulated debts of the 11th and 12th Dukes. The purchaser was recorded as J. B. Greenshields of The Kerse, Lanarkshire, who paid £640.10.0 (2022: £60,500) for it. Following the sale of The Kerse in 1913, Murray's *Apotheosis of Napoléon* was sold in August 1916 at a Sotheby's auction, when it was bought by a Monsieur Bacri of Paris. The next that is known of the bust, according to the online inventory of the Thorvaldsen Museum in Copenhagen (where it is catalogued as A867), was its acquisition by the museum in 1929 from an unidentified seller.

That would appear to be definitive as far as the original is concerned. The museum's online inventory specifies that it has two examples of the *Apotheosis*

CHAPTER FIVE

Apotheosis of Napoléon in the Napoléon Room, *c.*1900.

of Napoléon in addition to A867 just described: A909 is a plaster cast, bought from an unnamed private owner in 1974; and A252 is also a plaster cast, bequeathed to the museum by Thorvaldsen on his death on 24th March 1844, and put on display when the museum opened in 1848. However, according to a Christie's 1998 sale catalogue entry, the museum should have *four* examples of the work, the fourth one being a marble *Apotheosis of Napoléon* that 'was found unfinished in [Thorvaldsen's] atelier [after his death] and was completed under the supervision of H. W. Bissen for the Museum Thorvaldsen'. That being the case, either the museum has *two* marble versions of the bust – the Murray original and the one completed after the sculptor's death – or, if its online inventory is correct, then it may at some point after 1848 have disposed of the one completed 'under the supervision' of Bissen.

In trying to establish the authenticity of Madame Tussaud & Sons' Item 95, it is known that during his lifetime Thorvaldsen's workshop created at least five copies in marble of the *Apotheosis of Napoléon*, and several in plaster. The marble copies include the one that was sold at Christie's (Lot 121) on 16th October 1998 for $63,000 (2022: £92,393); a second, now in the Auckland Art Gallery, New Zealand; and a third in the Montreal Museum of Fine Arts in Quebec, Canada.

While it now seems clear that Madame Tussaud's *Apotheosis of Napoléon* was not the original, it could have been one of these workshop copies. It could even have been that completed by Bissen, which may have been disposed of by the museum after it received the Thorvaldsen bequest in 1844. This, after all, was the very time when Madame Tussaud's was busy acquiring Napoléonica; and the Bissen-finished bust may have been de-accessioned by the museum because it

[105]

≈ CHAPTER FIVE ≈

Madame Mère, photograph in the 1925 catalogue.

was not all the master's own work. As the bust's present whereabout is unknown, it can be assumed that it was destroyed in the 1925 fire. For the rest, as with so much of the Madame Tussaud & Sons' collection, the truth may never be known.

Before moving on to the rest of the Imperial Family, it is worth noting that Item 110, a pencil drawing of the Emperor 'placed between his two wives' in the Napoléon Room, was attributed in the 1925 catalogue to Baron Gérard. Nothing more is known about this image, which was not listed in the 1911 insurance catalogue. It was probably a working drawing for one of the Baron's paintings of Napoléon executed after 1799, when the artist received his first Bonapartist commission: to paint a portrait of Madame Mère.

Madame Mère was represented in the Napoléon Room at Madame Tussaud's with three images. The first was a portrait (Item 91), which was listed in the 1856 inventory, without an artistic attribution, as a half-length 'Picture of Napoléon's Mother' with a value of £50 (2022: £4,670). Devalued in the 1905 inventory to £25 (2022: £2,335), by the date of the 1911 inventory and the insurance catalogue it had been revalued at £250 (2022: £23,351). A photograph of it shown here was included in the 1925 exhibition catalogue. The second was a portrait, illustrated and catalogued as by David (Item 93~see Chapter 7); and a terracotta bust (Item 84) valued in 1911 at £30 (2022: £2,802). Unusually, the bust was comprehensively catalogued as follows:

> This striking bust of Napoléon's mother was completed from a plaster cast taken in Rome after death and was purchased … from Count Léon, a natural son of Napoléon I by a Polish lady. He bore a remarkable resemblance, both in form and feature, to his father, who conferred upon him the title he bore, and specially mentioned him in his last Will & Testament … In his later years, Count Léon settled in England, living in modest rooms in Camden Town, where one of the Messrs Tussaud was introduced to him by the Count de Lally Tollendaal [*sic*].

Although this entry would appear to be definitive as to the provenance of the bust of Madame Mère, it is riddled with contradictions, starting with the statement about Count de Lally Tollendal introducing the Tussauds to Count Léon.

Originally from Ireland, the de Lally-Tollendal's were Jacobites who moved to France after 1715. Once there, Thomas Arthur Lally followed his father into the military service of the French King and, in due course, was created a General, Comte de Lally and Baron de Tollendal by King Louis XV. In 1766, having lost the Indian city of Pondicherry to the English in 1761 and then been imprisoned in England, Thomas returned to France where – presumably *pour encourager les autres* – he was tried and executed for military incompetence. The sentence was unjust, and the execution was badly botched: the Marquis de Sade recorded that

[106]

CHAPTER FIVE

'de Lally-Tollendal danced around for half-a-minute trying to hold his head on'. In recognition of the injustice of Thomas's execution, he was posthumously pardoned by King Louis XVI in 1778. Thomas's son, the exotically named Trophime-Gérard de Lally-Tollendal, was a royalist politician who emigrated to England during the French Revolution in the 1790s. Following the restoration of the monarchy, and by then back in France, Trophime-Gérard was created a Marquis by King Louis XVIII in 1815. He died in Paris in 1830, without issue, at which point the de Lally-Tollendal titles became extinct.

Because the elder Count de Lally-Tollendal died when Madame Tussaud was five-years-old, if one of her sons had been introduced to Count Léon it must have been by the second Count (and first Marquis) Trophime-Gérard de Lally-Tollendal and *before* 1830. At that date, Count Léon – described by the historian, Andrew Roberts, as 'an argumentative, drunken wastrel' – was twenty-four-years-old and, therefore, not in his 'later years'. As for Madame Mère, she was still very much alive, only dying in 1836, making it impossible that the bust was cast from her death mask.

Count Charles Denuelle de la Plaigne Léon (1806–1881).

To throw further doubt on the catalogue's account of the bust's acquisition, Count Léon's mother was Napoléon's French (not Polish) mistress, Eléonore Denuelle de la Plaigne, and there is no official record of the Count, an inveterate and unlucky gambler, living in England after the abdication of his natural father. In fact, he spent his early adult life as an officer in the French National Guard, fought a duel in Paris in 1832 over a gambling debt with Captain Charles Hesse, a Waterloo veteran, and died in poverty in Pontoise, France, in 1881. He did, however, have two sons, Charles and Gaston, who successively inherited the title of Count Léon, but neither would have been known as such prior to the year of their father's death in 1881.

Taking these various facts together, the errors in the 1925 catalogue entry were either a result of sloppy drafting or were deliberately misleading. If the latter, then there can be no certainty about the authenticity of the bust's provenance, were it not for the following story in Chapter XXV, pages 149-150, of John Theodore Tussaud's *The Romance of Madame Tussaud's*. The account is set in the aftermath of the disastrous Franco-Prussian War of 1870, which resulted in the fall of Napoleon III and the end of the Second Empire:

> At about this time [John Randall Tussaud, Marie's grandson] met Count Léon, the natural son of Napoléon the Great. The Count was then nearing seventy years of age, and had taken refuge in this country after the great *debacle* of 1870. He lived in modest lodgings at Camden Town, and to pay his way set about selling the last remaining relics of the Imperial family he had in his possession.

CHAPTER FIVE

> In [Joseph Randall Tussaud's] diary I now have before me I find that my father visited him on 31st of January 1873, the Count having expressed a wish to show him the family heirlooms, with the view to their finding a permanent resting-place among many Napoléonic memorials at Madame Tussaud's.

The Count offered him a fine miniature of Napoléon's brother, Lucien; a terracotta bust of Napoléon's mother, 'Madame Mère'; and a snuff-box left by Napoléon with Count Léon's mother. The box contained a portion of the snuff which the Emperor had been using. There was also a lock of hair belonging to Napoléon's son, the Duc de Reichstadt, known in high Imperial days as the King of Rome. One or two of these relics were acquired for the Exhibition.

Unfortunately, although the text goes some way towards unravelling the erroneous cataloguing, it does not stipulate which items were acquired, so failing to provide a definitive provenance for the bust which, in any event, was lost in the 1925 fire.

Although not strictly relevant to the bust of Madame Mère, but for those readers interested in the fate of Count Léon, John Theodore Tussaud's account continued:

> The Count bore a striking resemblance to the Emperor, except in two particulars: his figure was cast in a larger mould, and his eyes were hazel, whereas Napoléon's were blue-grey. Count Léon returned to France, leaving behind him in London his son Charles, for whom I obtained a place in a City warehouse, where he remained engaged for several years, being at no pains to disguise his identity ... Count Léon finally settled at Pontoise, some twenty miles north-west of Paris, first at the Villa Davenport in the rue l'Hermitage and afterwards in the rue de Beaujon. This was his last stage. The room that he made his final refuge he adorned with four portraits of Napoléon, 'my glorious father'.
>
> To what depths had the Emperor's son fallen! The old man's shirts were in rags: he could not afford clean lines; he had to forgo tobacco. He died on 14th of April, 1881, and without pomp or ceremony his body was laid in a pauper's grave. His only memorial was a grassy mound and a little black wooden cross that soon rotted and fell to pieces.

How John Randall Tussaud knew what had happened to Count Léon after he returned to France was not explained, but he could have heard it from Léon's son, Charles, who may still have been stacking shelves in a City warehouse at the time of his father's death in 1881.

CHAPTER FIVE

The next member of the Imperial Family to be featured at Madame Tussaud's was Lucien Bonaparte. Catalogued as Item 75 in the Napoléon Room was a 'Bust of Lucien Bonaparte by Trentanove', the Italian sculptor whose image of Napoléon was in the Entrance Hall. In addition to that of the Emperor, Raimondo Trentanove is known to have sculpted two busts of Madame Mère, one contemporaneous with that of the Emperor and now in the Palais Fesch Musée des Beaux-Arts in Ajaccio, Corsica, and the other created in 1818 and now in the Galleria Nationale de Parma, Italy. Trentanove is not, however, known to have sculpted one of Lucien. Nonetheless, neither this, nor the paucity of the exhibition catalogue entry, invalidates the attribution of Item 75 to the Italian sculptor, although the 1911 insurance catalogue valued the bust at a mere £30 (2022: £2,802), which may cast some doubt.

A full-length portrait of 'Prince Lucien Bonaparte in the robes of a French Senator, by Lethière' (Item 104: Napoléon Room) may have been the work of Guillaume Guillon-Lethière, who was the illegitimate son of a French lawyer and a freed black slave; he was also Lucien's protégé and his art consultant in Spain from 1800 to 1802. There exists in a private collection a double portrait of Lucien contemplating his mistress, painted by Guillon-Lethière in 1802, and there is a second portrait of Lucien in civilian clothes painted by the artist in 1806. There is, however, no record – other than in the 1925 exhibition catalogue – of a portrait that matches the description of Item 104. In the 1911 insurance catalogue the painting was ascribed to 'Le Thier' and valued at £300 (2022: £28,022), but that is not definitive as to its artistic attribution.

below left Lucien Bonaparte Contemplating his Mistress by Guillaume Guillon-Lethière, 1802.

below Lucien Bonaparte, photograph in the 1925 catalogue.

[109]

CHAPTER FIVE

Bust of Napoléon in the Classical style by Guiseppe Rocchi.

None of this might have mattered because, although Item 104 was not described in the exhibition catalogue, it was illustrated. Unfortunately, the black-and-white photograph, labelled 'LUCIEN BONAPARTE (*From the Portrait by Lethière*)', was *not* that of Lucien. It was, actually, a well-known painting of Jérôme Bonaparte by Gérard, which was illustrated and discussed earlier in this chapter, the original of which now hangs at the Musée National du Château de Fontainebleau. It is, of course, possible that the 1925 catalogue's captions of the two paintings were inadvertently exchanged in production, although that would not explain why Item 104 was attributed to Lethière, but Item 89 was captioned as Jérôme and attributed to Lefèvre.

The catalogue entry for Item 96 in the Napoléon Room, labelled 'Louis Bonaparte, King of Holland', although long on the subject's biographical details gave no information about the painting. The 1911 insurance catalogue stated that it was a half-length portrait worth £25 (2022: £2,330). Slightly more informative as to attribution (but nothing else) was given by the 1925 catalogue entry for Item 72 in the Napoléon Room, described as a 'Bust of Murat by Rocchi'. Little is known about Guiseppe Rocchi, beyond the fact that he sculpted a bust of Murat's imperial brother-in-law in the classical style. The 1911 insurance catalogue called him merely 'Giuseppe' and assigned a value of £40 to the bust (2022: £3,736).

Madame Tussaud's no doubts as to attribution with Item 111 in the Napoléon Room, which the exhibition catalogue illustrated and unequivocally stated was 'The Empress Marie Louise, by the Baron Gérard'. The entry was equally unequivocal:

> This portrait of Napoléon's second wife, daughter of the Emperor of Austria, and mother of the King of Rome (Napoléon II), was painted by command of the Emperor, who was so pleased with it that he ordered it to be worked in tapestry, which was exhibited at the Louvre.

The clear implication of this catalogue entry was that the painting of Marie Louise was the original, an attribution underscored by the 1911 insurance catalogue which put a price on it of £1,200 (2022: £112,008), the third highest valuation in the catalogue after Napoléon's Waterloo carriage and the blade of the guillotine. At best, however, it may have been a studio copy, one of which today hangs in the Musée National du Château de Fontainebleau while the original hangs in the Kunsthistoriches Museum in Vienna. Less problematic was Item 136 in the same room, which was simply listed as 'The Coronation of Marie Louise (engraving)'. Although not listed in the 1911 insurance catalogue, this was almost certainly an engraving of Georges Rouget's *Marriage of Napoléon I and Marie Louise*.

The last two items relating to Empress Marie Louise at Madame Tussaud's

[110]

CHAPTER FIVE

far left Empress Marie Louise by François Gérard, photograph in the 1925 catalogue.

left Marriage of Napoléon I and Marie Louise by Georges Rouget, 1810.

were a pair of portraits, one of the Empress and the other of the Emperor, who was the first of her three husbands. However, although these paintings appear in the 1843 inventory, they were not listed in the 1925 catalogue or the 1911 insurance catalogue. Given that Madame Tussaud's paid the not inconsiderable sum of £144 (2022: £13,450) for the two pictures on 10th July 1842, and a month later paid a commission for their acquisition of £15.15.0 (2022: £1,475) to a Mr Bently [*sic*], the likelihood is that they were originals, although by whom is impossible to determine as they do not appear in any of the archive photographs. The aforementioned agent for the portraits' purchase may have been the publisher and printer, Richard Bentley, the founder of the periodical, *Bentley's Miscellany*, which was edited by Charles Dickens.

Last to be considered in this chapter are items at Madame Tussaud's that were associated with Napoléon François Joseph Charles Bonaparte, otherwise known successively as the Prince Imperial of France, the King of Rome, Emperor Napoléon II, the Duke of Reichstadt and 'L'Aiglon'. Born in 1811, Napoléon François Joseph Charles was Napoléon's longed-for legitimate male heir, and as such was showered with honours, property and gifts. The latter included a cot designed by the painter and draughtsman, Pierre-Paul Prud'hon, a baptismal present to the infant from the City of Paris. It was installed on a dais under a canopy in one of the State Rooms in the Tuileries Palace. Not intended for actual use, in 1814 it was taken to Vienna by Empress Marie Louise, where it remains on display in the Imperial Treasury at the Hofburg. Meanwhile, rather more practical cots for the King of Rome's use – all made by the leading furniture makers of the day – were commissioned for each of the imperial palaces. One of these cots can be seen in a portrait of the Empress and her son by Gérard, hanging at the Palace of Versailles. Another was acquired by Madame Tussaud's

CHAPTER FIVE

right Cot designed for the King of Rome by Pierre-Paul Prud'hon, at the Imperial Treasury, Vienna.

middle Empress Marie Louise and the infant King of Rome by François Gérard.

far right King of Rome's cot, photograph in the 1925 catalogue.

(Item 53: Napoléon Room) with the following attribution: 'It was made by the famous Jacob, of Paris, and its intrinsic value has been estimated at £500' (2022: £46,703). That said, the 1911 insurance catalogue gave it a value of only £300 (2022: £28,022) and did not ascribe a maker.

However, the cot was illustrated in the catalogue, and to judge from the photograph it could well have been the work of the master *menuisier*, Georges Jacob, or his son, François-Honoré-Georges Jacob-Desmalter, who took over the family workshop in 1796. The firm of Jacob-Desmalter in the rue Meslée, Paris, received many commissions from the Imperial Family and, in addition to their in-house designs, created furniture designed by Pierre-Paul Prud'hon and the leading architect, Charles Percier.

Placed with the cot in the Napoléon Room were what the 1925 catalogue admitted were 'facsimiles' of the infant King's sceptre and orb. As the cot, orb and sceptre were destroyed in the 1925 fire, and there is no mention of the cot's acquisition in the archives, there is no way now of verifying its provenance or authenticity.

Bust of the King of Rome, aged 10 months, after Henri Joseph Rutxhiel.

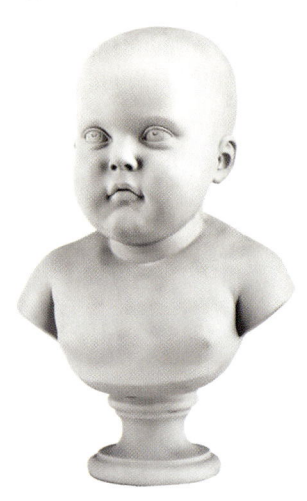

The second artefact associated with the Emperor's son was Item 164 in the Napoléon Ante-Room, described as a 'Bust of the King of Rome'. No description followed, but it may have been a likeness of the infant Napoléon François Joseph Charles Bonaparte, copies of which can still be bought in Paris for €550 (£468), as opposed to a bust of the more mature Duke of Reichstadt, as he was re-titled in 1818. In the 1911 insurance catalogue it was described as 'a Small Bronze' and valued at £15 (2022: £1,401).

Rather more was asserted in the exhibition catalogue about Item 105 in the Napoléon Room, described as 'Locks of the Hair of Napoléon and of his Son', which were valued in 1911 at £100 (2022: £9,340). It is well-established that during his lifetime the Emperor freely gave away locks of his hair as gifts. There are many examples in museums and public collections, and others regularly appear for sale

CHAPTER FIVE

at auction. That they were not all genuine is confirmed by the Emperor's former aide, Charles, Comte de Flahaut, who famously remarked that he had 'seen enough hair since Napoléon's death to carpet the floor of Versailles'.

In any event, prior to his death in 1821 Napoléon instructed his valet on St Helena, Louis-Joseph-Narcisse Marchand, that after his death the valet was to send a lock of hair from his son, the King of Rome, to Madame Mère. Marchand was also instructed to distribute clumps of Napoléon's hair to the Imperial Family and the suite-in-waiting on St Helena. This instruction was carried out. A lock of his master's hair retained by Marchand was later given by him to a friend, who in turn sold it to Madame Tussaud's. The lock of the King of Rome's hair acquired by Madame Tussaud's was, presumably, the one sold to her grandson, John Randall Tussaud, by Count Léon in 1873.

Count Louis-Joseph-Narcisse Marchand (1791–1876) by Jean-Baptiste Mauzaisse.

The loss of the imperial follicles in the 1925 fire may, at the time, have seemed more a matter of historical than financial regret. That would no longer be the case: a single strand of Napoléon's hair, attached by sealing wax to a piece of paper on which was written 'A Single Hair of Napoléon Bonaparte's head 29th Augt 1816', sold at auction in 2015 for £130. Further evidence of the value of the Emperor's barnet is provided by the prices paid for Lots 87 and 176 at the sale of the Monaco Collection of Napoléonica on Sunday 16th November 2014. The first lot, with a pre-sale estimate of €1,500-2,000, consisted of a glazed reliquary frame containing two locks of hair, one belonging to the First Consul and the other to Joséphine. It sold for €10,500 (£14,634). The second lot included two whisps of hair belonging to the Emperor and his second Empress; the pre-sale estimate was €2-3,000 and the hammer price was €8,500 (£11,847). Being much rarer, a lock of the infant King of Rome's hair would today be worth well in excess of those attributed to either of his parents.

Duke of Reichstadt by Carl von Sales.

The last item relating to the King of Rome in Madame Tussaud & Sons' Exhibition was Item 100 in the Napoléon Room. This was catalogued in both 1911 and 1925 as 'The King of Rome, by Sale' [sic], and was almost certainly a copy of the portrait of the Duke of Reichstadt by the Austrian imperial portraitist, Carl von Sales, which hangs in the Napoléon Room at Schönbrunn Palace, Vienna. The archives disclose that Madame Tussaud's paid £45.5.0 (2022: £4,250) for this painting in 1842, which seems rather excessive unless it was a studio copy; it was valued in 1911 at £100 (2022: £9,340).

[113]

CHAPTER SIX

NAPOLÉONICA

COLLECTORS HAVE ALWAYS BEEN interested in acquiring peripheral items associated with the theme of their collections. For example, a museum specialising in eighteenth century paintings will, whenever possible, acquire letters, furniture, items of clothing or artist's materials that belonged to, or were associated with, the painters whose works are on display. In the case of Madame Tussaud & Sons, this was particularly true when it came to items associated with Napoléon. Indeed, there seems to have been no limits to the parameters the Tussauds applied when making acquisitions, with the Emperor's toothbrush being every bit as desirable as his carriages.

Most of Madame Tussaud's pre-1925 collection has so far been grouped either thematically or chronologically. However, in this chapter the more general concept of Napoléonica encompasses items relating to the Emperor that are not specific to an artist or an event, although all have a Lucien Bonaparte provenance.

Doubts about these items relate more to the cataloguing than authenticity. Indeed, there is an interesting footnote in Madame Tussaud & Sons' 1883 exhibition catalogue, which stated that all the Napoléonica in the exhibition had either been 'affirmed' as genuine in front of a Master in Chancery (i.e. a judge), or had a 'certificate of genuineness that may be seen'.

Had the authenticity of the objects on display been challenged in the late-nineteenth century? The archives has no answer to that question. The footnote also made a statement which, 140 years later, is highly relevant to the current controversy surrounding the repatriation of museum items, but on which Madame Tussaud's self-evidently failed to act:

> ...everything connected with the first Emperor Napoléon...ought not be with propriety in private hands; but should take their place in the "INVALIDES" in Paris, where rest the remains of the great Soldier, General, Consul and Emperor of the French, amidst his companions in arms.

opposite Napoléon Crossing the Alps by Jacques-Louis David.

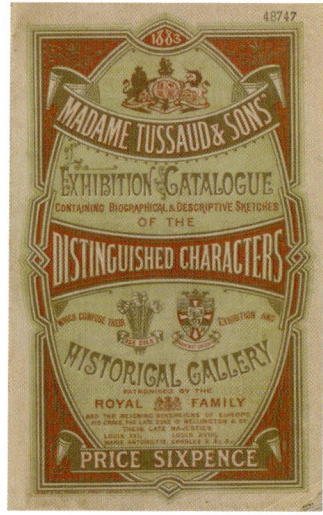

Madame Tussaud & Sons' 1883 exhibition catalogue.

≈ CHAPTER SIX ≈

above *Marengo* by Baron Antoine-Jean Gros.

above right *Sara* by Gottlob Alexander Sauerweid.

Item 150 in the Napoléon Ante-Room was described as a 'Bronze Equestrian Statuette of Napoléon – a beautiful example of the art of Mansion [*sic*], showing the Emperor on *Marengo*'. There are many different variations in bronze of this subject, usually based on a painting such as *Napoléon Crossing the Alps* by Jacques-Louis David (see Chapter 7). Interestingly, although not listed in the 1925 exhibition catalogue, the 1911 insurance catalogue stated that there was in the collection a 'Large Gallery Picture – *Napoléon Crossing the Alps* by Vernet', valued at £250 (2022: £23,351). This attribution was presumably to Carl Vernet (1758–1836), the son of the better-known Claude Joseph Vernet, who specialised in painting horses. As for the 'Bronze Equestrian Statuette of Napoléon' (Item 150: Napoléon Ante-Room), without a photograph it is impossible to know upon which picture it was based.

What is known about the bronze horse depicted in Item 150 is that Napoléon acquired *Marengo* from the El Naseri Stud in 1798 (although some sources state that the animal was the gift of Sheikh Khalil el Bakri, a member of the Great Diwan in Cairo). From that date onwards, the future Emperor was usually (but not invariably) depicted on a pale-grey Arab charger. But while the image was reasonably constant, there must be some doubt as to whether it was the same horse. This is because, at the height of his power, Napoléon had more than fifty horses for his exclusive use in the Imperial Mews, including several pale greys with names that included *Sheikh*, *Distinguished* and *Sara*.

According to Madame Tussaud's 1843 ledger, the bronze was acquired in May 1842 for £60 (2022: £5,604), and was valued in the 1911 insurance catalogue at a disappointing £30 (2022: £2,802). The 1843 ledger also stated that £3 (2022: £280) was paid by way of commission for its purchase to 'Mr Unsterdown'. It

CHAPTER SIX

is worth noting that the price *paid* by Madame Tussaud's for the bronze was, relatively speaking, rather more than the £3,200 being asked at the time of writing by The Armoury of St James's, a London dealer in militaria and Napoléonica, for a 21cm high 'Equestrian Bronze Figure of Napoléon I on *Marengo*'.

Not a lot more is known about the objects listed as Item 66 in the Napoléon Room, described in the 1925 catalogue as 'Napoléon's Girandoles – one of a pair of chandeliers, a gift from Napoléon to the Duchess of Canizaro, said to have cost £800' (2022: £74,725); the second was listed as Item 135 and cross-referenced back to Item 66. In the 1911 insurance catalogue, they were valued as a pair at £300 (2022: £28,022) with the additional information that they were 'with Trophies (on wall)'. Girandoles are, in fact, multi-branched candlesticks that are sometimes wall-mounted, and are not chandeliers, which always hang from the ceiling. Although not illustrated, the Emperor's gift to the Duchess would almost certainly have been militarily-themed – hence the reference to 'with Trophies' – and made of ormolu (gilded bronze) by Pierre-Philippe Thomire, Napoléon's favourite *bronzier*.

In a further example of 1925 miscataloguing, the Duchess's name is incorrectly spelt. But who was she? Born in England in 1785, Sophia Johnstone inherited a fortune from her natural father, George Johnstone, a Director of the East India Company. Described by the diarist Charles Greville, and confirmed in a cartoon by Landseer, as 'very short and fat with rather a handsome face, totally uneducated but full of humour', in 1814 Sophia married the impoverished Italian aristocrat Francis, Duke of Cannizzaro. The marriage gave him an income and her a title, but apparently there was little love between them. He soon returned to Italy with his mistress, and Sophia took up with a 'fiddler from a second-rate theatre in Milan'. How and if she came into Napoléon's orbit is unrecorded, but given the date of her marriage, she may have met him during his exile on Elba.

The girandoles were acquired by Madame Tussaud's from a Mr Russell on 1st May 1842 for £78 (2022: £7,285). As Madame Tussaud's 1843 ledger also includes an entry dated 18th May 1842, showing that Russell received commission and a £10 (2022: £934) advance on pictures, and two £50 (2022: £4,670 each) 'gratuities', he was probably the auctioneer of the Duchess's effects, or the agent for their sale, following her death in 1841.

Two display cases in the Napoléon Room were described as a mixed collection of 'Napoléon Relics' (Items 99) and 'Napoléon Mementoes' (Item 113). They included a gold repeater watch*, probably made by the Emperor's Swiss watchmaker, Abraham-Louis Breguet, which, according to the exhibition's 1925 catalogue, 'was used by Napoléon on St Helena, [and] was given by him to his valet'. Also

Napoléon I on Marengo, 1890.
© The Armoury of St James's

Duchess of Cannizzaro (1785–1841), c.1830, by Sir Edwin Landseer.

* It has recently emerged that this watch survived the 1925 holocaust, albeit 'badly damaged by fire'. It was offered for sale at Christie's in 2005 but failed to sell. It may still be in Madame Tussaud's uncatalogued archives.

[117]

CHAPTER SIX

above William Bullock (1873–1849) by Jean-Henri Marlet.

above right The Egyptian Hall, Piccadilly, *c*.1828.

included were a table knife, with the Imperial arms on the handle, and a 'diamond scarf pin'. Both had both been found in Napoléon's campaign carriage after the Battle of Waterloo by a Prussian infantry officer, Major Freiherr (Baron) Heinrich Eugen von Keller (see Chapter 8). The table knife would have been of *vermeille* (silver-gilt) and made by goldsmith Martin-Guillaume Biennais, who created all the silverware and *nécessaires de voyage* for this carriage. The Tussaud 1843 ledger recorded that the watch and the scarf pin were acquired from 'Mr Bullock' on 24th July 1832 for £50 (2022: £4,670), and the table knife was acquired on 29th May 1842 for £4.10.0 (2022: £400) 'at Mr Bullock's sale'. In the 1911 insurance catalogue, the watch was valued at £350 (2022: £32,692); the knife at £20 (2022: £1,868); and the diamond pin £50 (2022: £4,670). In addition, it listed two empty *nécessaires de voyage* cases at £10 (2022: £934) each, and assorted silver, silver-gilt and plate worth £465 (2022: £43,434), all of which had the same provenance as the knife and diamond pin.

William Bullock started life as a Birmingham-based jeweller. By the end of the eighteenth century, he was better known for his Cabinet of Curiosities, which he moved into the newly-built Egyptian Hall in Piccadilly, London, in 1812. After the Battle of Waterloo in 1815, Bullock became a prolific collector of Napoléonica, all of which he added to his exhibition at the Egyptian Hall. However, in 1819 he disposed of it all at an auction that he conducted himself. So successful was this sale that Bullock used the empty Hall for further auctions, with himself as the auctioneer. Interestingly, the 1883 exhibition catalogue included the text of a letter sent by Bullock to Madame Tussaud's dated 12th November 1832, which contradicted the 1925 catalogue entry concerning the watch:

The French Repeating Watch which you had of me I had from Monsieur Mati, of Paris, who was Valet of the late Emperor of France and accompanied him in his

CHAPTER SIX

Russian Campaign, and declared it to have been presented to him by Napoléon on his leaving him, after the battle of Leipzig [1813].

The letter, and a separate entry in the 1883 catalogue, also makes clear that Napoléon's 'diamond scarf pin' was actually created by Bullock using a diamond he had acquired from the noted mineralogist, John Mawe, then a diamond merchant in The Strand. This was one of the many diamonds found in a jewel box (Item 112: Napoléon Room) in Napoléon's campaign carriage, which were later bought by Mawe from the Prussian Freiherr who captured it.

The remainder of the objects displayed under Items 99 and 113, and some other pieces to be described further on, all had a Lucien Bonaparte provenance. According to the 1883 catalogue footnotes, and has already been mentioned, some of these items were bequeathed by Napoléon to his son the King of Rome, but failed to reach him in Vienna. They were instead given to Madame Mère, who in turn bequeathed them in 1836 to Lucien; the remainder were sent to Lucien from St Helena in 1822, following the death of Napoléon.

Lucien Bonaparte, Prince of Canino and Musignano.

In whichever way they reached him, the 1883 catalogue claimed – despite no supporting historical evidence – that all the Napoléonica was in Lucien's London house, Etruria Lodge in St John's Wood, in the 1830s. Apparently, when he moved permanently to Viterbo in Italy in 1832, the house and its contents were placed in the care of Messrs Stafford, Gee & Stafford of 1 Buckingham Street, The Strand, London, a firm of solicitors which conveniently also acted for Madame Tussaud's. Following Lucien's death in 1840, Messrs Stafford, Gee & Stafford then disposed of the collection to Madame Tussaud's, albeit that the acquisitive lady and her sons had to buy some of the items at an auction conducted by 'the famous Mr Robins'. George Henry Robins had a family-owned auction house, located at the Great Piazza, Covent Garden, London.

Before moving on, it is worth noting that the Tussauds do *not* explain was why Madame Mère's bequest was sent to Lucien's London house *five years after* he had left England. Although their first footnote was at pains to point out that the authenticity of these objects was affirmed in front of a Master in Chancery, that might imply some doubt about the provenance the Tussauds claimed for them. So, what were these Lucien-related Napoléonic relics? Under Item 99 was listed a cameo ring, a toothbrush, a pair of silk stockings, and a pocket handkerchief; and under Item 113 were a Napoléonic tooth and the instrument that extracted it; a dessert knife, fork and spoon; a gold presentation snuff box; and the sword and sword belt of the King of Rome.

The cameo ring and the gold snuff box, both of which would almost certainly have borne images of Napoléon, were apparently given to Lucien by his brother

≈ CHAPTER SIX ≈

right A typical Napoléonic presentation snuff box.

far right An example of a cameo ring bearing an image of Napoléon. ©Royal Collection Trust/His Majesty King Charles III 2023

at the time of 'one of their reconciliations', according to the 1883 and 1925 exhibition catalogues. This assertion was repeated in the 1911 insurance catalogue, with the two items being given a value of £10 (2022: £934) and £75 (2022: £7,005) respectively.

Although initially a close ally of Napoléon's, in 1804 Lucien and his brother fell out over the latter's imperial project, and Lucien went into self-imposed exile in Italy. He returned briefly to France in 1809, before attempting to leave for the United States, only to be caught by a British warship and allowed to settle in England. Following Napoléon's first abdication in 1814, Lucien again returned to France where he remained for the Hundred Days, during which he threw his support behind his brother. In grateful thanks, Napoléon elevated him to the status of an Imperial Prince and admitted Lucien's wife and children to the Imperial Family. Under the circumstances, the ring and snuff box were probably given to Lucien at this time rather than in 1809. Either way, his support for the Emperor in 1815 ensured Lucien's second exile following Napoléon's defeat at the Battle of Waterloo and the restoration of King Louis XVIII, hence his London property.

In an 1842 inventory of items at Madame Tussaud's, an entry dated 16th January refers to the settlement of a debt of £105 (2022: £9,870) to a Miss Gordon of St John's Wood, London. Known to have been friendly with Lucien Bonaparte, press cuttings of the time reveal that she owned one of Napoléon's snuff boxes, a cameo ring, three of his handkerchiefs, a toothbrush, a clock and a portrait of Madame Mère; and according to the Tussauds' ledger, she sold all these items to them in 1842 for £260 (2022: £24,285). Given that these pieces included a picture of Napoléon's mother, it is likely that she had acquired them from Lucien, or from the sale of his effects by Messrs Stafford, Gee & Stafford in 1840. Although not mentioned in the exhibition catalogue of 1925, the 1883 version listed a

CHAPTER SIX

Napoléonic 'Under Neckerchief used by the Emperor at St Helena, late the property of Prince Lucien' and a 'singular secret clock, containing a small figure of Napoléon, late the property of Lucien', these no doubt being two of the items sold to them by Miss Gordon, as listed above.

By 1925, the Madame Tussaud's catalogue was claiming that the toothbrush had 'been purchased at the sale of Prince Lucien's collection' by Robins in 1840, as opposed to being bought from Miss Gordon two years later, as recorded in their 1842 ledger. However, they were certain in claiming that it belonged to one of Napoléon's dressing cases made by Biennais, in this case from the *nécessaire de voyage* 'which the Empress Marie Louise arranged when her husband was about to set out on the Russian campaign' in 1812. This identifies it as part of the equipment inside Napoléon's campaign carriage, which was a gift to the Emperor from his second wife, and is described in detail in Chapter 8.

In addition to oral hygiene, Napoléon was also obsessed with bodily cleanliness. An habitually early riser, he spent the first hours of the day working with his personal staff, before taking a hot bath, in which he would lie for up to two hours, while dictating orders and instructions. This was followed by a cup of tea and his *toilette*, which included scraping his tongue, brushing his teeth, and shaving himself. Then, after a second bath and before being dressed, he liberally doused his body with Eau de Cologne, up to sixty bottles of which he used every month.

As Emperor, and in the days before dry cleaning, Napoléon was able to avoid wearing clothes that reeked of stale sweat and camphor by indulging in the luxury of putting on new uniforms on an almost daily basis. In his wardrobe, as well as the elaborate but infrequently worn *petit habillements* used on State occasions, were the Emperor's iconic green and red uniform of a Colonel of the Chasseurs à Cheval of the Imperial Guard; the blue and white uniform of a Colonel of the Foot Grenadiers of the Imperial Guard; and the blue and white

An example of a Napoléonic toothbrush, *c*.1795, Science Museum, London.

far left Napoléon as Colonel of the Foot Grenadiers of the Imperial Guard by François Gérard.

middle Napoléon as Colonel of the Chasseurs à Cheval of the Imperial Guard by Robert Lefèvre.

left Napoléon in the uniform of the National Guard.

[121]

CHAPTER SIX

uniform of the National Guard. His valet, Louis-Joseph Marchand, recorded that all these uniforms were ordered in very considerable quantities and delivered in bulk on the quarter days by the imperial tailors, Chevallier until 1812, and Lejeune thereafter.

Napoléon's conspicuous consumption of Eau de Cologne and uniforms also applied to the imperial shirts, silk stockings and underwear, which were ordered in huge quantities from the workshop of Mademoiselles L'Olive and de Beuvry of Paris. In their memoirs, the ladies stated that they delivered two hundred-and-forty muslin shirts to the Imperial wardrobe between January and April 1813 alone, although in the inventory taken after the Emperor's death on St Helena in 1821, there were a mere forty-seven shirts.

Nothing is known about the 'silk stockings and the pocket handkerchief from Prince Lucien's collection' that were acquired by Madame Tussaud's, and valued in 1911 at £40 (2022: £3,750) in total. However, the sword and sword belt of the King of Rome, were bought by Tussaud's in 1842 for £13 (2022: £1,214) and were described in the 1883 catalogue as 'of exquisite workmanship, the mounting of fine gold'. Valued in 1911 at £15 (2022: £1,401), the items were probably inherited by Lucien from his mother, given their appearance in the sale at the Robins auction house.

The Madame Tussaud's 1843 ledger records that the exhibition acquired Napoléon's deathbed on 27th October 1841, paying £400 (2022: £32,842) for 'the bedstead, Mantle, clothes etc'. Displayed as Item 193 in the Hall of Tableaux, it was described in the 1883 catalogue as:

> THE CAMP BEDSTEAD used by Napoléon during seven years' incarceration at St Helena, with the mattress and pillow on which he died, and on which he is represented lying in state in his Chasseurs uniform, covered with the cloak he wore at Marengo, left expressly by will to his son, the King of Rome.

The cloak presumably was acquired from Lucien's collection, another of the items he had inherited from his mother. The 1925 catalogue included a reproduction of the painting by Sir George Hayter in Tussaud's collection (Item 168: Napoléon Ante-Room), depicting the 1st Duke of Wellington viewing the Napoléonic deathbed tableau. This was accompanied with the information that it was the last painting for which the Iron Duke ever sat, and the rather mawkish note: 'The Duke was a frequent visitor to the Exhibition, and always when he came to the figure of his great antagonist on the camp-bed he would pause and reverently uncover' [i.e. remove his hat]. A fuller, and somewhat fanciful, account appears in John Theodore Tussaud's *The Romance of Madame Tussaud's*:

CHAPTER SIX

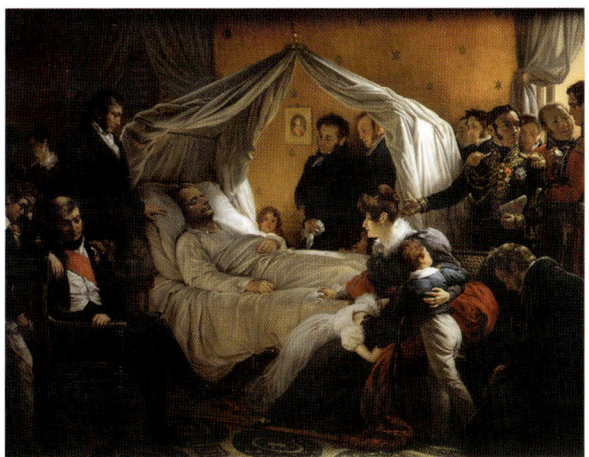 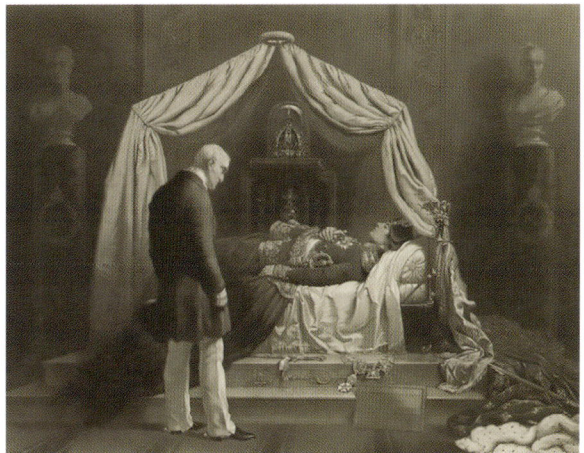

Early one morning, soon after the Exhibition had been opened for the day, Joseph, Madame Tussaud's son, who had been wandering through the rooms, as was his habit, perceived an elderly gentleman in front of the tableau representing the lying-in-state of Napoléon I.

The model of the dead exile rested – as it does down to this very day – on the camp bedstead used by Napoléon at St. Helena, and was dressed in the favourite green uniform, the cloak worn at Marengo (bequeathed by Napoléon to his son) lying across the feet. In the hands, crossed upon the chest, was a crucifix. In those days it was the custom to lower at night the curtains that enclosed the bed, in order to exclude the dust, whereas now the whole scene is encased in glass.

Observing that the visitor was desirous of seeing the effigy, and no attendant being at hand, Joseph Tussaud raised the hangings, whereupon the visitor removed his hat, and, to his great surprise, Joseph saw that he was face to face with none other than the great Duke of Wellington himself.

There stood his Grace, contemplating with feelings of mixed emotions the strange and suggestive scene before him.

On the camp bed lay the mere presentment of the man who, seven-and-thirty years before, had given him so much trouble to subdue. No feeling of triumph passed through the conqueror's mind as he looked upon the poor waxen image, too true in its aspect of death; he rather thought upon the vanity of earthly triumphs, of the levelling hand of time, and how soon he, like his great contemporary, might be stretched upon his own bier.

Mr. Joseph Tussaud used frequently to recall this dramatic meeting between the Iron Duke and the effigy of his erstwhile foe, and to imagine the feelings of the old General as he gazed upon the couch. It was probably the first of the Duke's many visits to the Exhibition.

above left Death of Napoléon by Charles de Steuben.

above The Duke of Wellington (1769–1852) viewing the Napoléon deathbed scene in the Hall of Tableaux at Madame Tussaud's, by Sir George Hayter.

≈ CHAPTER SIX ≈

A few days after this most interesting visit Mr. Tussaud, who was an old friend of Sir George Hayter, related the incident to that artist.

Hayter was immediately struck with the potential value of the event for the production of a painting of the historic scene, and the Tussaud brothers at once commissioned him to execute the work for them.

Sir George thereupon communicated the idea to the Duke, who readily responded, and offered to give the necessary sittings ... Hearing that the artist was making progress with the painting, the Duke visited his studio, and, having expressed himself warmly in appreciation of the picture (the figures had been but lightly limned in at the time), said: "Well, I suppose you'll want me to sit for my picture here?"

Hayter has given us a most characteristic portrait of Wellington as he then appeared. He is dressed in his usual blue frock-coat, white trousers, and white cravat, fastened with the familiar steel buckle. He stoops a little as was his wont, his head is lightly covered with snow-white hair, and his manly features are marked with an expression of mingled curiosity and sadness as, hat in hand, he looks upon the recumbent Napoléon. The picture was completed early in December 1852 and has been on view in the Napoléon Rooms at the Exhibition ever since.

Napoléon's death bed counterpane, photograph in the 1925 catalogue.

The painting by Hayter, valued in 1911 at £200 (2022: £18,750) perished in the 1925 fire, but it is clear from all extant images that the bed had a collapsible metal frame and was similar to other examples of the Emperor's campaign beds in national and private collections. The 1925 catalogue was at pains to point out that, while the Emperor's uniform was a copy, the bedstead, mattress, pillows and the cloak were all the originals; the 1883 catalogue further stated that these items were 'attested' as such. The 1911 insurance catalogue did *not* list the bedstead, but valued the pillows and mattress at £500 (2022: £46,703) and the Marengo cloak at £500 (2022: £46,708). Remarkably, 'A Campaign bed, reputedly one of Napoléon's beds from St Helena' was sold by Madame Tussaud's at a Christie's auction on 19th October 2005 for £9,840 against a pre-sale estimate of £4-6,000. It may have survived the 1925 fire because it was, as indicated by the 1911 insurance catalogue, no longer on display.

Both the 1883 and the 1925 exhibition catalogues, and the 1911 insurance catalogue, but not the 1843 ledger, listed separately as Item 173 in the Napoléon Ante-Room: 'Counterpane from the Camp Bed on which Napoléon died (stained with his blood)'. Not to be confused with the Marengo cloak, which acted as the funeral pall, the 'Counterpane' does not appear in any of the illustrations of the Emperor's death. However, the photograph in 1925 exhibition catalogue shows it in an elaborate glazed frame, with the bloodstain surrounded by a wreath of dried flowers or embroidered beads. The catalogue also gave the counterpane

[124]

CHAPTER SIX

a Lucien Bonaparte provenance, although whether he acquired it direct from St Helena or via Madame Mère's estate was not specified; in the 1883 catalogue its authenticity was listed as 'affirmed'. In 1911 it was valued, like the Marengo cloak, at £500 (2022: £46,703).

The rest of the Napoléonica covered in this chapter was a mixed bag, albeit one that would be of considerable interest to collectors were the items available today. Unfortunately, some were very inadequately described. A good example of such cataloguing was a 'Gun presented by Napoléon to a favourite General' (Item 151: Napoléon Ante-Room). No further clues as to the type of gun, the identity of the recipient, or the reason for its presentation were given. Nonetheless, the 1911 valuers clearly thought it was genuine and gave it a value of £100 (2022: £9,340). Similarly, Item 139 in the same location was merely described as 'Napoléon's Hunting Crop', valued in 1911 at £25 (2022: £2,335).

Slightly more was related in the 1925 catalogue about Item 158, listed as 'Napoléon's signature', but with the added information that it was on a patent document nominating Sieur Leclerc to the Legion of Honour. In all probability, this was Général de Division (Major General) Charles Victoire Emmanuel Leclerc (1772–1802), who was the first husband of Napoléon's sister, Pauline. Leclerc, along with twenty-five of his most senior officers and 25,000 soldiers, died of yellow fever in the French Caribbean colony of Sainte-Domingue, where he had been sent to supress an uprising of freed slaves led by the Governor General of the island of Haiti, Toussaint L'Ouverture. Documents bearing the Emperor's signature today command prices from £2,000 to £5,000, although Item 158, had it survived, might be worth more given its association with a figure so close to Napoléon. In 1911 it was valued at £25 (2022: £2,355).

Item 107 in the Napoléon Room was described in the 1883 catalogue as 'The Celebrated Atlas used by the Emperor, in which are Plans of several battles, drawn with his own hand'. This document was valued in 1911 at a substantial £1,000 (2022: £93,407), and illustrated in the 1925 catalogue with some additional information:

> After the Battle of Montmirail, in the Marne Department, on February 11th, 1814, when the allied Russian and Prussian armies commanded by Blücher were defeated by him, the atlas was inadvertently left at the Hôtel de la Poste aux Chevaux, at Château Thierry, a small town hard by, where Napoléon rested for a short time. It was attested by numerous witnesses before the Mayor of the town in the same year.

The 1883 catalogue stated that there was also a pocket handkerchief with the atlas. This was not mentioned in the 1925 catalogue entry, although the box

General Charles Victoire Emmanuel Leclerc (1772–1802) by François Kinson, and Napoléon's signature.

Napoléon's Atlas, photograph in the 1925 catalogue.

CHAPTER SIX

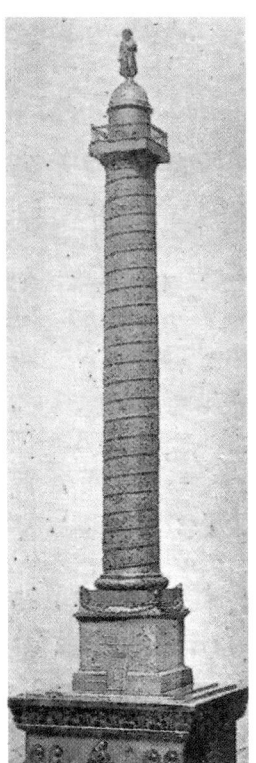

Model of the Vendôme Column, photograph in the 1925 catalogue.

containing the atlas also held a 'pair of Napoléon's boots, eagles from his flags, and his leathern bottle-case'. No further information was provided about these relics, although the 1883 catalogue stated that there were 'THREE ORIGINAL EAGLES taken at Waterloo' in the collection. The 1911 insurance catalogue stated that the boots were 'worn by Napoleon during the Russian Campaign', and gave them a value of £10 (2022: £934) and the leather bottle case £5 (2022: £467). The authenticity of all these items is considered in Chapter 8.

Also illustrated in the 1925 catalogue was a 'Model of the Vendôme Column' (Item 85: Napoléon Room), surmounted by a statue of Napoléon. The 1911 insurance catalogue stated that it was to a scale of 'half inch to the foot'. The original, which still stands in the Place Vendôme, Paris, was erected to celebrate the Battle of Austerlitz in 1805. Completed in 1810 to a design based on that of Trajan's Column in Rome, it was clad in bronze *bas reliefs* depicting Napoléonic battle scenes, and was cast from 1,200 captured Russian and Austrian cannons. Originally topped by a bronze statue of Napoléon in Roman robes, after the restoration of the monarchy in 1814 the statue was destroyed on the order of the Allies, although the iron model from which it was cast survived. It was sold at Bullock's 1819 auction (Lot 105 on the first day of the sale) to a Mr Hume for £32.12.0 (2022: £3,250), just £2.12.0 (2022: £200) more than its scrap value. According to the auction catalogue, Bullock had obtained the two-ton model from the 'Museum of Antiquities', but where that was located or when it was acquired was not explained.

The plinth at the top of the Vendôme Column remained vacant until 1831, when a replacement statue of Napoléon in his iconic uniform and bicorne hat was installed. This, in turn, was replaced by his nephew, Emperor Napoléon III, in 1863 with a statue of Napoléon I once more in classical attire. The entire column was dismantled during the Paris Commune of 1871, although the *bas reliefs* were preserved, and it was re-erected in 1873–75 with a copy of the original statue once more at the apex.

It is clear from the 1925 Tussaud's photograph that the figure at the top of the column was in uniform, which dates the model to the period 1831 to 1863. Depending on size, these models are currently priced at around £2,500, although in 1911 Madame Tussaud's column was valued at £75 (2022: £7,005). Interestingly, the insurance catalogue of that year also included a 'Fragment of the Column of the Place Vendôme', valued at £5 (2022: £467), which was not listed in the 1925 catalogue.

In addition to a large collection of engravings, most of which depicted the Emperor on a variety of different battlefields and none of which were exceptional enough – or described in sufficient detail – to merit consideration here, there was a *verre églomisé* (reverse painting on glass) in the Napoléon Ante-Room (Item 145). Entitled 'The Apotheosis of Napoléon, by Lagrenée', the picture depicted

[126]

CHAPTER SIX

Napoléon as a Roman Emperor and was described by Joseph Bonaparte as 'the most perfect likeness of the Emperor' he had ever see, which dates it after 18th May 1804. Acquired in 1845 by Madame Tussaud's at the sale of John Sainsbury's collection, according to Christie's records Sainsbury had paid £500 (2022: £46,703) for it at the auction of The Duke of Sussex's collection two years earlier. There is no record of the price it achieved in the Sainsbury sale. Despite being valued in 1911 at £200 (2022: £18,750), the 1925 catalogue entry boasted that 'since [1845], like everything else connected with the history of Napoléon, its value has been considerably enhanced... This example of [Lagrenée's] art, bold in conception and admirable in execution, has been pronounced by some authorities his *chef d'oeuvre*.' This optimistic view was in direct contrast to the valuer of Madame Tussaud's collection, who listed it a much reduced sum of £200 (2022: £18,644). Another piece attributed to Jean Jacques Lagrenée (1739-1821), albeit that the 1925 catalogue was (unusually) clear that it was a copy, had a self-explanatory description:

> In this magnificent table the Emperor is shown surrounded by his famous Marshals ... The original, by Lagrenée, the artist who painted the *Apotheosis of Napoléon*, was for some time in this Exhibition, having been lent to Madame Tussaud & Sons by its owner.

The Austerlitz or Marshals Table.

The original is known either as the Marshals or the Austerlitz Table, although it was listed in the 1925 catalogue as 'A Napoléon Table in Facsimile' (Item 55: Napoléon Room). It was commissioned by the Emperor from the Sèvres factory in 1806, to celebrate his victory over the Austrians and Russians at the eponymous battle of the previous year. Delivered in 1811 it was, with unconscious irony given the reason for its existence, placed in the Austrian-born Empress Marie-Louise's salon in the Tuileries Palace. In 1812, the table was exhibited briefly at the Paris Salon, but was sold sometime after 1815 by King Louis XVIII. After passing through many hands, including being exhibited on loan at Madame Tussaud's, it was bought in 1929 by the Musée de Malmaison at the auction of the effects of a descendant of Marshal Ney.

Although disclosing that Item 55 was a copy, the 1925 catalogue entry incorrectly attributed the painted panels of the original to Jean-Jacques Lagrenée, when they were actually painted by Jean-Baptiste Isabey. However, as Jean-Jacques Lagrenée was a ceramics artist at the Sèvres factory, it is possible that he was responsible for copying Isabey's originals onto the porcelain plaques of the

[127]

※ CHAPTER SIX ※

Interior of the Château de Malmaison, 2022.

copy. In any event, the 1911 insurance catalogue gave it a value of only £10 (2022: £934).

By contrast, the information about a pair of candelabra, listed as 'Ornament from Malmaison' (Items 73 & 78: Napoléon Room), and 'A 'Napoléon Timepiece' (Item 106: Napoléon Room) all from Empress Joséphine's house, the Château de Malmaison, was almost non-existent and so defies examination. All that can be said is that these objects would have been in the Empire-style, and in the manner of the furnishings and fittings on display in the house-museum today. Two Empire clocks, one with a pair of candelabra, in the Napoléon Room, were valued in 1911 at £60 (2022: £5,593) and may have been these items. Although not listed in the 1925 exhibition catalogue, the 1911 insurance catalogue also stated that there was in the collection 'A Tassel from the Bed at Malmaison, in which Napoléon I slept'. It gave this fragment of *passementerie* a derisory value of £1 (2022: £93).

The last two items to be considered in this chapter relate to one of Napoléon's 'favourite chargers', *Jaffa*. A picture of the horse and its tail were listed under Item 101 in the Napoléon Room, with the additional information that the tail had been lent to Madame Tussaud's by Winchcombe Hartley Esq. In somewhat typical Tussaud style, this entry poses more questions than it answers. First, there is the question whether or not there was ever a Napoléonic charger called *Jaffa*.

Napoléon (on a horse that might be *Jaffa*) and his Generals by Ludwig Elsholtz.

[128]

CHAPTER SIX

In the grounds of Glassenbury Park in Kent there is a stone pillar marking the grave of *Jaffa* believed to have been ridden by Napoléon at the Battle of Waterloo, brought back to England, and then retired at Glassenbury Park, where it died at the age of thirty-eight in 1829. Given the number of Napoléonic chargers in the Imperial Mews, it is perfectly possible that the horse identified as *Marengo* was not the only pale grey Arab charger used by the Emperor during the Waterloo campaign. It is equally possible that, like *Marengo* who was rescued from the battlefield, returned to England, and ended his days as a skeletal exhibit at the National Army Museum, *Jaffa* was brought back to England by a British officer. However, in 1829 the owners of Glassenbury Park were the absentee Irish Roberts family, not Winchcombe Hartley. The property was managed by the agent, Thomas Redford, although a 'Mr Green', possibly one of the many short-term tenants of the estate, was in possession in the year of *Jaffa*'s death. In the eighteenth and nineteenth centuries, the eldest son of the Hartley family of Bucklebury House in Berkshire, and Lyegrove House in Little Sodbury, Gloucestershire, was invariably called Winchcombe. The last Winchcombe Hartley died in 1881 and his estate was divided between his sister and three nieces. However, as there were no familial connections between the Hartleys and the Roberts of Glassenbury Park, their agent, or the possible tenant, 'Mr Green', how or why *Jaffa*'s tail came into the Winchcombe Hartley family, and was then lent to Madame Tussaud's remains just another Tussaud mystery. The 1911 insurance catalogue listed that the tail was 'on loan', without stating from whom, and gave it a value of £50 (2022: £4,670).

CHAPTER SEVEN

THE PAINTINGS BY JACQUES-LOUIS DAVID

THE MOST CONTENTIOUS GROUP of items in Madame Tussaud & Sons' Exhibition prior to the fire, at least as far as this book is concerned, were the twelve paintings attributed in the 1925 exhibition catalogue to the French artist, Jacques-Louis David (1748-1825). So important were they considered by Madame Tussaud's that the artist was given his own brief biography in every edition of the exhibition catalogue:

> [David] was born in Paris on the 31st August, 1748. From his earliest childhood his artistic instincts manifested themselves, and at school he was always drawing. When the Revolution broke out, the National Assembly charged him with several commissions at the expense of the State, and in 1792 he was nominated deputy for Paris in the Convention. Imbued with rigid republican principles, and believing himself another Brutus, he was one of the judges who sent Louis XVI to the scaffold. Besides designing official dresses for public functionaries, he introduced the style of furniture known as "the Empire". During the Revolution he was violently attacked by the enemies of Robespierre, to whom he had attached himself, and twice he was imprisoned. But his pupils presented a petition to the Convention praying that he might be set at liberty, and it was probably his great popularity as an artist that saved him from going the way of Robespierre to the scaffold. After his assumption of the Imperial crown Napoléon made David his chief painter, and for some years the artist was occupied in decorating the hall at Versailles with representations of his coronation and of other scenes in his career. On the restoration of the Bourbons, David retired to Brussels, and there he spent the rest of his industrious life, dying in 1825.

In places fanciful, this account omitted to mention David's facial deformity, an important aspect of his life which is clearly visible in his self-portrait. The

opposite Self-portrait by Jacques-Louis David.

CHAPTER SEVEN

catalogue may have omitted it, but Madame Tussaud, who met him in the house of her 'uncle' in Paris, remembered it well in her *Memoirs*: 'his countenance [was] the most repulsive; he had a large wen on one side of his face, which contributed to render his mouth crooked'.

In addition to the text of the exhibition catalogues, the David pictures were also listed, with their then values, in the inventory of 1856, then again in those of 1880/81, 1884/5, 1901, 1905 and 1911. They are considered here in the order in which they appear in those inventories, with a note as to their values in the successive listings, and with extracts from the 1925 exhibition catalogue, along with some images. Importantly, however, there are some discrepancies between the artistic attributions in the 1911 stock inventory and the much fuller insurance catalogue of that year. These are highlighted, although it is not possible to explain how they occurred, other than to assume that the stock list was compiled by the Tussauds and the insurance catalogue by an external valuer.

However, even with the available information, the question of the paintings' authenticity is a difficult one. For, although Tussaud's 1925 exhibition catalogue stated unequivocally that the pictures were 'the work of this celebrated artist', unlike the Napoléonica in 1883 catalogue they were never 'affirmed' or otherwise certified. To make authentication even more difficult, there is no *catalogue raisoné* of David's work against which the pictures can be checked.

All of this is important, because if the collection was genuine and had survived the fire, it would now be worth – in the opinion of Philip Mould, the celebrated dealer in historical portraits – in excess of £100 million. That said, the present-day value does not mean that at the time of purchase they would have been beyond the financial means of the Tussauds. Following his death in 1825, David's works fell out of fashion and could be obtained for relatively little money. Indeed, his paintings have only risen steeply in value since the first quarter of the twentieth century.

below Sketch of Madame Mère for the Coronation painting by Jacques-Louis David, Museum of Fine Arts, Boston.

below right Madame Mère at Napoléon's Coronation (detail from the painting by Jacques-Louis David).

CHAPTER SEVEN

The first work by David to be considered here is a portrait of Madame Mère 'by David', which was listed as Item 93, but with no further information beyond a cross-reference to Item 91 (see Chapter 5). Perhaps significantly, it did not feature in any of the Tussaud inventories, although it may have been the 'favourite picture belonging to Prince Lucien', which Tussaud's acquired from Miss Gordon in 1842. Although not in the inventories, this full-length portrait was listed in the 1911 insurance catalogue, with a value of £750 (2022: £70,055), but it was attributed to Baron Gérard *not* David.

The second work attributed to David in the 1856 inventory was 'Entry of Napoléon into Vienna', with a note in parenthesis that it was not at first identified as a painting by the artist. Listed as Item 147 in the Napoléon Ante-Room in the 1925 catalogue, and illustrated with a photograph showing its very elaborate carved frame, it was attributed to David in the 1883 catalogue, but without descriptions or the historical notes in the 1925 edition:

below left Napoléon's Entry into Vienna (1805) attributed to Jacques-Louis David, photograph in the 1925 catalogue.

below Madame Mère by François Gérard.

In this picture the principal figures are portraits. Napoléon, led on by a soaring eagle, is accompanied by his most famous Marshals and Generals, whose names appear at the bottom of the frame. It was in November, 1805, that the French army entered the Austrian capital; the decisive battle of Austerlitz took place a few days later, and then Austria was forced to accept the humiliating treaty of Presburg.

Although there exist, in public and private collections, two different coloured engravings depicting Napoléon's entry into Vienna in 1805, neither is based on the Madame Tussaud's picture and there appear to be no working sketches by

CHAPTER SEVEN

above Cardinal Fesch (far right) at Napoléon's Coronation (detail from the painting by Jacques-Louis David).

above right Cardinal Fesch (1763–1839) attributed to Jacques-Louis David, photograph in the 1925 catalogue.

David for this painting. The work was valued in 1856 at £45 (2022: £4,203), but was not revalued thereafter and is not even listed in the 1911 insurance catalogue. This may indicate that Madame Tussaud's had second thoughts after 1856 as to its authenticity.

The painting of Napoléon's maternal uncle, titled 'Cardinal Fesch by David' (Item 71: Napoléon Room), included another short biographical essay and a photograph, but no clue as to provenance. Cardinal Joseph Fesch 1763–1839) assisted at the imperial Coronation in 1804. The image of him in the Coronation picture, and a full-length pencil sketch now in the Harvard Museum collection, also by David, show the Cardinal in profile and bear some resemblance to his full-face image in the 1925 catalogue. These, however, do not prove that the Tussaud's picture was either an original or by David, a problem exacerbated by the fact that there are no working sketches or studies of the Cardinal by David for the Tussaud painting.

Nor was a specific value ascribed to the painting until the 1911 insurance catalogue, when it was described as a half-length portrait, attributed to David and valued at £300 (2022: £28,022). The 1880/81 and 1905 valuations merely group the portrait of Fesch with those of 'Pauline Bonaparte' and 'Marshal Duroc' (Items 70 & 69: Napoléon Room) with a combined value of £15 (2022: £1,401) in 1880/81 and £45 (2022: £4,203) in 1905. By the time of the 1911 insurance catalogue, the portraits of Pauline and Duroc had been revalued to £75 (2022: £7,005) each, but without artistic attributions.

Pauline was considered one of the most beautiful women of her generation, and was painted by most of the leading portraitists of her day and immortalised in marble by Canova as his *Venus Victrix* now in the Galleria Borghese in Rome. By 1925, the Tussaud's catalogue entry for Pauline and her portrait 'by David' ended with the following:

> This portrait is [now] attributed to the French painter Tugnes [*sic*], a pupil of David, and was formerly in one of the palaces in Italy occupied by the Princess after her separation from her second husband [Prince Camillo Borghese].
> No pupil of David's with the name of 'Tugnes' (or anything like it) has been identified, nor is there a record of an artist of that name working in Europe in the early nineteenth century.

CHAPTER SEVEN

The portrait of 'Marshal Duroc by David' (Item 69: Napoléon Room) is equally problematic, despite being given a valuation of £75 (2022: £7,005) in the 1911 insurance catalogue, albeit without an artistic attribution, and a lengthy, anecdotal biography in the 1925 exhibition catalogue. Gérard Christophe Michel Duroc was Napoléon's First Grand Marshal of the Palace, head of his military household, and was present at the Coronation in 1804. However, the only known image of Duroc by David is a sketch in oils of the Marshal's head in profile, now in the Musée Léon Bonnat in Bayonne, France. It was clearly a study for David's Coronation painting, for which there is also a pencil sketch.

The next portrait attributed to David in the 1880/81 inventory was of 'Prince Poniatowski' (Item 83: Napoléon Room), which was valued then, with those of Caroline and Joseph Bonaparte, at a combined sum of £25 (2022: £2,335). In the 1905 ledger it was individually valued at £25, rising to £50 (2022: £4,670) in that of 1911. The picture was not included in the 1883 catalogue, was not attributed to David in the 1911 insurance catalogue, and nor was it illustrated or its provenance stated in the 1925 exhibition catalogue. Prince Józef Poniatowski was an interesting man. Born in 1763, he was the nephew of King Stanislaus II Augustus, last King of Poland, and became a professional soldier in the Austrian army. At the request of his uncle, he returned to his homeland in 1789 to head the Polish army but, following the partitioning of his country by the Russians in 1792, he returned to Austria. In 1794 he led a Polish uprising against Russian rule, which resulted in his second exile in 1798. In 1807 he was appointed Minister of War in the Napoléon-created Grand Duchy of Warsaw, and when the Emperor launched the invasion of Russia in 1812, Poniatowski volunteered to join him. Wounded during the fighting for Moscow, he returned home to raise new Polish forces to help cover Napoléon's retreat from Russia. Shortly before the Battle of Leipzig on 17th October 1813, Poniatowski led two heroic cavalry charges, actions for which he was promoted to the rank of Marshal of the Empire. But in the withdrawal

left Pauline Borghese, née Bonaparte, Princess Consort of Sulmona and Rossano, sovereign Duchess of Guastalla, by Antonio Canova.

above Pauline Bonaparte in 1803 by Robert Lefèvre.

Prince Józef Poniatowski (1763–1813) *c.*1810 by Josef Grassi.

[135]

CHAPTER SEVEN

Death of Prince Józef Poniatowski (1763–1813) by January Suchodolski.

that followed Napoléon's defeat at that battle, and before his baton could be delivered to him, he was, in the words of the 1925 Tussaud's catalogue:

> … ordered to cover the retreat of the French army. The enemy [the Russians] were already in possession of the suburbs of Leipzig, and had thrown troops over the [River] Elster, when, on the 19th October, 1813, the Prince arrived with a few followers at the river. The bridge had by this time been blown up by the French, and the brave Pole, already wounded, deliberately spurred his horse into the stream and was drowned.

What the 1925 catalogue did not state was that Poniatowski's fate was guaranteed by the large money belt that he always wore under his tunic: the weight of the gold in it was so great that he sank like a stone. The subject of many contemporary portraits by Polish artists, Prince Poniatowski does not appear to have either sat for David or been the subject of one of his paintings.

The portrait of 'Caroline Bonaparte' (Item 82: Napoléon Room) attributed to David did have a slight provenance, in as much as the Tussaud's 1925 exhibition catalogue stated it was 'formerly in one of the palaces in Naples, whence it was removed after her husband's deposition', but that is all – although the entry does

[136]

CHAPTER SEVEN

explain why Caroline had spent time in Naples. Born in 1782, the third of Napoléon's sisters, Caroline married one of his military commanders, Joachim Murat, in 1800. By 1804 Murat was a Marshal of the Empire, and in 1808 Napoléon appointed him King of Naples. Murat's wife, Queen Caroline, acted as a highly effective Regent while her husband was away fighting. Following Napoléon's defeat at Leipzig in 1813, Murat attempted to save his throne by switching sides to the Coalition of Allies ranged against his brother-in-law; and then in 1815 declared war against Austria in order to strengthen his rule in Italy. However, he was defeated at the Battle of Tolentino in May and fled into exile, but was captured by the forces of the Bourbon King Ferdinand IV of Naples, shortly to be returned to his throne, and executed by firing squad on 13th October 1815. His widow Caroline fled initially to Austria, where she married again, and then retired to Florence, where she died in 1839.

The lack of detail about portrait's provenance is not the only tantalising fact about Item 82. For, as well as an image in the 1925 catalogue, and an artistic attribution in the 1883 catalogue, the inventories also tell an interesting story. According to the ledgers, in 1905 the painting was valued at £75 (2022: £7,005), but in the 1911 inventory the value had jumped tenfold to £750 (2022: £70,055), making it the most valuable painting 'by David' in the Madame Tussaud & Sons' collection. It is possible that whoever revalued the picture in 1911 was convinced of its authenticity and, by implication, doubtful that the others were by David. That said, there is no evidence in the archives to support this theory, and the 1911 insurance catalogue – as opposed to the inventory of the same date – gave no artistic attribution.

above left Princess Caroline Murat, née Bonaparte, Grand Duchess of Berg and Cleves, Queen of Naples, attributed to Jacques-Louis David, photograph in the 1925 catalogue.

middle 'Squared', working drawing of Princess Caroline for the Coronation painting, by Jacques-Louis David.

above Princess Caroline (on the left) at Napoléon's Coronation, detail from the painting by Jacques-Louis David.

CHAPTER SEVEN

When identifying an image of Caroline Murat, there is plenty of choice in terms of attributing an artist to the work. All the usual suspects painted her, including Ingres, Isabey, Gérard (multiple times), and Vigée Lebrun. Indeed, David painted her – full length and in profile – for the Coronation picture. This multiplicity of painters has caused some problems for art historians. Take for example the painting of Caroline hanging at Attingham Park in Shropshire. According to the National Trust's guidebook:

> ... the picture was bought by Thomas Henry Noel-Hill, 8th Lord Berwick (1877-1949), at the sale of the Empress Eugénie's pictures, at Christie's in 1927. It was catalogued as by Vigée Lebrun, and although close to the work of Gérard, it is more likely to be by Louis Ducis, who was court artist to the Murats in Naples.

Whatever conclusions are drawn from the steep increase in the valuation of the Madame Tussaud's portrait of Caroline between 1905 and 1911, it remains a fact that there are no extant references to the work being by David, and there is no record of him travelling to Naples. So, while it may well have come from one of the lady's Neapolitan palaces, as stated in the 1925 catalogue, it is more likely to have been the work of another hand. Without being able to examine the original, it is impossible to take a definitive view.

The third of the pictures grouped together in the 1880/81 inventory with a combined value of £25, that of 'Joseph Bonaparte, King of Spain' (Item 81: Napoléon Room). This, too, was revalued in 1905, with an uplift to £25 (2022: £2,335), and further increased in value to £50 (2022: £4,670) in 1911, albeit without an attribution to David in the 1911 insurance catalogue. However, without a photograph in the 1925 exhibition catalogue, or a mention in that of 1883, it is difficult to form a definitive judgment, beyond noting that the only known painting of Joseph by David is, as with Caroline and so many of the others considered here, a vignette in the Coronation picture.

The last group of portraits attributed to David, listed in the Tussaud inventories, and displayed in the Napoléon Room were those of Prince Eugène, Marshal Soult, and the picture of Madame Mère, the latter addressed earlier in this chapter. They were given a combined value of £37.10.0 (2022: £3,500) in the 1880/81 inventory. In 1901, this group was joined by two late entries: Marshal Macdonald and Queen Hortense, the former valued in 1911 at £25.10.0 (2022: £2,400) and the latter at £150 (2022: £14,011). With the exception of the portrait of Madame Mère, the other pictures were accompanied by biographical sketches and, in the case of Soult and Hortense, photographs. None of them, however, was given a provenance and only the half-length painting of Soult was attributed to David in the 1911 insurance catalogue.

Prince Joseph Bonaparte (on left) at Napoléon's Coronation, detail from the painting by Jacques-Louis David.

CHAPTER SEVEN

The biography of Eugène de Beauharnais at Item 92 in the Napoléon Room was particularly gushing – and incomplete:

> Eugène de Beauharnais, Duke of Leuchtenberg, Prince D'Eichstedt, was born in Paris on September 3rd, 1781, son of Joséphine and her first husband, the Vicomte de Beauharnais [who lost his head during the Revolution]. When tranquillity had become re-established after the excesses of the revolutionary period, young Eugène came under the notice of Napoléon, the then Governor of Paris [sic], to whom he presented himself to beg that his father's sword, which had been deposited in the Arsenal prior to his decapitation, might be restored to him. This act of filial piety made a lively impression on Napoléon, who granted the youth's petition, and ever afterwards took the liveliest interest in him. Joséphine hastened to thank the General, and thus it was [according to his romanticised version] that she made the acquaintance of the man who was to raise her to an Imperial throne.

What the Tussaud biography overlooked was Eugène's stellar career during the Empire, which included his adoption as Napoléon's son, his elevation to the style and title of an Imperial Prince, his appointment as Viceroy of Italy and heir presumptive to that throne, and the fact that his children married into the royal families of Sweden, Portugal, Brazil and Russia.

Like the other Tussaud portraits attributed to David in the 1925 exhibition catalogue, the image of Eugène de Beauharnais was included in David's Coronation painting. There is also a pencil study by the artist of the Prince for his painting, *The Presentation of the Eagle Standards*, albeit it in a more heroic pose and in a different uniform. Hanging at the Hôtel Beauharnais in Paris there is a half-

below left 'Squared', working drawing of Prince Eugène de Beauharnais (1781–1824) for the Coronation painting by Jacques-Louis David.

middle Prince Eugène de Beauharnais (centre, in profile, with moustache) at Napoléon's Coronation, detail from the painting by Jacques-Louis David.

below Prince Eugène de Beauharnais, attributed to Jacques-Louis David, but probably by or after Joseph Karl Stieler.

CHAPTER SEVEN

right Marshal Jean-de-Dieu Soult, Duke of Dalmatia (1769–1851), attributed to Jacques-Louis David, photograph in the 1925 catalogue.

far right Jean-de-Dieu Soult by an unknown artist c.1804.

length portrait of the Prince, attributed to 'the workshop of David', and another copy of the same painting hanging in the Musée de l'Armée at Les Invalides. Although it is possible that Madame Tussaud's might have had the original, a cursory examination of Eugène's portrait at the Hôtel Beauharnais, and the one at Les Invalides, shows that they are both copies of a portrait of him *not* by David, but by the German artist, Joseph Karl Stieler. Nonetheless, Eugène's portrait was valued at £25 (2022: £2,335) in the 1905 ledger, and £50 (2022: £4,670) in both the 1911 revaluation and the insurance catalogue.

The painting of 'Marshal Soult' (Item 94: Napoléon Room) attributed to David in both the 1925 exhibition catalogue and the 1911 insurance catalogue, was similarly revalued To £25 (2022: £2,405) in 1905, but in the 1911 ledger it overtook that of Prince Eugène's portrait by £150, giving it a value of £200 (2022: £18,681). There is no recorded reason for this disproportionate increase (unless it was the 1911 attribution), nor are there any working drawings of Soult by David. The photograph of the portrait of the Marshal in the 1925 catalogue showed him as a young man, wearing the uniform of a Revolutionary Army General, a rank which he reached at the age of twenty-five in 1794. He was appointed a Marshal of the Empire in 1804. The catalogue biography tactfully omitted that Soult had a reputation both as a political intriguer, and as a looter on the grand scale: while in Portugal in 1809 he plotted to acquire the throne, and as Military Governor of Andalusia in 1810 he is credited with appropriating for himself Francs 1.5 million (2022: £4.5 million) worth of art, making him a 'plunderer in the world class'. Judging from later images of the Marshal by other artists, he *is* the subject of Madame Tussaud's painting, although by which portraitist is uncertain and will now never be definitively established.

CHAPTER SEVEN

In 1901, Madame Tussaud's ledger showed that two further portraits attributed to David had entered the collection. These were of 'Queen Hortense' and 'Marshal Macdonald' (Items 97 & 98: Napoléon Room). However, they were not valued until 1911, when they were given values of £150 (2022: £14,011) and £25 (2022: £2,335) respectively in both the inventory and the insurance catalogue, but without an attribution to David in the latter. Only the image of Hortense was illustrated in the 1925 exhibition catalogue, but both were given the customary biographies.

Despite there being no photograph of the Macdonald portrait in the 1925 catalogue, there is an image of a 'study [in oils] by David' of the Marshal's head in Oleg Sokolov's *L'Armée de Napoléon*. There are also two almost identical portraits of him, attributed to Gros and Gérard, in the Musée de la Légion d'Honneur in Paris. The only difference between the latter two portraits is the colour of the riband over Macdonald's right shoulder – and both are remarkably similar, facially, to the study attributed to David. Given that this image does not appear in any other publication as a work by David, the likelihood is that it was misattributed to the artist by Sokolov. Furthermore, unlike the pencil studies by

below left Marshal Etienne Jacques-Joseph-Alexandre Macdonald, Duke of Taranto (1765–1840), by Antoine-Jean Gros.

middle Marshal Macdonald by François Gérard.

below Marshal Macdonald, study by Jacques Louis David.

David referred to above in connection with the other Tussaud's portraits, this portrait – if it was by David – was not executed as a preparatory image for his *Coronation* or the *Presentation of Eagle Standards* pictures, because Macdonald was not present at either event: he was, in fact, in disgrace with the Emperor, as the 1925 catalogue entry recounted:

Etienne Jacques Joseph Macdonald...was descended from a noble Scottish family which followed [King] James II into exile [in 1689]. At the age of nineteen...he joined

CHAPTER SEVEN

above Hortense de Beauharnais, Queen of Holland, attributed to Jacques-Louis David, photograph in the 1925 catalogue.

above right Hortense de Beauharnais, Queen of Holland (centre), holding the hand of her son, Napoléon-Louis Charles Bonaparte (1802–1807) at Napoléon's Coronation, detail from the painting by Jacques-Louis David.

the Irish Legion. [During the Revolutionary Wars he rose to the rank of General but,] faithful to his old friend [General] Moreau, who was exiled [to the USA in 1804] on a [trumped-up] charge of plotting to overthrow Napoléon, he fell into disgrace, and was refused a [new] command; but, after six years, he was again summoned to active service, and bore himself with great distinction at the Battle of Wagram [1809], receiving a wound in the leg, but refusing to dismount until victory was complete. Napoléon then hastened to his side, embraced him, appointed him Marshal and a Duke of the Empire. At Fontainebleau, in 1814, when quitting France for Elba, Napoléon gave him as a souvenir Mourad Bey's sabre which he had always worn on the battlefield.

Which just leaves Item 97, the illustrated portrait of Napoléon's step daughter, Queen Hortense. As with the rest of the collection, there is no surviving documentation to prove that this picture was either by David's hand or a copy from his studio. The only known portrait of Hortense by David is, once again, that in the Coronation picture, where she is depicted holding the hand of her son, the ill-fated Napoléon-Louis Charles Bonaparte who died aged four as the 1925 catalogue recounted.

If the circumstantial evidence relating to the portraits that were lost in the 1925 fire at Madame Tussaud's were not enough to question their attribution to David, there are two other factors that should be taken into account. The first is evident in the photograph the Napoléonic tableau at Madame Tussaud's in 1900. This shows that, most unusually, all the paintings attributed to Jacques-Louis David are the same size. Second, in the *Romance of Madame Tussaud's* by John

CHAPTER SEVEN

The Napoléon group at Madame Tussaud's, 1900.

Theodore Tussaud, there is – most curiously given their artistic importance – no mention of the Davids, nor does he mention Madame Tussaud's personal recollection of David, as recounted in her *Memoirs*.

Given all of the above, and the fact that only the half-length portraits of Cardinal Fesch and Marshal Soult were attributed to David in the 1911 insurance catalogue, it seems reasonable to assume that – on the balance of probability – *none* of the oil paintings attributed to David at Madame Tussaud's were by that artist. Fortunately, no such issues of attribution or provenance arise in the next chapter.

CHAPTER EIGHT

ELBA, WATERLOO & WELLINGTON

Following the disastrous Russian Campaign of 1812, and the subsequent invasion of France by the Allied armies of Russia, Prussia, Austria and – from the south – the United Kingdom, Napoléon was forced to abdicate on 11th April 1814, although not before he had unsuccessfully attempted suicide A reproduction of the table on which the abdication was signed was listed under Item 79 in the Napoléon Room and valued in 1911 at a mere £5 (2022: £467).

Banished to the island of Elba, the Emperor was permitted to keep his title and maintain a personal guard, drawn from soldiers of the Imperial Guard who had chosen to go into exile with him. On 28th February 1815, Napoléon landed back in France and so commenced the Hundred Days, which ended with his final defeat by the Allies at the Battle of Waterloo on 18th June, and his subsequent exile to St Helena. The principal focus of this chapter is on Madame Tussaud's collection of memorabilia taken at or after Waterloo, along with three items that pre-date the battle in origin.

The first was 'Napoléon's State Carriage' (Item 57: Napoléon Room), built for his Coronation in Milan as King of Italy in 1805. This did not rate more than a paragraph in the 1925 exhibition catalogue, but merits a slightly longer explanation here. Since the establishment of the Consulate in 1799 and then the French Empire in 1804, Napoléon had been at pains to construct a narrative that gave imperial Roman legitimacy to his role. Even after his Coronation as Emperor of the French, France was still technically a republic. So, on the face of it, Napoléon's decision on 17th March 1805 to appoint himself King of Italy was against the grain.

opposite Napoléon signs his Abdication at Fontainebleau 11th April 1814 by Gaetano Ferri.

below Napoléon's farewell to the Imperial Guard, 1814, by Antoine Montfort.

CHAPTER EIGHT

Napoléon as King of Italy by Andrea Appiani.

below The Flag of Elba, photograph in the 1925 catalogue.

middle Napoléon returns from Elba by Charles de Steuben.

below right Ceremony on the Champs de Mai, 21st March 1815.

Unlike the Emperor's Coronation at Notre Dame in Paris, the one in Milan Cathedral on 26th May 1805 seems to have been a less well organised and somewhat lower key event, although a new carriage was ordered for the occasion, emblazoned on the doors with the Iron Crown of Lombardy. After the ceremonies were over, this coach joined those in the Imperial Mews, before becoming permanently attached to the French *Grande Armée* on its travels. It was seized in the wake of Waterloo and later ended up in the collection of Madame Tussaud's. The only record relating to its acquisition appears in the 1838-1843 ledger, which stated that on 23rd January 1842, Madame Tussaud's acquired 'Napoleon's carriage' for £52 (2022: £4,857). By 1911 it was valued at £500 (2022: £46,703).

The second pre-Waterloo item was 'The Flag of Elba' (Item 62: Napoléon Room), actually an Eagle Standard *drapeau* and *cravat*, which was illustrated in the 1925 exhibition catalogue and rated a lengthy entry, here edited:

The Flag of Elba ... is composed of tri-coloured silk ... elaborately embroidered in silver; the reverse side with the inscription "Champ de Mai, 1815". The Flag and sash were both worked by Princess Pauline, the Emperor's favourite sister, who resided on the island during a part of his exile there. It was this flag which Napoléon displayed when, on his return from Elba, he harangued the troops sent to oppose him.

Shortly after his arrival in Paris, and on the morning of 21st of March, 1815, Napoléon held a grand review in the Place Carousel, and at the termination of the review General Cambronne entered the square at the head of the officers of the battalion of Elba, carrying the Imperial Eagles and the Flag which Napoléon had presented to them. It was on the Champ de Mars – denominated on this occasion the "Champ de Mai" ... that the Flag was more formally presented by the Emperor to his Guards. Surrounded

by a brilliant assemblage of his Marshals and Generals, he advanced and solemnly gave into the keeping of the Guards who had voluntarily shared his exile, and had followed him back to France, the Flag which he had presented to them in the days of his adversity. Gallantly did they fight under it at Waterloo, but it was at last taken by the Prussians, and was presently purchased of them by an English collector.

According to the 1843 ledger, it had been purchased the previous year for £56 (2022: £5,230) from an undisclosed source, and in 1911 it was valued at £750 (2022: £70,055). The purchase price was a fraction of its value today, even adjusting for inflation, although the 1911 insurance value is broadly in line with current prices. For example, in 2014 two Eagle Standard *drapeaux* with excellent provenances sold at auction for €75,000 (2022: £64,000) and €50,000 (2022: £42,750) each.

The Old Guard at Waterloo, detail from the painting by Robert Hillingford.

While on the subject of Imperial Eagles, possibly the most valuable of all the seventy-six Eagle Standards believed to have survived the Restoration of the Bourbon monarchy, is the 1815-pattern Eagle finial, *cravat* and *drapeau* of the 1st Regiment of Foot Grenadiers of the Imperial Guard, the most senior regiment of Napoléon's *Grande Armée*. Originally in the collection of Count Anatoli Nikolaievich Demidov, Principe di San Donato, the Eagle Standard of the 1st Foot Grenadiers was not lost in battle. Instead, it probably came into the Russian's possession through his rather unsatisfactory marriage in 1840 to Princesse Matilde-Letizia Bonaparte, the daughter of Napoléon's brother, Jérôme Bonaparte. The Eagle Standard, complete with its well-preserved *cravat* and *drapeau*, was placed on display by the Prince in his fourteen-room museum at the Villa San Donato in Florence and remained there until the rump of the Demidov collection of artworks was sold in March 1880, ten years after his death. At this point it was bought for US$300 (1880: £60 / 2022: £7,500) by the wealthy American collector, Isabella Stewart Gardner, of Boston, Massachusetts. In 1903, she placed it on display in the Short Gallery of her eponymous mock-Venetian-Renaissance museum in Boston. There it remained until 18th March 1990, when the Eagle finial (but not the *cravat* and *drapeau*) was stolen, along with twelve other unique works

CHAPTER EIGHT

Napoléon's campaign carriage, known as *La Dormeuse*, photograph in the 1925 catalogue.

of art, including Rembrandt's only known seascape. These items were worth an estimated US$500 million in total and the theft, which took just eighty-one minutes, is the largest art heist ever recorded. Despite a reward of US$10 million remaining on offer, none of these stolen items has ever been recovered.

The third item that pre-dates Waterloo was the most significant and important of all the Napoléonica in Madame Tussaud's collection. Listed as 'Napoléon's Military Carriage taken at Waterloo' (Item 48: Napoléon Room), this campaign carriage was known as *La Dormeuse* ('The Sleeper'), was illustrated in the 1925 exhibition catalogue, and merited a long and often inaccurate entry. The correct story follows.

In an age when armies moved at the speed of their slow baggage trains, Napoléon's moved at the pace of a marching soldier: it was one of the secrets of his success. However, while the comfort of the Emperor's ordinary soldiers and officers was to some extent compromised on the altar of speed, Napoléon and his Marshals managed to maintain a high standard-of-living in the field. This was particularly true of the Emperor himself. During his reign, Napoléon spent more time abroad than he did in France. It was, therefore, vital for him to be able to maintain his administrative grip wherever he happened to be, without sacrificing his high standards of comfort and personal cleanliness. To achieve this required a considerable wheeled infrastructure.

During the Russian Campaign of 1812, the Emperor's personal convoy consisted of fifty vehicles, five hundred horses and six hundred men. Once deployed, his

[148]

CHAPTER EIGHT

La Cuisine Roulante.

personal staff were able to set up every aspect of the Emperor's mobile palace in a matter of minutes, whether in a soggy field or in a commandeered castle. Behind this efficiency lay the application of clever design and engineering to every component of the convoy, from the folding pavilion-tent and the collapsible bed ingeniously stored on a specially designed vehicle, to the extraordinary kitchen on wheels, *La Cuisine Roulante*, that is now on display at Les Invalides in Paris.

These arrangements perpetuated several myths connected with the capture of the Emperor's personal carriages in the immediate aftermath of the Battle of Waterloo. To set this in context, by the time the Emperor left Paris on 12th June 1815 to face Wellington and Blücher at Waterloo, his personal wheeled infrastructure had – for reasons of speed and economy – been reduced from the fifty carriages and waggons of the Imperial Convoy that set off for Moscow, to three much smaller groups. In the first group were six vehicles carrying Napoléon's wardrobe, linen, food, stores, the imperial tent, furniture and other equipment required for his daily routine of work, eating, bathing and sleeping. This was followed, at an interval allowing sufficient time for the first group to do their set-up work, by the second element of the convoy. In these carriages travelled his personal office staff, with all their equipment from maps to ink. Allowing enough time for Napoléon's personal staff to unpack their desks, the third part of the convoy then departed. This comprised *La Dormeuse*, which the Emperor shared on the move (but not at night) with his Chief of Staff, Marshal Berthier; a second coach, a *berline*, carried his ADCs; and a *bastardelle* (a closed, lightweight carriage), was

[149]

CHAPTER EIGHT

occupied by his personal secretary. These three carriages were escorted by Chasseurs à Cheval of the Imperial Guard.

As previously noted, *La Dormeuse* was ordered in 1812 for Napoléon by his second wife, Empress Marie Louise, at a cost of F34,000 (2022: *c.* £94,180) from Jean Simons of Brussels and Paris. Simons was a *nouveau riche* coachmaker, who had prospered during the French Revolution and whose Paris workshop had earlier built Napoléon's French Coronation coach. The coachmaker had acquired that contract when his singer-actress wife, Amélie-Julie Candeillé, introduced him to the Empress Joséphine. This doubtless cost Simons a hefty commission to the then Empress. However, *La Dormeuse* was constructed not in Paris, but in the unfashionable rue de la Blanchisserie in Brussels. These workshops were immediately adjacent to a house which Simons had been obliged to acquire because of a lack of property in the more fashionable centre of the city. In 1814, and safely out of harm's way in Paris, Simons let his property in Brussels to Charles, 4th Duke of Richmond and Lennox, who initially took the house as part of an economy drive. However, in 1815 the property at 23 rue de la Blanchisserie also provided the Duke, at this time also a British General, with a base for his command of Wellington's reserve troops in the city and allowed him to be near his son and heir, Charles Lennox, Earl of March, who, having been badly wounded in the closing stages of the Peninsular War the previous year, was then serving as ADC to the Prince of Orange. With unintentional historic irony, the Duchess

The Duchess of Richmond's Ball by Robert Alexander Hillingford.

of Richmond used the showroom of the empty coachworks, where *La Dormeuse* had been made, as the setting for her ball on Thursday 15th June 1815, three days before the Battle of Waterloo. The Duchess's party was rated by the noted historian, Elizabeth Longford, as 'the most famous ball in history'.

Back to the carriages: Napoléon had a second campaign carriage, made by Getting of Paris at a cost of F10,282 (2022: circa £28,481), but it was not available during the Hundred Days. In any event, it was Simons' *La Dormeuse*, drawn by six brown Normandy-bred horses, with two postillions and driven by the Emperor's personal coachman, Jean Hornn (a Belgian born in Bergen-op-Zoom in 1788), that carried the Emperor from Paris to Moscow and back in 1812. During the retreat in the snow, the carriage's wheels were removed, and it was strapped onto a sled. *La Dormeuse* had also accompanied Napoléon to exile in Elba in 1814 (without Hornn), and returned with him to France in 1815 for the Hundred Days. Given the fate of this carriage and its contents after Waterloo, it is worth quoting a contemporary description of it, written shortly after the battle and reproduced in William Bullock's 1819 auction catalogue:

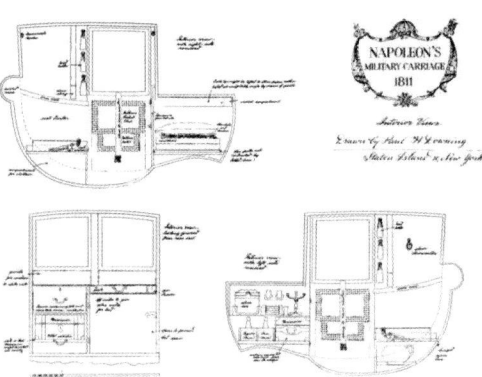

La Dormeuse interior.

> The exterior of the carriage is, in many respects, very like the modern English travelling chariots. The colour is a dark blue, with a handsome border ornamented in gold... the Imperial arms are emblazoned on the bullet proof pannels [sic] of the doors. It has a lamp at each corner of the roof, and there is one lamp fixed at the back which can throw a strong light into the interior.
>
> In the front there is a great projection; the utility of which is very considerable. Beyond this projection, and nearer to the horses, is a seat for the coachman: this is ingeniously contrived, so as to prevent the driver from viewing the interior of the carriage; and it is also placed so as to afford those within, a clear sight of the horses, and of the surrounding country...
>
> The pannels [sic] of the carriage are bullet proof; at the hinder part is a projecting sword case, and the pannel [sic] at the lower part of the back is so contrived, that it may be let down, and therefore facilitate the addition or removal of conveniences [chamber pots], without disturbing the traveller.
>
> The under-carriage, which has swan-neck iron cranes, is of prodigious strength; the springs are semi-circular, and each of them seems capable of bearing half a ton; the wheels, and more particularly the [iron] tires, are also of very great strength. The pole is contrived to act as a lever, by which the carriage is kept on a level on every kind of road. The undercarriage and wheels are painted in vermillion, edged with the colour of the body, and heightened with gold. The harness... bears strong marks

CHAPTER EIGHT

of its service in the Russian Campaign and is [recognisable as Imperial equipage] only by the bees, arms and eagles, which are to be seen in several places.

The interior ... is adapted to the various purposes of an office, a bed-room, a dressing-room, a kitchen, and an eating-room.

The seat has a separation [to prevent the Emperor and Berthier being thrown together by a jolt] ... In front of the seat are compartments for every utensile [*sic*] of probable utility; of some there are two sets, one of gold and the other of silver. Among the gold articles are a teapot, a coffee pot, sugar basin, cream ewer, coffee cup and saucer, slop basin, candlesticks, wash-hand basin, plates for breakfast etc. Each article is superbly embossed with the imperial arms and engraved with an 'N'. By the aid of a lamp, anything could be heated in the carriage.

Beneath the coachman's seat is a small box about two and a half feet long, and about four inches square: this contains a [folding] bedstead of polished steel, which could be fitted-up within one or two minutes. The carriage also contains mattresses and other requisites for bedding, of very exquisite quality; all of them commodiously arranged. There are also articles for strict personal convenience [chamber pots] made of solid silver, with silver gilt interiors, fitted into the carriage [below the passenger seat].

A small mahogany case, about ten Inches square by eighteen inches long, contains the peculiar *nécessaire de voyage* of the ex-Emperor. It is somewhat in appearance like an English writing desk [slope?], having the imperial arms most beautifully engraved on the cover. It contains nearly one hundred articles, almost all of them in solid gold.

The liquor case, like the *necessaire*, is made of mahogany: it contains two bottles; one [containing] rum, the other some fine old Malaga wine. Various articles of perfumery are among the luxuries which remain [including] Windsor soap, and some English court-plaster, eau de Cologne, eau de Cavande, salt spirit etc.

There is a writing desk, which may be drawn out so as to write while the carriage is proceeding; an inkstand, pens, etc were found in it ... and the Emperor's portfolio.

In the front there are also many small compartments, for maps and telescopes; on the ceiling of the carriage is a net for carrying small travelling requisites.

On one of the doors of the carriage are two pistol holsters, in which were pistols manufactured at Versailles; and in the holster, close to the seat, a double-barrelled pistol also was found ... all were loaded. On the side there hung a large silver chronometer with a silver chain ... by Mugnier of Paris.

The doors of the carriage have locks and bolts: the blinds, behind the windows, shut and open by means of a spring, and may be closed so as to form an almost impenetrable barrier.

On the outside of the window[s] [are] roller blind[s] made of strong painted canvas: when pulled down [they prevent rain, snow and damp] from penetrating.

CHAPTER EIGHT

Napoléon's *berline*.

The second carriage in the third part of the Emperor's convoy has often been promoted by many authorities, most of whom should know better, as Napoléon's principal campaign carriage. It was not. This smaller and less well-equipped carriage, a *berline*, still exists and can be viewed at the Napoléonic National Museum at the Château de Malmaison. It was made by Getting in 1812, specifically – like *La Dormeuse* – for the Russian Campaign. Instead of a fixed top, it had two folding roofs, fore and aft, that allowed it to be used in fine weather as an open-topped carriage. To put these vehicles into a modern context, today *La Dormeuse* would be a Winnebago, parked up for the duration of a holiday, and the *berline* would be the small 'runabout' car used by the family to make short trips to the supermarket and the beach.

As the light started to fail over the battlefield at Waterloo on Sunday 18th June 1815, by 8pm the only French soldiers still holding their ground around the Emperor's command post, near the inn known as La Belle Alliance, were the two regiments of the Foot Grenadiers of the Old Guard, formed-up in squares. Their job was to guard Napoléon, who commanded the unit on the left of the inn, and who had by that time realised that the day was lost and that his place was in Paris. With his iconic charger, *Marengo* (if that was its name), lying wounded in a ditch on the battlefield, Napoléon withdrew from the affray on a spare horse. Escorted by the Chasseurs à Cheval, he made his way to a farmhouse called Le Caillou, between La Belle Alliance and Genappe, where he had spent

CHAPTER EIGHT

the previous night and where the three coaches of the third element of his personal convoy awaited him. Once there, he clambered aboard *La Dormeuse*, and accompanied by the Chasseurs à Cheval and the Getting-made *berline*, Napoléon's campaign coach then trundled off in the direction of Genappe, hotly pursued by Prussian light infantrymen and British cavalry.

At around 11 pm the remains of the imperial convoy had to make a detour through a field just north of Genappe, in order to get around the village which was blocked with fleeing Frenchmen. What happened next is recounted in an affidavit, sworn by Hornn in London in 1816 before the Lord Mayor; a first-hand, legally binding account, it is more reliable than others, which differ in substance and detail. It is possible, but perhaps understandably not mentioned in the affidavit, that by going off-road the carriage became stuck in the water-logged ground and that is why it was overtaken by the Prussians. It had been raining heavily the previous night and that morning.

The Incident at Genappe, engraving in the auction catalogue of the contents of the Bullock Museum, 1819.

For whatever reason, the off-road detour around Genappe allowed the Prussians, led by Baron von Keller, to catch up with the coaches. Von Keller's fusiliers immobilised Napoléon's escape vehicle by bayonetting *La Dormeuse*'s two lead horses and their postillion, while the Baron hacked at Hornn the coachman, before moving to the offside door to seize the occupant of the coach. Hornn later recorded that he was left for dead by the side of the road, stripped of his clothes by Belgian scavengers, and then rescued six days later by a British officer, who took him to Brussels where his wounds were dressed, and his right arm was amputated.

CHAPTER EIGHT

Meanwhile, in the time that it had taken the Prussian officer to inflict ten sword cuts on the unfortunate Hornn, Napoléon had jumped out through the nearside door of *La Dormeuse*. Such was his haste that his hat fell off and he had no time to put on his greatcoat and sword, but mounted one of his escort's chargers and, 'with tears streaming down his face', continued his headlong flight back to Paris leaving *La Dormeuse* and the *berline* stuck in the mud.

In accordance with the usage and practice of war, von Keller claimed both carriages and their contents as spoils of war, and therefore his property, before leading his men off south to Millet. There they captured the baggage train of the French Army of the North, three thousand Frenchmen (including many senior officers), eighty cannon and a huge stash of diamonds hidden in gunpowder kegs. For this action, and the capture of Napoléon's carriages, von Keller was awarded the prestigious Prussian decoration, *Pour le Mérite*.

On the day after the battle, von Keller was re-united with his spoils of war. Presumably after sorting through the contents of both carriages, he sent Napoléon's hat, sword, and an elaborately embroidered Mameluke burnous to his commander, Marshal Blücher, who later presented the latter to the Prince Regent. Found in *La Dormeuse*, and used as a dressing gown by the Emperor, in some accounts this burnous is erroneously referred to as a 'mantle' or a 'mantle of state', which it obviously was not. Von Keller also sent Blücher the *berline*, in which he had found a large collection of Napoléon's foreign Orders and decorations. To Wellington's considerable irritation, von Keller sent *him* only three minor souvenirs from *La Dormeuse*, including a soiled napkin embroidered with the imperial cypher. This the Iron Duke later gave to a Waterloo veteran, for unspecified 'services rendered' in connection with the Duke's close friendship with Harriet Arbuthnot. The grandson of the recipient of this piece of linen later presented it to Madame Tussaud's, along with an account of its acquisition. The napkin, which was not separately listed in the 1925 exhibition catalogue or in the 1911 insurance catalogue, was lost in the 1925 fire, but the correspondence escaped the flames.

While Wellington was grumbling at the slim pickings he had been sent by the Prussian Major, Marshal Blücher forwarded Napoléon's hat, sword and decorations to King Frederick William III of Prussia, who put them on display at the Prussian Hall of Fame in the Zeughaus Museum in Berlin. Blücher sent the by-now-empty *berline* to his wife at their house at Kreiblowitz, near Breslau, in what is currently

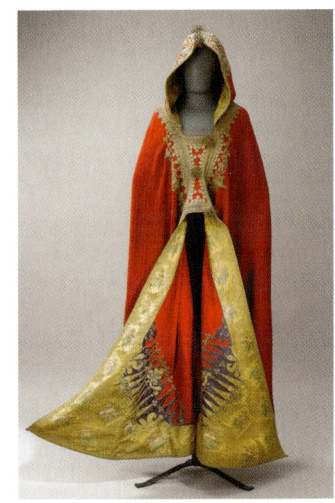

Napoléon's burnous
©Royal Collection Trust / His Majesty King Charles III 2023

Treasures from Napoléon's *berline* at the Zeughaus Museum, Berlin.

CHAPTER EIGHT

The Prince Regent (1762–1830) by Henry Bone after Sir Thomas Lawrence.

Poland but was then East Prussia. There the *berline* remained until 1973, when Graf Blücher von Wahlstatt gave it to the Napoléonic National Museum at the Château de Malmaison, since when it has been incorrectly identified as the carriage in which the Emperor fled from Waterloo.

In the meantime, von Keller dispatched *La Dormeuse* and the rest of its contents to Düsseldorf, where they were put on display from 25th June 1815. The contents in particular attracted a great deal of attention, for they constituted a veritable Aladdin's cave of treasures. Besides an annotated copy of Machiavelli's, *The Prince*, *La Dormeuse* contained: 'a diamond head dress (tiara), [a] diamond snuff box ... [and] several boxes of mounted and unmounted diamonds', in addition to the items already described.

After displaying the campaign carriage in Düsseldorf, von Keller took it to London, along with the four remaining horses, Jean Hornn (who had recovered from his wounds), and a second imperial coachman called William Jonsen, who had driven *La Dormeuse* on Elba and during the return to Paris at the start of the Hundred Days, and may have been driving the *berline* at Waterloo.

Once in London, these spoils, and the remaining contents of *La Dormeuse*, were presented to the Prince Regent. Accounts differ as to the specific arrangements of this transfer, variously stating that the campaign carriage was either a gift to the Prince Regent from the Prussian government or was bought from the Prussians by the British government and then given or sold to the Prince Regent. None of these accounts is correct. What actually happened was recorded by William Bullock, in the sale catalogue of the contents of his museum in 1819:

> In consequence of some dispute between the [Prussian] ambassador and the officer [von Keller], who considered the carriage and contents to be his private plunder, the Prince Regent refused to accept them as a present [from the Prussian government] but purchased them of the officer for 3,500 guineas (2022: £343,271) – understanding ... that Mr Bullock had previously offered [von Keller] 2,500 guineas (2022: £245,193), with the intention of exhibiting them to the public. He [the Prince Regent] [then]

CHAPTER EIGHT

agreed to part with them [to Mr Bullock] for 3,000 [guineas] (2022: £294,232), one party losing 500 [guineas] (2022: £49,038) and the other advancing 500 [guineas], which offer was accepted by Mr Bullock.

This rather convoluted transaction between von Keller, the Prince Regent and Bullock, has led to much misunderstanding ever since. Excluded from the deal were the loose diamonds and the diamond-encrusted snuff box, which Bullock had bought separately from von Keller. This is confirmed by an annotation in the auction catalogue, which stated that the snuff box (decorated with one hundred and forty brilliants) was never the property of the Prince Regent. It was later included by Bullock in the 1819 sale, when it was bought by a Mr Davies for £166.10.0 (2022: £15,600).

Before any of this happened, and having banked the Prince Regent's cheque, von Keller invested the proceeds in a spa in Breslau. William Bullock collected the carriage and its horses from the Royal Mews, where – on the order of Henry Bathurst, 3rd Earl Bathurst, the Secretary of State for War and the Colonies – they had been stabled since their arrival in London. This was an arrangement for which Bullock was billed by the Master of the Horse, the Duke of Montrose, 'as His Grace cannot include the [expense] in His Account without an Order from the Treasury' (according to correspondence held in the Letter Books of the Master of the Horse). On payment of the stabling costs incurred at the Royal Mews, Bullock put *La Dormeuse*, the horses, the coachman and the contents on

La Dormeuse at Bullock's Museum.

CHAPTER EIGHT

display in his museum on Piccadilly. As already noted, when von Keller brought the carriage to London, but before he sold it to the Prince Regent, he disposed of the loose Napoléonic diamonds to Mr John Mawe in The Strand.

Once at Bullock's Museum in Piccadilly, the contents of the carriage were arranged in several display cases, and – as in Düsseldorf – the *tout ensemble* created a sensation. Every day, upwards of ten thousand gawpers flocked to see the coach and sit where the Emperor had parked his rump. When the London public had finished admiring *La Dormeuse*, the entire *equipage* went on a tour around the United Kingdom, during which more than 800,000 people paid to see it. By the time it returned to London, William Bullock had more than offset the purchase price by banking in excess of £33,000 (2022: £3.08 million) from the entry fees, which must have somewhat irked the ever-short-of-cash Prince Regent.

After the UK tour, the four horses were sold at Tattersall's on 1st December 1818, as reported in a clipping from the *Essex County Chronicle* found recently in the Madame Tussaud archives. Sadly, Tattersall's records for the period were destroyed by bombing during the Second World War, so who bought the horses and what was paid for them has been lost. Not so the details of *La Dormeuse* and its contents, which were disposed of at the 1819 auction of Bullock's Museum for a total of £901.6.0 (2022: £84,159), further adding to Bullock's net profit. Mr Bullock's own copy of the sale catalogue still exists and is helpfully annotated by him, in his role as the auctioneer, with the names of the purchasers of the items from his collection (Sir Walter Scott and Captain Clark of The Royals, amongst many others) and the prices that they paid. *La Dormeuse*, was sold for £168 (2022: £15,692) to a Mr Hopkinson, who said he intended to tour it around the USA. The tour never happened, and the carriage was sold again to a new owner, who had the same intention. Later, the carriage was seized in lieu of a debt by a carriage maker, Robert Jeffreys of Gray's Inn Road, who in turn sold it in 1842 for £2,500 (2022: £233,517) to Joseph, son of Madame Tussaud. Its insured value in 1911 was £4,000 (2022: £373,628).

Once at Madame Tussaud's, *La Dormeuse* continued to be a significant money-spinner, as part of a special exhibition about Napoléon, advertised as follows in *The Times* in 1843:

> Napoléon's celebrated military carriage, taken at Waterloo … his watch, gold snuff box, ring, one of his teeth, the instrument that drew it, tooth-brush, Madras worn in exile, dessert service used by him at St Helens, a counterpane stained with his blood … Madame Tussaud & Sons' Exhibition at the Bazaar, Baker-Street: open from 11 till dusk, and from 7 till 10. Great room, 1s; Napoléon relics and chamber of horrors, 6d.

≈ CHAPTER EIGHT ≈

La Dormeuse on display at Madame Tussaud's.

top La Dormeuse after the 1925 fire and *above* The axle of *La Dormeuse*.

The juxtaposition of 'relics' with the 'chamber of horrors' may not be accidental, as Napoléon remained both a revered and a hate figure in British culture for much of the nineteenth century: the 'boneyman' was often substituted for the 'bogeyman' in tales told to frighten children. In the 1925 fire, as *The Times* reported, the Emperor's campaign carriage was reduced to 'scrap iron'. So intense was the wax-fuelled fire that the only recognisable remnant of *La Dormeuse* was its main axle, which was displayed once the exhibition was rebuilt and in 1978 lent to Malmaison, where it remains.

Unlike the portraits by David, there is no doubt about the authenticity of *La Dormeuse* and its fitted contents, which – in addition to the items already mentioned – included a silver provision box containing a half-eaten portion of roast chicken, valued in 1911 at £50 (2022: £4,670); a rosewood case containing six razors and a strop, also valued at £50; a book of post roads, and a telescope, valued in the insurance catalogue at £25 (2022: £2,335) each. All of these items were illustrated in the 1925 exhibition catalogue and were for the most part displayed in 'The Gillingham Case' (Item 127: Napoléon Room), along with saddlery and postillions' whips with an imperial provenance and a combined 1911 value of £80 (2022: £7,472). The catalogue entry recorded that they had all been acquired by Madame Tussaud & Sons when offered for sale following the death of Baron von Keller.

It has recently emerged that there was an important piece of Napoléonica

[159]

≈ CHAPTER EIGHT ≈

that survived the 1925 fire and was sold by Madame Tussaud's at Christie's in 2005. This was a glass scent bottle of bulbous form, engraved in gilt with the imperial-crowned *N*, and with a facetted stopper. Christie's gave it a pre-sale estimate of £2,000 to £4,000, but it sold for £8,400. Although – as Christie's noted – it did not appear in any of the exhibition's ledgers, catalogues or insurance

right Silver provision box, photograph in the 1925 catalogue.

far right Nécessaire de voyage, photograph in the 1925 catalogue.

right Napoléon's telescope, photograph in the 1925 catalogue.

far right The Gillingham Case, photograph in the 1925 catalogue.

inventories, the auctioneers had no doubt about its provenance and suggested that it 'was probably among the relics acquired from Miss Gordon, who acquired them from the late Prince Lucien Bonaparte'. It could also have been an item from *La Dormeuse*, as scent bottles are mentioned among 'Napoléon Mementoes' (Item 113: Napoléon Room). Either way, it was self-evidently not in the exhibition in 1925 and its absence from the ledgers, inventories and catalogues, suggest that it may have been kept at the home of a Tussaud family members, before joining the main collection in time to be sold off by later owners of madame Tussaud's in 2005. This scent bottle can be viewed at *www.christies.com/en/lot/lot-4587484*.

Although the provenance of the foregoing Napoléonica was well-established,

CHAPTER EIGHT

there must be considerable doubt regarding the claim in the exhibition catalogues that Madame Tussaud's owned 'three Eagles taken at Waterloo', and another Eagle listed under Item 107 in the Napoléon Room, although the latter may have topped the Flag of Elba and been separately displayed. To add further doubt, the 1911 insurance catalogue listed only one 'Eagle', stated that it was 'taken at Waterloo' and valued it at £10 (2022: £934). Given that the fate of all the Eagles captured by, or otherwise lost to, the British (and other nations) is well recorded,* this assertion must be challenged as inaccurate. Only two Eagles were captured at Waterloo, those of the French 105th and 45th Infantry Regiments of the Line. Today, they are displayed respectively at the National Army Museum, London, and the Museum of the Royal Scots Dragoon Guards at Edinburgh Castle. At no point were they exhibited at Madame Tussaud's.

* See Christopher Joll and Penny Cobham, *The Imperial Impresario: The Treasures, Trophies & Trivia of Napoléon's Theatre of Power* (Nine Elms Books, 2022).

There must also be some doubt about the authenticity of two other items in the Gillingham Case (Item 127). First, the 'Sword of Honour ... the gift of Napoléon to [Marshal] Junot [which] was among the spoil found on the battlefield'. The entry in the 1911 insurance catalogue repeated that provenance and added that 'Junot's name [was] on the hilt'. Although the inscription on the hilt is irrefutable, it is very doubtful that the sword was found 'on the Field of Waterloo' as Junot was not there, having died on 29th July 1813. Nonetheless, the 1911 insurance catalogue valued the sword at £50 (2022: £4,670), along with a copy, not listed in the 1925 exhibition catalogue, but valued at £10 (2022: £934).

Marshal Jean-Andoche Junot, Duke of Abrantes (1771–1813), by Andrea Appiani.

The second item in the Gillingham Case (Item 127) of dubious authenticity was one of Napoléon's bicorne hats. The 1911 insurance catalogue merely listed it with a value of £200 (2022: £18,681), but the 1925 exhibition catalogue asserted that it 'was purchased at the sale in Vienna of the effects of Hippolite Bellange [*sic*], a French artist, who is best remembered by his pictures of Napoléon's battles.' Hippolyte Bellangé was as described, but it is extremely unlikely that he owned a genuine Napoléonic bicorne hat, as he would have been only fifteen in 1815 when Napoléon was finally defeated. To add further doubt as to the hat's provenance, Bellangé died in Paris not Vienna. The likelihood is that it was a studio prop.

Less problematic is 'the sabre worn by Napoléon in Egypt', also displayed in the Gillingham Case, which according to the 1925 catalogue entry:

> ...was highly prized by him, for it is believed to have originally belonged to Sobieski, the great Polish warrior-king (John III)...The weapon was particularised in Napoléon's will; it was bequeathed to Prince Lucien, his brother, and after the Prince's death was sold, with the rest of his possessions, in London.

There is some documentary evidence that Sobieski's sword was found during the Italian Campaign, which commenced in 1797, so it could have come into

Hippolyte Bellangé (1800–1866).

[161]

≈ CHAPTER EIGHT ≈

Joseph Bonaparte's carriage captured after the Battle of Vitoria, 1813.

Napoléon's possession before the invasion of Egypt the following year. The 1843 ledger recorded that it was acquired by Madame Tussaud's in May 1842 for £13 (2022: £1,214), although whether it was bought at the auction of Lucien's estate or direct from Miss Gordon was not specified. It was valued in 1911 at £50 (2022: £4,670).

Similarly, there is no reason to doubt the authenticity of the 'gold embroidered waistcoat of Joseph Bonaparte, King of Spain… captured at Vittoria [*sic*]', given that in the aftermath of the battle in 1813, British cavalry seized Joseph's campaign carriage, and its entire contents (less a bagful of diamonds kept by the ex-King and later used to buy Point Breeze in the USA). A full account of this incident can be found in *Spoils of War: The Treasures, Trophies & Trivia of the British Empire* (Nine Elms Books, 2020). The waistcoat was valued in 1911 at £10 (2022: £934), although there is no record of how the Tussauds acquired it, or from whom.

More problematic is one of the last items listed in the Gillingham Case, which was described as a 'Bronze Statuette of Napoléon', but was self-evidently from the text of the 1925 exhibition catalogue a death mask:

> … It was executed from a plaster cast taken by Dr. Antomarchi [*sic*], which the doctor preserved with jealous care, and with which he consistently refused to part, although as much as £6,000 [2022: £541,336] was offered for it. One statuette in bronze was presented to the Emperor's mother, the other is the one here exhibited.

The whole subject of Napoléon's death mask is fraught with controversy. Suffice it to say here that Dr Antommarchi, who was present at Napoléon's death, started making bronze and plaster-cast copies from his original gypsum mould after 1828, and that two, possibly five, such original castings still exist. The rest, including almost certainly that at Madame Tussaud's, are later copies of copies. This conclusion is not entirely reinforced by the 1911 insurance catalogue, which gave the death mask a relatively high valuation for the time of £25 (2022: £2,335), while only valuing a second death mask – on loan and without the Antommarchi provenance – at £10 (2022: £934).

An Antommarchi-signed death mask of Napoléon.

The remaining items to be considered in this chapter belonged to or were associated with the 1st Duke of Wellington. Given his visits to Madame Tussaud's, as noted and illustrated in Chapter 6, it is unlikely (but not impossible) that the items on display in 1925 were fakes. Those that were facsimiles were listed as such, and included the 'Case of Wellington Orders' (Item 166: Napoléon Ante-Room), and the magnificent silver-gilt 'Wellington Shield' (Item 54: Napoléon Room), the original of which had been presented to him by the Corporation of the City of

CHAPTER EIGHT

Wellington on the field of Waterloo by Benjamin Robert Haydon.

London. This last was listed in the 1911 insurance catalogue as a copy worth £15 (2022: £1,401). However, the Iron Duke's 'Orders, Stars and Bâtons' were valued at that time as though they were the originals at £500 (2022: £46,703). This may have been because they were 'costly facsimiles in gold, silver enamel etc'.

In addition to these items, Madame Tussaud's also owned and displayed some of the Duke's personal possessions, including the 'Coat and Waistcoat of the Duke of Wellington' (Item 156: Napoléon Ante-Room) that he had worn for a painting by Benjamin Robert Haydon, who – like Sir George Hayter – later gave them to the Tussauds. Although not listed as such, these clothes were probably those given a value in 1911 of £250 (2022: £23,438). The portrait itself was commissioned to hang in Liverpool's Town Hall, but is now in the collection of the National Portrait Gallery, London.

[163]

CHAPTER EIGHT

The duel between the Duke of Wellington and the 10th Earl of Winchelsea (1791–1858), *Illustrated London News* cartoon.

The rest of the Wellingtonia, valued in 1911 to a total of £410 (2022: £38,296), was described in full in the 1925 catalogue:

> Wellington Relics [Item 90: Napoléon Room] – The mementoes of the great Duke preserved in this case include a toothbrush, a swordstick, various garments, and the pistols used by the Duke and the Earl of Winchilsea and Nottingham in the duel in Battersea Fields – now Battersea Park – on the 21st of March, 1829.

The entry then goes on to describe at length the reasons for the duel (Catholic emancipation) and what happened on the day: Wellington fired and almost certainly deliberately missed, although he was a notoriously bad shot; Lord Winchilsea then deloped [fired in the air] and apologised. A pair of the Duke's duelling pistols, made by W. Jones of London and presented to him by the East India Company in 1815, are held in the Museum of London. That does not mean, however, that the pair on display at Madame Tussaud's were not authentic. Wellington probably had more than one pair, as may also have been the case with Item 149 in the Napoléon Ante-Room, described in the 1925 catalogue:

> The Duke of Wellington's Camp Bedstead – This, though not the camp bedstead on which the Iron Duke died – for that is treasured at Apsley House – is the one on which he slept the night before Waterloo.

The 1911 insurance catalogue was less specific, merely stating that the bedstead and a piece of the mattress had belonged to the Iron Duke and together were worth £110 (2022: £10,274). In fact, Wellington died at Walmer Castle, Kent,

CHAPTER EIGHT

seated in a chair – and the bed from which he had just risen was that which he had used 'throughout his military career'. It is still at Walmer Castle. Meanwhile, a smoke-blackened plaster mould and cast, made of the Iron Duke's profile in death, has recently been unearthed in the Madame Tussaud archive. It was listed in the 1911 insurance catalogue with a value of £20 (2022: £1,868).

above left Death of the Duke of Wellington; *above* The room in which Wellington died at Walmer Castle.

CHAPTER NINE

ST HELENA

IN THE WAKE OF THE debacle at Waterloo, Napoléon abandoned *La Dormeuse* outside Genappe, and returned to Paris. There he found his position was untenable, leaving him with no choice but to abdicate on 22nd June 1815 for the second time. Three days later the ex-Emperor settled at Malmaison, the former home of his late first wife, Joséphine. However, when he heard that the Prussian troops, already on the outskirts of Paris, had orders to capture him dead or alive, he fled to Rochefort, with the intention of taking ship to the United States. With the British Royal Navy blockading all French ports, this plan failed and Napoléon finally surrendered to Captain Frederick Maitland on HMS *Bellerophon* on 15th July. There then followed a series of unsuccessful negotiations with the British government, including a direct appeal to the Prince Regent, which ended with the decision that the ex-Emperor should be banished to the island of St Helena in the South Atlantic. He was conveyed there on the British battleship, HMS *Northumberland*, HMS *Bellerophon* being insufficiently seaworthy for the long voyage.

Madame Tussaud's commemorated this final voyage with a display of 'Napoléon Relics from the *Northumberland*' (Item 50: Napoléon Room). These included the wash-stand and towel-horse he used during the voyage, which had been presented to Madame Tussaud by the officer in command of HMS *Northumberland*, Captain (later Vice Admiral) Charles Bayne Hodgson Ross, who wrote of his passenger:

> He is fat, rather what we call pot-bellied, and although his leg is well-shaped, it is rather clumsy, and his walk appears rather affected, something between a waddle and a swagger – but probably not being used to the motion of a ship might have given him that appearance. He is very sallow and [has] quite light grey eyes, rather thin, greasy-looking brown hair, and altogether a very nasty, priestlike-looking fellow.

The HMS *Northumberland* bathroom furniture was valued in 1911 at £10 (2022: £934). However, the insurance catalogue but not the 1925 exhibition catalogue, listed a second 'Washing Stand and Towel Horse', which it asserted was 'used

opposite Napoléon onboard HMS *Bellerophon* by William Quiller Orchardson.

Napoléon on HMS *Northumberland* by Denzil Ibbetson.

CHAPTER NINE

above Napoléon on St Helena by Franz Josef Sandman;

below Longwood House, St Helena.

by Napoléon at St Helena'. It was valued higher at £50 (2022: £4,670), albeit without any information as to provenance or acquisition.

After ten weeks at sea, the ex-Emperor spent two months living with the Balcombe family at the Briars pavilion, before moving into Longwood House, a large damp wooden bungalow. There, his substantial retinue was later reduced on the orders of his antagonistic jailor, Sir Hudson Lowe, the Governor of St Helena.

In exile, Napoléon passed the time dictating his memoirs, learning English, and playing cards. He died at Longwood on 5th May 1821 and was buried on the island. In 1840, by command of the French monarch, King Louis Philippe, his body was exhumed and the remarkably well-preserved corpse was returned to France. Once there, Napoléon I was accorded a State Funeral on 15th December of that year, and re-buried in a red quartzite sarcophagus in an open crypt under the dome of Les Invalides.

As with the St Helena-related items described in previous chapters, and the Napoléonic Waterloo-related items detailed in the last chapter, there is no reason to believe that most if not all of the relics of the ex-Emperor's exile at Madame

≈ CHAPTER NINE ≈

above left Carriage used by Napoléon on St Helena, photograph in the 1925 catalogue.

above middle Remains of the St Helena carriage after the 1925 fire.

above General Count Charles Tristan de Montholon (1783–1853) by Édouard Pingret.

left Napoléon dictating his memoirs to Count Emmanuel de Las Casas (1766–1842) by William Quiller Orchardson.

Tussaud's were anything other than genuine. These included the 'Carriage used by Napoléon on St Helene' (Item 49: Napoléon Room). Like *La Dormeuse*, this much smaller vehicle, described as an 'open barouche' in the 1911 insurance catalogue, was illustrated in the 1925 catalogue and accompanied by a lengthy entry that included the relic's provenance:

> This was the carriage commonly used by Napoléon during his years of exile on St. Helena, and is the last he ever entered. Its authenticity is certified by the Counts Montholon and Las Casas. It was purchased by Messrs. Tussaud from Mr. John Blofield, who furnished the following particulars and verifications, addressed to Messrs. Tussaud, and dated London, January 8th, 1851:
>
> DEAR SIRS, In accordance with your request I send you the following brief particulars of the carriage used by the Emperor Napoléon at St. Helena. I purchased it in 1848 at that island, of Major Charles Sampson, an officer who had lived highly respected there for more than fifty years, and who gave the following certificate:
> "Received from Mr. John Blofield, for Bonaparte's old carriage, used by him on

[169]

CHAPTER NINE

the Island of St. Helena" [Here follows the amount paid] MAJOR C. SAMPSON"

In 1850 I went to Paris. I showed it to General Count Montholon and Count Emmanuel de las Casas. These gentlemen immediately recognised it, and both said they had frequently ridden in it with the Emperor, and they most kindly gave me the following certificates, which, as you purchased the carriage, I enclose. General Montholon informs me that the Emperor always used it drawn by four horses, ridden by two postillions, with the head of the carriage down.

CERTIFICATES

"I hereby certify that the carriage shown to me at Paris, by Mr. John Blofield, is the actual carriage used by the Emperor Napoléon at the Island of St. Helena. GENERAL MONTHOLON."

"I hereby certify that the carriage shown to me by Mr. John Blofield, and purchased by him of Major C. Sampson, of St. Helena, is the actual carriage used by the Emperor Napoléon on that island. EMMANUEL DE LAS CASAS."

I remain, dear Sirs, yours faithfully, JOHN BLOFIELD

Neither Madame Tussaud's archives, nor the ledgers, record what was paid for this vehicle, but in 1911 it was valued at £300 (2022: £28,022). The 1911 insurance catalogue also stated that the St Helena carriage was displayed with a 'Riding Whip, in a Case', which it valued at £25 (2022: £2,355). This implied that it had belonged to the ex-Emperor.

In the wake of the 1925 fire at Madame Tussaud's, the charred remains of their three Napoléonic carriages make brief *post-mortem* appearances in the Minutes Book for Madame Tussaud's (1926) Ltd, No.3, which covers the Minutes from 1929 to 1933, as follows:

6th June 1929: Mr Wild reported that he had received an offer of £5.5.0 (2022: £263) for Napoléon's Coach, and it was resolved not to accept this offer but to leave the matter over.

18th July 1929: Mr John Tussaud reported on the goods in storage at Edmonton, and it was resolved that the burnt remains of 3 Napoléonic carriages be brought to the Exhibition and stored in Studio No.3 and that the 2 gaol gates be disposed of.

1st August 1929: A letter from Messrs Scammell Ltd. dated 10th July was read repeating their offer of £5. Mr Maxwell [Chairman] agreed to take over the coach for the sum of £10 (2022: £502).

To which of the carriages the last of the Minutes refer is unclear, although it was probably not the axle of *La Dormeuse*, the fate of which was noted in the last chapter.

CHAPTER NINE

above left Napoléon in exile on St Helena.

above Napoléon's grave on St Helena.

Meanwhile, even less clarity was provided by the 1925 catalogue entries for four items related to the ex-Emperor's enforced leisure on St Helena. These were all displayed in the Napoléon Room and comprised a 'fender' from Longwood, presumably a club fender from around one of the fireplaces (Item 50); 'Napoléon's Drawing-Room Chair' (Item 112), possibly taken from the same room; a 'Chair made from Napoléon's Willow' (Item 121), although whether it was made from the branches and used by Napoléon or made after his death was not stated; and a 'Piece of Napoléon's Willow' (Item 59), described as a 'fragment of the trunk of the willow-tree in whose shade Napoléon was wont to sit … and under which he was buried … the gift of the owner of the land'). It was given a value in 1911 of a mere £5 (2022: £467). Regarding this last item, at the time of the Emperor's exile, Longwood House and the valley in which he was buried were the property of the East India Company. However, in 1854 Napoléon's nephew, Emperor Napoléon III, acquired both properties for the French nation for £7,000 (2022: £653,849), in which ownership they remain.

Another souvenir of St Helena, described in the 1925 catalogue as 'Napoléon's China Service' (Item 103: Napoléon Room) apparently consisted of a 28-piece dessert service 'used by the Emperor at St. Helena'. The 1901 and 1925 catalogues both omitted the name of the maker or the pattern of the plates, but included helpful information about the item's provenance, stating that the service was 'purchased by Captain Sheppard [*sic*], of His Majesty's ship *Brazen*, and presented by him to a friend; and was finally acquired [by Madame Tussaud's] from Messrs Emanuel, Bond Street.' The purchase price was recorded in the 1842 ledger as

[171]

CHAPTER NINE

£20.10.0 (2022: £1,900), again without any information about the maker or the pattern. Although this provenance was repeated in the 1911 insurance catalogue, it stated that there were '36 pieces' and gave it a value of £150 (2022: £14,011).

HMS *Brazen* was indeed stationed at St Helena in the period 1820–1821, under the command of Captain William Shepheard RN. Furthermore, in 1830 Charles Town and Emanuel Emanuel founded Town & Emanuel at 103 Bond Street, London, where they dealt in 'antique furniture, curiosities and pictures'. The pair remained in business in Bond Street until 1849, when their stock was sold in two separate auctions at Christie's. So, given the data in the exhibition catalogues, the 1842 ledger and the 1911 insurance catalogue, the acquisition by Madame Tussaud's in May 1842 of a 28 – or possibly 36-piece dessert service used by the Emperor at St. Helena from Mr Emanuel of Bond Street is perfectly feasible.

According to the Fondation Napoléon,* the most important imperial porcelain taken to St Helena was that known as the *Quartiers Généraux* service. Made for Napoléon's personal use, it was commissioned from the Sèvres porcelain factory in 1807 and delivered in 1811. In addition to soup plates, serving dishes, fruit baskets, cups, ice cream buckets and centrepieces, the 270-piece set included seventy-two green-and-gilt bordered dessert plates, each painted with a different landscape or townscape connected with Napoléon's Italian, Egyptian, Austrian, Prussian and Polish campaigns. In 1807, each of these plates cost Francs 425 (2022: £1,177) and the bill for the whole service was Francs 65,499 (2022: £181,423), making it the most expensive manufactured by Sèvres to that date. In 2022, auctioneers Fraysse et Associés in Paris sold a *single* Quartiers Généraux dessert plate for €200,000 (£170,000) plus premium. However, French government archives record that only sixty plates from this service were taken by the ex-Emperor to St Helena, and that once on the island they were *not* used. Instead, according to the Fondation Napoléon, they were kept as gifts for his entourage. At the time of Napoléon's death in 1821, fifty-four of these plates remained ungifted. Pending their disposal in accordance with his written wishes, they were displayed in the billiard room at the north end of Longwood, on the orders of Lady Lowe, the Governor's wife.

A dessert plate from the *Quartiers Généraux* service.

* The Fondation Napoléon exists to encourage and support the study of the First and Second French Empires. It maintains a comprehensive and reliable online database on the subject (*www.napoleon.org*).

[172]

≈ CHAPTER NINE ≈

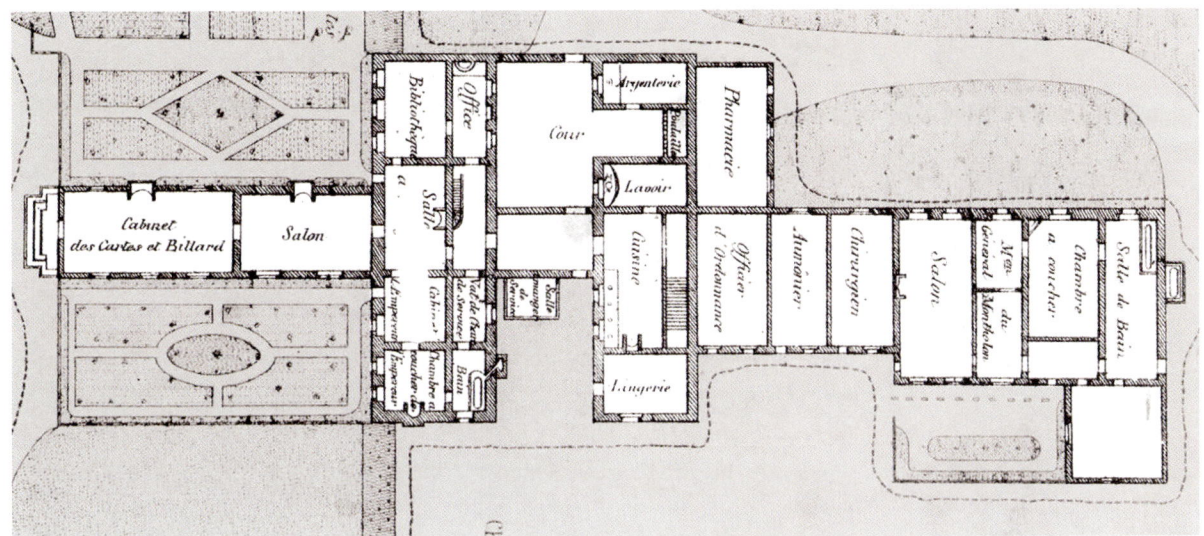

In his Will Napoléon left instructions for his attendant, Count Montholon, 'to keep these items and pass them on to my son when he is sixteen years old'. However, when the Austrian authorities in Vienna, where the boy lived, refused to allow him to accept this legacy, Montholon retained the plates and later distributed them as he pleased. This did *not* include selling twenty-eight or thirty-six of them to Captain Shepheard of His Majesty's ship *Brazen*. For the Fondation Napoléon has compiled an inventory of the *Quartiers Généraux* service, which demonstrates conclusively that, of the dessert plates not now in public or private collections, only *eight* remain unaccounted for. So, the twenty-eight or thirty-six dessert plates destroyed in the fire at Madame Tussaud's in 1925 were clearly not from the *Quartiers Généraux* service.

Fortunately, that does not invalidate the provenance of the dessert plates listed as Item 103. For, although Napoléon did not use the dessert plates from the *Quartiers Généraux* service on St Helena, he must have had other chinaware for daily use at his dining table. Although there is no inventory of the porcelain used at Longwood, plates from the so-called *Grand Maréchal* service are known to have gone with him to St Helena. That service was supplied to the Tuileries Palace in 1806 by the Imperial Porcelain factory, and featured a dark blue-and-gilt border, decorated with leaves, within which was a garland of flowers. One plate is preserved at Napoléonic National

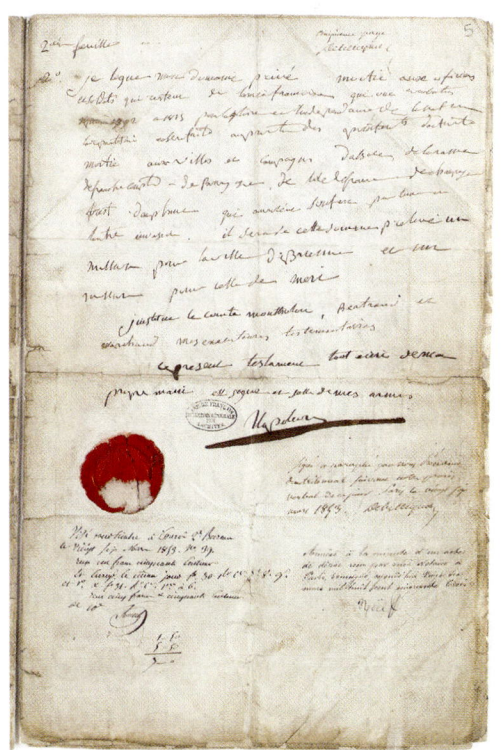

top Longwood House floorplan.

above Napoléon's last Will.

[173]

CHAPTER NINE

Dr Barry O'Meara (1786–1836).

Museum at the Château de Malmaison, and others come onto the market from time to time. So, the plates in 'Napoléon's China Service' at Madame Tussaud's may have originated from that service.

While on the subject of dining, Napoléon's obsession with oral hygiene led to the large number of his toothbrushes now in public and private collections. On St Helena he was frequently troubled with toothache. The 'Napoléon Mementoes' (Item 113: Napoléon Room) included one of the Emperor's teeth, along with the information that Napoléon 'had three teeth extracted by his physician, Dr Barry O'Meara on St Helene'. O'Meara was the exile's British-appointed Irish physician, who later criticised the way his patient was treated on St Helena, both in letters to the Admiralty and in his book, *Napoléon in Exile, or A Voice from St Helena* (1822). The letters resulted in his removal from the island in 1818, and the arrival of Dr Antommarchi. According to the Madame Tussaud's 1925 catalogue, on visiting Italy after Napoléon's death, O'Meara gave one of the three extracted teeth to Madame Mère, and another to the ex-King of Spain, Joseph Bonaparte, but kept the last one for himself. This, together with the instrument with which the teeth were extracted, was consigned to the sale of Prince Lucien's effects, conducted by Robins in 1840, from where Madame Tussaud acquired them. As O'Meara had died in 1836, these Napoleonic relics were presumably sold in 1840 by one of his descendants. Madame Tussaud paid £10 (2022: £934) for the tooth and the 'Two Dental Instruments used by Dr O'Meara to extract teeth of Napoléon I'. In 1911, the former was valued at £50 (2022: £4,670) and the latter at £5 (2022: £467). The dessert knife, fork, and spoon also listed under 'Napoléon Mementoes' (Item 113), for which Tussaud's paid £27 (2022: £2,521), were bequeathed by the Emperor to his brother, Joseph, but are mentioned here because Joseph gave them to Dr O'Meara when presented with the imperial molar. They were valued in 1911 at £100 (2022: £9,375).

The remaining 'Napoléon Mementoes' listed under Item 113 included scent bottles, a snuff box made from the Emperor's outer coffin, an onyx ring given by him to his secretary, Louis Antoine Fauvelet de Bourienne, a 'favourite' razor, wallpaper from Longwood House on St Helena, and a box made from a timber of HMS *Bellerophon*.

Separately itemised in the 1911 insurance catalogue, together with the black silk lining from Napoléon's coffin and the pen with which the ex-Emperor corrected his *Memoirs*, these items had a combined value of a mere £74 (2022: £6,912). The scent bottles, like the toothbrush, were from *La Dormeuse* and were acquired at the Bullock sale; they are not shown in the 1843 purchase ledger. The other items all had a St Helena provenance, although how they came to be acquired or what

CHAPTER NINE

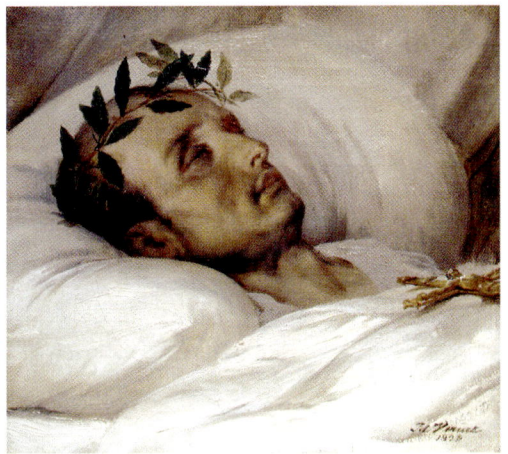

they cost was not stated. What is known is that when the ex-Emperor's body was exhumed on St Helena on 14th October 1840, the wood of the outer mahogany casket had to be cut away to allow full access to the lead, wood and tin coffins within, and from it was made a snuff box and other souvenirs.

Before the 1925 fire, Madame Tussaud's also had a specific exhibit named 'St Helena Relics' (Item 133: Napoléon Room), described in the exhibition catalogue as follows:

above left Napoléon on his deathbed, 5th May 1821, by Horace Vernet.

above The Exhumation of Napoléon, 14th October 1840, by Nicolas-Eustache Maurin.

> The underclothing exhibited here was worn by the Emperor at St. Helena, and, together with the Madras handkerchief, passed into the possession of Prince Lucien, at whose death they were purchased at the sale of his effects to which reference has already been made. Here also is the sword which Napoléon carried during his years of exile, and the stock which he wore at Waterloo.

These pieces were itemised in the 1911 insurance catalogue with a combined worth of £205 (2022: £19,148). Collectors have always placed an extraordinary value on even the humblest item of the Emperor's clothing. One pair of 'Cashimeer [sic] small-clothes' (i.e. underpants) were among the items of clothing in *La Dormeuse* that were offered for sale in the Bullock auction (Lot 99) on Friday 11th June 1819; they sold to a Mr Shipley for £1.18.0 (2022: £170).

Even at today's values, this is considerably less than a pair of Napoléon's silk drawers worn on St Helena, which were auctioned by the French auctioneer, Osenat, in 2014 with a pre-sale estimate of €15,000–20,000. In the same year a sweat-stained cotton nightshirt, worn by Napoléon as he lay dying, and two sleeves from the nightshirt that the imperial exile was wearing when he actually died on 5th May 1821, were estimated to sell respectively for €40,000 (£34,188)

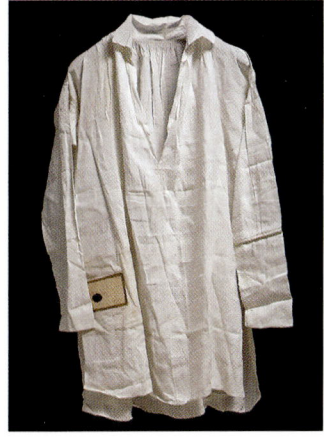

above A shirt worn by Napoléon on St Helena.

[175]

CHAPTER NINE

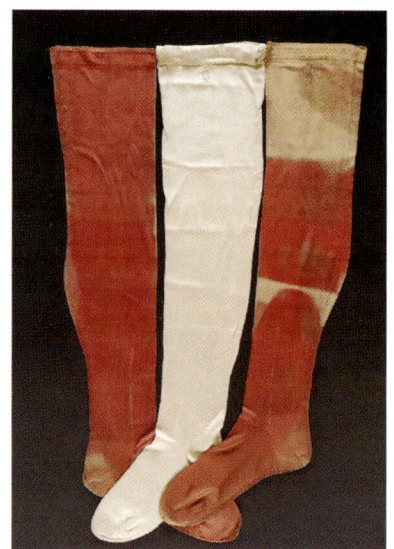

above Napoléon's nightshirt in the Achille Archambault collection.

above right Napoléon's stockings.

below Napoléon at St Helena with a Madras scarf on his head.

and €18,000 (£15,384). These items came from the collection of Achille Archambault, one of Napoléon's former coachmen, who accompanied him to St Helena as head groom, and who later labelled them:

> This shirt was removed from the Emperor Napoléon the 4 May 1821. As the Emperor's linen was bleached at my home, I gave the order to the staff responsible for this to give it to me and only me, the last items taken from His Majesty.

During his lifetime, the ex-coachman was offered Francs 100,000 (2022: £277,000) for his collection, but turned it down, and kept the items as heirlooms for his family. They were only rediscovered in 2014, lying in a dusty box in Corsica. However, when the collection was offered for sale by Osenat, a descendant of Archambault objected on the grounds that the items were of such historical importance that any risk they might leave France had to be blocked. The auction house concurred, and the entire Archambault collection was withdrawn, although a pair of Napoléon's white silk stockings, with an Archambault provenance, sold at Osenat's Napoléon Bicentennial sale in April 2021 (Lot 203) for €9,200 (£7,820).

Still on the theme of the ex-Emperor's linen, and with particular reference to Madame Tussaud's 'St Helena Relics', it is worth noting that three coloured and a pair of white silk stockings, a cotton *chausette*, a cotton batiste shirt (worn on St Helena and bequeathed to General Bertrand), and a printed cotton scarf, were sold in the Monaco Collection auction in 2014 for €146,000 (£124,786) in

[176]

CHAPTER NINE

total. The shirt alone sold for £59,829, with the coloured stockings re-appearing on the market for a second time as Lot 200 at the Osenat Napoléon Bicentennial sale with a pre-sale estimate of €12,000 (£10,256). They sold on that occasion for €21,500 (£18,275), while at the same auction Lot 182, a single, embroidered handkerchief of Napoléon's sold for an impressive €15,000 (£12,750), and a shirt worn by him 'after Waterloo' (Lot 199) sold for €80,000 (£68,000).

CHAPTER TEN

THE BOURBON RESTORATION & THE SECOND FRENCH EMPIRE

Although in the Madame Tussaud's 1925 catalogue there were frequent references to the restoration of the Bourbon monarchy in 1814, and again in 1815 following the hiatus of Napoléon's brief return to power during the Hundred Days, there were no relics in the collection directly or indirectly associated with King Louis XVIII, and only two relating to his brother, King Charles X, and their cousin, King Louis-Philippe I. This lack of royal (post-imperial) relics may have been because neither of the last two Bourbon monarchs, nor their Orléanist cousin, reigned for long – or their reigns largely coincided with the period that Madame Tussaud was constantly travelling throughout the United Kingdom, before finally settling in London in the 1830s.

opposite King Louis XVIII (1755–1824) in Coronation robes by François Gérard.

Allegory of the Restoration of the Bourbons by Louis-Philippe Crépin.

CHAPTER TEN

right King Charles X (1757–1836) photograph in the 1925 catalogue.

far right King Charles X by Sir Thomas Lawrence.

above King Charles X by Robert Lefévre.

The relatively liberal Louis XVIII accepted a constitutional settlement in 1814 that curtailed the absolutist imperial power of his predecessor and the equally illiberal royal powers of the *Ancien Régime*. In consequence, he survived on the throne for ten years until his death in 1824. Louis's ultra-conservative younger brother, Charles X, lasted for only six years before being toppled in the July Revolution of 1830, a violent response to his attempt to overthrow the political *status quo* agreed in 1814 and return to pre-revolutionary absolutism. Unlike his eldest brother, Louis XVI, Charles X succeeded in fleeing to England with his family, while the French Chamber of Deputies appointed his Orléans cousin as King, Louise-Philippe, the first and only King of the French.

At Madame Tussaud's, the Hall of Kings featured a full-length portrait of Charles X (Item 12), in uniform standing in front of a throne, thus indicating that it dated from after 1824. Despite a photograph and a lengthy entry, which ended with the comment that while in exile Charles X 'made an ineffectual attempt to persuade Madame Tussaud to part with the shirt which his ancestor, Henri IV, was wearing at the time of his assassination (see Item 137)', no artist is attributed to the work. However, in the 1911 insurance catalogue it was attributed to Robert Lefévre and valued at £200 (2022: £18,681).

Judging from the photograph in the catalogue, the painting bore some resemblance to a full-length depiction of Charles X by Sir Thomas Lawrence, dated 1825, in which he wears the same uniform and the breast star of the Order of the Garter, albeit his face is turned to the left rather than the right; and a half-length portrait

[180]

CHAPTER TEN

far left King Louis Philippe I (1773–1850) by Franz Xaver Winterhalter.

left King Charles X in Coronation robes by François Gérard.

by the aforementioned Lefèvre, dated 1826, in which the facial aspect is to the right and bears a much stronger similarity to the King's appearance in the picture at Madame Tussaud's. The probability is that the painting in the Hall of Kings was a combination of the two images executed by an unnamed artist.

The second relic, the breast star and ribband of a Grand Cross of the Legion of Honour, belonged to King Louis Philippe I and was depicted in a painting of the King by Winterhalter. It was listed, without explanation as to its provenance, in the 1901 catalogue and, in an historically mystifying juxtaposition, was included in the 1925 catalogue with 'Memorials of Marie Antoinette and Louis XVI' (Item 171: Napoléon Ante-Room). It was valued in 1911 at £15 (2022: £1,401), along with four other Bourbon Restoration items that did not appear in the exhibition catalogue: Louis Phillippe's 'Dress of the Order of the Garter', insured for £40 (2022: £3,736), a 'Ribbon' (presumably of an Order) and a 'Pair of Gloves', together worth £5 (2022: £467); and Charles X's 'Under-dress worn at his Coronation' i.e the clothes he wore under his robes, as in the painting here by François Gérard, worth £50 (2022: £4,670)*, and a 'Medallion of the Order of the Garter', presumably the Lesser George worn at the lower end of the Order's ribbon. It was valued at £15 (2022: £1,401).

In 1848, Europe was swept by a series of revolutions that led to wide-spread constitutional reforms and toppled the then reigning monarchs of Naples, Austria, Bavaria and France. On 24th February of that year, the throne of King Louis-Philippe was the first to fall. Fearing for his life, the ex-King of the French fled Paris

* The 'Under-dress' survived the 1925 fire, presumably because it was in storage, and was sold at Cooper Owen in 2005 for £1,100 (2022: £1,814).

CHAPTER TEN

right Emperor Napoléon III (1808–1873) by Franz Xaver Winterhalter.

far right Empress Eugénie (1826–1920) by Franz Xaver Winterhalter.

Copies of both of these paintings, which were not listed in the 1925 catalogue, survived the 1925 fire and the pair were valued by Sotheby's in 1983 at £500–£700 (2022: £1,815–£2,220).

in an ordinary cab, heavily disguised and using the name of Mr. Smith. He spent his last years in England, calling himself the Comte de Neuilly. Madame Tussaud's may well have acquired his Legion of Honour insignia following his death in 1850.

Meanwhile, the National Assembly of France, which had initially planned to accept Louis-Philippe's son, the Comte de Paris, as his royal replacement, rejected that idea in deference to violently expressed public opinion. Instead, on 26th February 1848, the Second Republic was proclaimed. Ten months later, Prince Louis Napoléon Bonaparte, nephew of Napoléon I, was elected President of the Republic, declaring himself Prince-President for Life after his coup d'état in 1851, and Emperor Napoleon III in 1852.

A number of items belonging to Napoléon III and his family found their way to Madame Tussaud's. Although not in the 1925 exhibition catalogue, the 1911 insurance catalogue included the 'Riding Habit of the Empress Eugénie', valued in 1911 at £10 (2022: £934), and a 'Facsimile of [a] Necklace presented to her', worth £5 (2022: £467). Other Second Empire items included in the exhibition were a pair of majolica busts of the Emperor and his wife (Items 126 & 129: Napoléon Room), which were described in the 1911 insurance catalogue as 'large' and valued at £15 each (2022: £1,401), although the catalogue gave no further information about the maker or the provenance. However, for the most part, the items relating to Napoléon III's and his family at Madame Tussaud's focussed on the end of his (mostly successful) eighteen-year reign in 1870, and its aftermath.

The reign itself started to unravel when, in a cynical act of statecraft, Prussian

CHAPTER TEN

Chancellor, Prince Otto von Bismarck, used the disputed candidacy of a Hohenzollern Prince for the vacant throne of Spain to provoke the French into declaring war on Prussia. He did this in order to induce four hitherto independent southern German states to join the North German Confederation. France mobilised its army on 15th July 1870, leading the North German Confederation to respond with its own mobilisation later that day. On 16th July 1870, the French parliament voted to declare war on Prussia, and France invaded German territory on 2nd August. The German coalition in turn invaded France two days later. A series of swift German victories in eastern France culminated on 1st September in the Battle of Sedan, and the capture of Napoléon III the following day. On 26th October, following the siege of Metz, the French commander, Marshal Bazaine, surrendered with 173,000 soldiers.

Prince Otto von Bismarck (1815–1898), studio photograph in 1890 by Jacques Pilartz.

CHAPTER TEN

Keys of the Fortress of Metz, photograph in the 1925 catalogue.

These events were commemorated at Madame Tussaud's, *inter alia*, with a case containing 'Relics of the Franco-Prussian War' (Item 157: Napoléon Ante-Room), which held items from 'the village of Bazeilles, a suburb of Sedan'. The 1925 exhibition catalogue did not list what they were, although the 1911 insurance catalogue listed the items as 'Curiosities & Relics of the late Franco-Prussian War' and the 'Dial, of the Clock of the Church of Bazeille, near Sedan'. The former were valued somewhat arbitrarily in 1911 at £75 (2022: £7,005) and the latter at £25 (2022: £2,335).

Separately displayed were The Keys of the Fortress of Metz (Item 19: Grand Saloon). An entry in the 1925 catalogue which explained how and why they came to be in the exhibition:

At the beginning of the war Napoléon III made his entry into Metz at the head of a brilliant Staff, and amid the enthusiastic acclamations of the populace and cries of '*À Berlin, à Berlin!*' The keys of this virgin fortress, placed on a velvet cushion, were ceremoniously presented to him, and re-consigned to the Governor. When, not many months after this ceremony, the King of Prussia, soon to be crowned German Emperor at Versailles, made his victorious entry into Metz it was intended, by way of spicing his triumph, that these same keys should be presented to him, but they had been secreted too well, and the design was frustrated. Many months after the capitulation they were smuggled out of the city, and eventually brought to London and offered to Madame Tussaud and Sons, who were glad to add to their collection this interesting memento of the war.

The keys were given a generous valuation of £250 (2022: £23,351) by the 1911 insurance valuers.

The other principal relic that commemorated the disaster of the Franco-Prussian War was the Carriage used by Napoléon III at Sedan (Item 192: Hall of Tableaux). Unfortunately, it was not illustrated in the 1925 catalogue, nor was it listed in the 1911 insurance catalogue. However, an engraving of it exists and is here reproduced, along with the catalogue entry for the carriage:

On the last days of August, a series of bloody battles was fought around Sedan, and it was from this carriage that the Emperor, too feeble to sustain the fatigue of riding on horseback, witnessed the defeat of his arms and the ruin of his fortunes. At last, on 2nd of September, he gave the order to surrender …

The Emperor then had a message sent to King Wilhelm I of Prussia, who was at Sedan with his army: 'Monsieur my brother, not being able to die at the head

CHAPTER TEN

Emperor Napoléon III surrenders to Otto von Bismarck.

Napoléon III in his carriage, accompanied by Otto von Bismarck, after his surrender following the battle of Sedan.

of my troops, nothing remains for me but to place my sword in the hands of Your Majesty.' After the war, when accused of having made a 'shameful surrender' at Sedan, Napoléon III wrote:

> Some people believe that, by burying ourselves under the ruins of Sedan, we would have better served my name and my dynasty. It's possible. Nay, to hold in my hand the lives of thousands of men and not to make a sign to save them was something that was beyond my capacity.

[185]

CHAPTER TEN

At six o'clock on the morning of 2nd September, in the uniform of a General and accompanied by four Generals from his Staff, Napoléon III was taken to the German Headquarters at Donchery. He expected to see King Wilhelm, but instead was met by Bismarck and the German commander, General von Moltke. They dictated the terms of the surrender to Napoléon, who asked that his army be disarmed and allowed to pass into Belgium, but Bismarck refused. They in turn asked Napoléon to sign the preliminary documents of a peace treaty, but he refused, telling them that the French government headed by the Regent, his wife Empress Eugénie, would need to negotiate any peace agreement.

The Emperor was then taken to the Château de Bellevue near Frenois where he was visited by King Wilhelm. Napoléon told Wilhelm that he had not wanted the war, but that public opinion had forced him into it. That evening, the Emperor wrote to his wife:

> It is impossible for me to say what I have suffered and what I am suffering now... I would have preferred death to a capitulation so disastrous, and yet, under the present circumstances, it was the only way to avoid the butchering of sixty thousand people. If only all my torments were concentrated here! I think of you, our son, and our unhappy country.

Released from Prussian captivity on 19th March 1871, the ex-Emperor and his family followed in the wake of his two royal predecessors and settled in England, which may explain how Madame Tussaud's acquired 'Napoléon III's Chemical

Copy of the Empress Eugénie's Crown and Jewels, photograph in the 1925 catalogue, see following page

[186]

CHAPTER TEN

Case' (Item 80: Napoléon Room). Although the 1925 exhibition catalogue gave no provenance, it noted that 'Chemistry was one of the hobbies of the late Emperor', and asserted that the case held 'appliances with which he made his experiments'. It was contradictorily described in the 1911 insurance catalogue as a 'Medicine Chest' and valued at £5 (2022: £467).

To support his family in exile, Napoléon III was forced to sell property and jewels. Madame Tussaud's marked the abdication with a display entitled 'Copy of the Empress Eugénie's Crown and Jewels' Item 51: Napoléon Room). They were not separately identifiable in the 1911 insurance catalogue, and their description in the 1925 catalogue was flawed: neither Napoléon III nor his consort had a Coronation, although a crown was commissioned for the Emperor but not the Empress. Instead, during her husband's reign, Eugénie acquired a collection of tiaras, which she wore on State and formal occasions.

far left Empress Eugénie wearing her emerald tiara, 1862.

left Victoria Eugenie of Battenberg (1887–1969), Queen of Spain wearing the Eugénie emeralds as a bandeau, by Philip de Laszlo.

So, far from being Empress Eugénie's 'crown', the paste on display at Madame Tussaud's was in fact a copy of Eugénie's famous emerald and diamond tiara, and its accompanying suite of jewels. These rocks were not sold by the cash-strapped ex-Emperor after 1870 but were retained by Eugénie. After her death in 1920, the tiara was broken up and the massive emeralds were bequeathed to Queen Ena of Spain. She – like Princess Diana in 1985 with the Cambridge emeralds – had them reset as a fashionable bandeau. Following the abdication of her husband, Alfonso XIII, in 1931, and the creation of the Spanish Second Republic, Ena was forced into exile. In 1961, the emeralds were once again broken up and this time sold at auction, ironically to help finance Queen Ena in her exile.

CHAPTER TEN

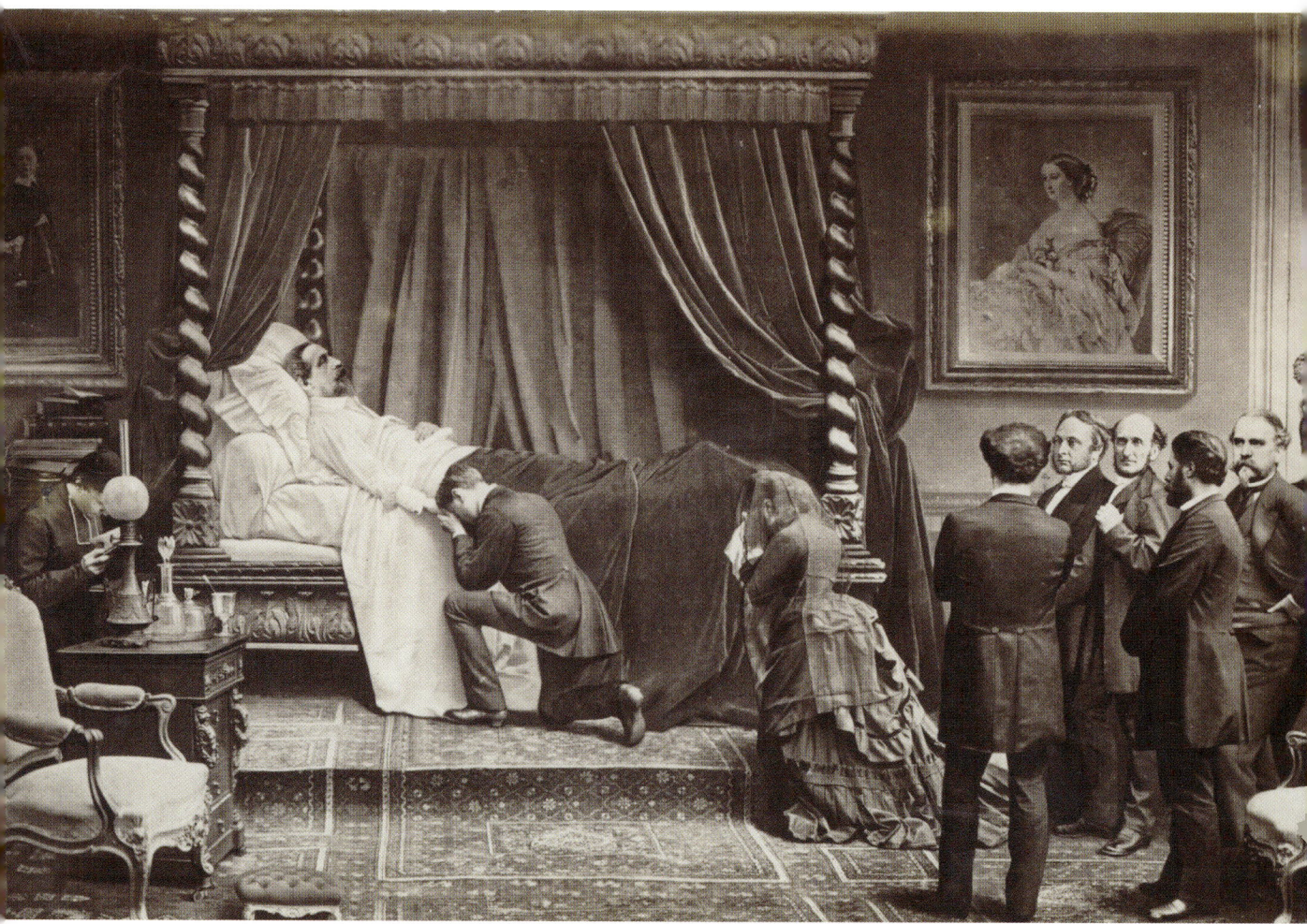

Deathbed of Napoléon III.

Napoléon III died at his house in Chislehurst on 9th January 1873, although not before Queen Victoria (who had happy memories of her State Visit to Paris in 1855) had paid the Bonapartes an official visit. The remaining Second Empire relics at Madame Tussaud's were connected with the ill-fated Prince Imperial, Louis-Napoléon, the only child of Napoléon III and Empress Eugénie. Born at the Tuileries Palace, in Paris, on 16th March 1856, the long-hoped-for heir to the imperial throne of the French was christened Napoléon Eugène Louis Jean Joseph, but was known within the family as Loulou. Despite being only fourteen at the outbreak of the Franco-Prussian War, he accompanied his father to the front in the uniform of a Sub-Lieutenant. However, when the tide of the war started to turn, the Prince Imperial's father ordered him first to Belgium and then to England, where he arrived on 6th September 1870 .

CHAPTER TEN

above left The Prince Imperial (1856–1879) aged 14 in 1870.

above The Prince Imperial in South Africa, 1879.

    Following his father's death, Loulou applied to join the British Army and to train (like his father and great-uncle before him) as an artillery officer. This he did at the Royal Military Academy Woolwich, then the school for future Royal Engineer and Royal Artillery officers. At the outbreak of the Anglo-Zulu War in 1879, he demanded to be allowed to serve there. At first Loulou's request was refused, until he prevailed upon his mother to intercede with Queen Victoria, with whom she had maintained friendly relations after her husband's death. The Queen, somewhat reluctantly given the massacre by Zulu *impis* of British troops at Isandlwana on 22nd January 1879, eventually sanctioned the posting and the Prince Imperial set sail for South Africa at the end of February of that year.

    Once there Loulou joined the Staff of the hopelessly inept Expeditionary Force commander, (acting) Lieutenant General Lord Chelmsford. His role was

CHAPTER TEN

CHAPTER TEN

that of an 'observer', and Chelmsford had orders from the War Office to keep him strictly out of harm's way. Unsurprisingly, as the heir of Napoléon I, Loulou chafed under the restrictions placed upon him for his safety. Eventually, he managed to get himself attached to a mounted force, whose job was to reconnoitre the route of the Expeditionary Force's advance on the Zulu capital, Ulundi.

On the morning of 1st June 1879, his understrength patrol, nominally under the command of Lieutenant Jahleel Brenton Carey, was once again ahead of the advancing force, this time in what was believed to be Zulu-free territory. The troop halted around midday at a deserted *kraal*, where they lit a fire to boil water for tea; but, in defiance of standing orders, no lookout was posted. As Loulou and his men were preparing to leave, about forty rifle- and spear-bearing Zulus rushed them. The Prince Imperial's horse, *Fatum*, bolted as he was trying to mount it, leaving him clinging to a holster on the saddle.

After about 100 yards, the holster strap broke, Loulou fell under *Fatum* and his right arm was trampled. Nevertheless, he leapt up, drawing his revolver with his left hand, and started to run, but the Zulus outpaced him and speared him in the thigh. As he turned and fired on his attackers, another assegai pierced his left shoulder. Despite these wounds he fought on, using the assegai he had pulled from his leg. Eventually, Loulou was overwhelmed. When recovered, his naked body was found to have eighteen assegai wounds, including one through the eye that had penetrated his brain.

opposite The Prince Imperial tries to mount *Fatum*.

top Death of the Prince Imperial by Paul Joseph Jamin.

above The Prince Imperial's Memorial, KwaZulu-Natal, South Africa.

[191]

CHAPTER TEN

above The sarcophagus containing the remains of the Prince Imperial in the Imperial Crypt, St Michael's Abbey, Farnborough.

above right The Prince Imperial's statue at RMA Sandhurst.

below The Prince Imperial Memorial, Chislehurst, Kent.

The recriminations that followed in South Africa, Paris and London were considerable, but as nothing to the grief of the ex-Empress. She later made a pilgrimage to the site of her son's death, where Queen Victoria had commanded the erection of a memorial that she funded personally. In the meantime, while a Court of Enquiry and a Court Martial sought to blame Lieutenant Carey for the death of the Prince Imperial, Loulou's decomposing body was brought back to England. On arrival, it lay in State at Woolwich Arsenal, before being taken to Chislehurst for the funeral, in a procession that included, in defiance of royal protocol, Queen Victoria.

That, however, was not the end of the story. In 1881, Empress Eugénie established an Imperial Crypt at St Michael's Abbey in Farnborough to which her husband's remains were transferred, along with those of Loulou. In 1920, Eugénie herself was buried there. The burghers of Chislehurst erected a monument on their common to the Prince Imperial; and a twice-life-size statue of Loulou was cast and installed at the Royal Military Academy Woolwich. It was moved to the Royal Military Academy Sandhurst when the two military institutions were merged in 1947. A familiar sight to all officers who have trained there, it still stands in front of New College, a building designed by Harry Bell Measures, great-great-grandfather of Christopher Joll, one of the authors of this book.

Not to be outdone by Queen Victoria, the War Office and the citizens of Chislehurst, Madame Tussaud's duly acquired its own mementoes of the Prince Imperial. These included 'Relics of the Prince Imperial' (Item 114: Napoléon

Room), a case apparently containing 'the uniform worn by him when taken by his father to the Franco-German War', valued in 1911 at £80 (2022: £7,472), and a lock of his hair worth £2 (2022: £186). No explanation of the acquisition of these objects was given in the text, nor was any reference made in the 1925 exhibition catalogue to an 'Evening Dress Coat & Vest' and a complete 'Hunting Costume' belonging to the Prince Imperial that are listed in the 1911 insurance catalogue with a combined value of £25 (2022: £2,335).

This was in contrast to a full-length painting of 'The Prince Imperial by Pichat' (Item 118) in the same room. This was illustrated in the 1925 catalogue and described as follows:

> This picture was painted expressly for Madame Tussaud and Sons' Exhibition by gracious permission of the ex-Empress Eugénie, and represents the young Prince at the moment when he was attacked by Zulus in South Africa, having with those who accompanied him, fallen into an ambuscade in which, unhappily, he was killed.

It was valued in 1911 at £150 (2022: £14,011). To add colour to this unhappy event, Madame Tussaud's displayed a 'Painting of the Head of *Fatum*' (Item 76: Napoléon Room), also by Oliver Pichat and worth £25 (2022: £2,335) in 1911, and a 'Statuette of the Prince Imperial attacked by Zulus' (Item 175: Napoléon Ante-Room), probably in bronze. Neither were illustrated or described in the 1925 catalogue, and the statuette was not listed in the 1911 insurance catalogue.

The Prince Imperial by Oliver Pichat, photograph in the 1925 catalogue.

CHAPTER ELEVEN

KING GEORGE IV TO QUEEN VICTORIA

KING GEORGE IV (1762-1830), formerly the Prince Regent from 1811 to 1820 during his father's mental illness, was in every sense of the word a larger-than-life character. Towards the end of his reign, he convinced himself that he had led a cavalry charge at the Battle of Waterloo in 1815, and was so fat, and stricken with gout, that he required a crane in order to mount his horse. As he was unable to climb stairs, he had his private rooms at the Royal Pavilion in Brighton rearranged so that he could live entirely on the ground floor. His girth, even in middle age, provided the caricaturists of the day with ample opportunities to lampoon him, while portraitists struggled to obey the royal command to slim his profile.

In 1925, Madame Tussaud's boasted a full-length portrait captioned in the exhibition catalogue 'George IV by Sir Thomas Lawrence PRA' (Item 2: Entrance Hall) which hung opposite a portrait of Queen Victoria by Sir George Hayter, to be considered later. Unlike the Napoléonic portraits attributed to Jacques-Louis David by the Tussauds, there is every reason to believe that this picture was, at the very least, a studio copy. In 1818, the Prince Regent commissioned Lawrence to paint his portrait wearing Garter robes, and then presented the painting to the Mansion House in Dublin. Following his Coronation in 1821, the image was frequently reproduced by the artist's studio, with a crown replacing the plumed hat of the Garter on the table. The Royal Collection Trust owns four such versions, all similar to the one illustrated with a photograph in the 1925 exhibition catalogue.

opposite The Prince Regent *attempting to mount a horse*, attributed to Charles Williams.

below left King George IV in Garter robes by Sir Thomas Lawrence, photograph in the 1925 catalogue.

below King George IV in Garter robes by Sir Thomas Lawrence.

CHAPTER ELEVEN

above Coronation portrait of King George IV by Sir Thomas Lawrence.

above right Tableau at Madame Tussaud's showing King George IV (centre) in his Coronation robes.

* Roger Fulford, *Royal Dukes* (1933).

Although not listed in the 1911 insurance catalogue as a copy, it was valued at £300 (2022: £28,022), which would seem to confirm the studio attribution. The 1925 Tussaud's catalogue stated that this particular portrait had been presented to 'General Sir William Nicholay [*sic*], shortly after the latter's retirement from active service'. Nicolay, who had fought at Waterloo as a Colonel, only reached the rank of Major general in George IV's lifetime. It is not clear how the painting passed from his ownership to Madame Tussaud's, although it may have been purchased following Nicolay's death in 1842.

In addition to his obsession with the favourable artistic treatment of his image, George IV both loathed Napoléon and was in awe of the trappings of the Imperial Court. Determined to outshine the Emperor at his own Coronation in 1821, 'he was pulled in here and stuffed out there to try and suggest ... something of his youthful beauty. Every available part of his person – his hands, his gloves, his white kid trousers – was flashing with imitation jewellery.'* The result was a bill for £400,000 (2022: £37,362,831), making it the most expensive Coronation to that date and forty times the cost of King George III's big day in 1761. Included in the 1821 sum was £44,939 (2022: £4,197,620) for 'uniforms, costumes, and robes'.

'The Coronation Robes of George IV' (Item 153) and the 'Front of Tunic, worn by George IV at his Coronation' (Item 162) at Madame Tussaud's were displayed, initially, on the right-hand side of the so-called Large Room, together with a waxwork of the King, wearing the Coronation tunic and robe, as can be seen in the engraving here. Sometime before 1883, these items were moved to the Napoléon Ante-Room and in the catalogue for that year were given a reasonably full description:

CHAPTER ELEVEN

In consequence of the Robes of His late Majesty George IV being in a state of decay from age and exposure to the air, they have been removed and placed under glass to prevent total loss.

The Crimson Robe on the right was worn by the King in the procession to Westminster Abbey, and was borne by nine eldest sons of peers. The robe opposite is the Purple Robe in which he was attired on his return from the Abbey. On the left is the one which he wore at the opening of Parliament. The three robes together contain 567 feet of velvet and embroidery, and with the ermine hangings [*sic*], are believed to have cost £18,000 [2022: £1,560,939].

The 1911 insurance catalogue stated that the robes were then worth £500 (2022: £46,703) and the 'Front of the Tunic' £100 (2022: £9,340).

Unlike the Napoléonic Coronation robes considered in Chapter 5, George IV's robes at Madame Tussaud's probably were the originals. In order to defray the vast cost of the Coronation, many items were sold off after the event, and there is circumstantial evidence in the archives that Madame Tussaud was one of the buyers. Furthermore, a report written by the then Tussaud's archivist, relating to a proposed Madame Tussaud's tour of Japan in 1992, stated:

King George IV in procession to Westminster Abbey for his Coronation.

[197]

CHAPTER ELEVEN

artefacts that she obtained with special associations to the famous and infamous ... The visitor will be able to see the Coronation train of George IV, [of] royal purple decorated with ermine and solid silver applique ... They were originally exhibited on his figure for many years, and have been restored by the Royal College of Needlework.

George IV's Coronation robes are not listed in the items held by the Royal Collection Trust, nor were they worn by his successor King William IV in 1831 or by their niece, the petite Queen Victoria at her Coronations in 1838. As the Madame Tussaud archivist's report of 1992 indicates, the robes appear to have survived the 1925 fire. Fortunately, recent research in the archives has unearthed the Minutes for a meeting of Madame Tussaud's & Co Ltd on 18th February 1937:

Relics: The Managing Director reported that the following relics had been found in the Wardrobe:- two Coronation robes of George IV, a shirt of George IV, and a Garter dress [*sic*] given by George IV to Charles X of France.

He further stated that a request had been received from the London Museum that we should loan these garments to them for a special exhibition of Coronation relics, and for an indefinite period at the end of the exhibition. He proposed that we should accede to this request, and this course was approved by the Board.

At the time of writing, Madame Tussaud's are negotiating with the Museum of London for a return of at least some of these items, for their own display to commemorate the Coronation of King Charles III in 2023.

The crown of King George IV carried by John Ireland (1761–1842), the Dean of Westminster, by James Stephanoff.

Madame Tussaud's Facsimile of Crown, Sceptre, etc., of George IV (Item 13: Hall of Kings) were, according to the 1925 exhibition catalogue, copied direct from the originals, made specially for the King by Rundell, Bridge & Rundell, who had supplied much of his silver-gilt plate for the Royal Pavilion and Carlton House. The crown was sixteen inches high and fitted with 12,314 diamonds, rented from the crown's makers, at a cost of £24,425 (2022: £2,281,467); it was said to make the King look like a 'gorgeous bird of the East'. After the Coronation, George IV was reluctant to part with his new crown and lobbied the government to buy it outright, so he could use it for the annual State Opening of Parliament. The King's request was refused, the crown was dismantled in 1823 and, although the frame still exists, it has never been used since. None of the facsimiles at Madame Tussaud's were listed in the 1911 insurance catalogue, suggesting that they may have been commissioned

[198]

CHAPTER ELEVEN

Queen Victoria (1819–1901), wearing the Diamond Diadem, detail from a painting by Franz Xaver Winterhalter.

after that date and copied from the bare frame held in the Jewel House at the Tower of London.

The Diamond Diadem, also made by Rundell, Bridge & Rundell, was worn by George IV over his Cap of Maintenance on the way to the Abbey. Despite costing £8,216 (2022: £767,432), including the rental of the diamonds, it did not suffer the same fate as his new crown. However, it was only in the reign of Queen Victoria that diamonds from the royal collection were set permanently in its frame. Rather less expensive was a piece in 'Miscellaneous Relics' (Item 155: Napoléon Room), described as a shirt 'from the wardrobe of George IV' and valued in 1911 at £10 (2022: £934). This was clearly one of the items placed on indefinite loan at the Museum of London in 1937. The 'Case of Sussex Relics' (Item 88: Napoléon Room) included a pocket-handkerchief belonging to George IV, acquired by Madame Tussaud's at the auction of the effects of the Duke of Sussex (see Chapter 2), and given a value in 1911 of £5 (2022: £467).

CHAPTER ELEVEN

The Marriage of George, Prince of Wales, and Princess Caroline of Brunswick (1768–1821), oil sketch by William Hamilton.
©Royal Collection Trust/His Majesty King Charles III 2023

In 1795, while still Prince of Wales, the future King George IV entered into an arranged marriage with Princess Caroline of Brunswick. She was said to be uncouth and careless of her personal hygiene. On first seeing her, the Prince reputedly whispered to James Harris, 1st Earl of Malmesbury, who had accompanied the Princess from Brunswick: 'Harris, I am not well, get me a glass of brandy', as he retreated to a far corner of the room. The 'Marriage of George IV by William Hamilton' (Item 33: Grand Saloon), one of several depictions of the event, was given a glowing report in the Tussaud's 1925 catalogue:

> The painter of this scene was … commissioned to paint for the nation this important work, which has been valued at 3,000 guineas [2022: £218,338]. Its interest is enhanced by the circumstance that every one of the portraits was painted from life.

Contrary to this entry, the picture had in fact been valued in the 1911 insurance catalogue at only £500 (2022: £46,703). An oil sketch for this painting was acquired by Queen Victoria in 1885; the inventory of the Royal Collection Trust states that the finished work was twelve feet wide and had been acquired by Madame Tussaud's sometime before 1856. That would seem to be conclusive as to the painting's authenticity; like so much else it was destroyed in the 1925 fire.

The disastrous union of George and Caroline produced, almost nine months to the day from the wedding and after only three nights spent together, Princess

[200]

CHAPTER ELEVEN

Charlotte of Wales who was born on 7th January 1796 and died on 6th November 1817 shortly after giving birth to a still-born son. Her relatively short life and role as Heir Presumptive, were commemorated at Madame Tussaud's in their 'Hanoverian Relics' (Item 152: Napoléon Ante-Room), which included 'a frock worn by the Princess Charlotte', valued in 1911 at £12 (2022: £1,120), with the additional information that it was a 'Baby Frock'. The 'Case of Miscellaneous Relics' (Item 67: Napoléon Room) also included a lock of her hair. It was dated 7th November 1817, thus indicating that it had apparently been taken *post-mortem*, and was valued in 1911 at £1 (2022: £93).

No explanation as to how Madame Tussaud acquired the relics was given. Writing in *The Romance of Madame Tussaud's*, her great-grandson John Theodore Tussaud, stated that she modelled in wax a copy of Princess Charlotte's so-called 'Nuptial Bust', carved in marble by Peter Turnerelli in 1816 and now in the National Portrait Gallery. As Madame Tussaud's copy was not 'from life', it seems unlikely that she met Princess Charlotte. However, the Princess's death in childbirth the following year no doubt added to Madame Tussaud's profits, as people flocked to see the late Heir Presumptive's waxwork. The canny Madame Tussaud may have acquired the lock of hair to enhance the exhibit, along with a number of Princess Charlotte's letters, a pair of her slippers, a pair of her gloves and a 'Piece of Silk Robe'. These last items were not listed in the 1925 catalogue, but appeared in the 1911 insurance catalogue with a collective value of £6 (2022: £560). Equally, as Madame Tussaud was still touring the United Kingdom in 1817, the relics of Princess Charlotte may have been acquired much later, by her sons, once the business had settled in London in the 1830s.

The only other George IV-related exhibits at Madame Tussaud's, included in the 'Hanoverian Relics' (Item 152: Napoléon Ante-Room), were listed in 1925 as 'the night-cap and night-shirt in which George IV died', valued in 1911 at £25 (2022: £2,335) without the death bed provenance, and the King's 'State sword'. Using funds from the Privy Purse, George IV commissioned two

The 1816 'Nuptial Bust' of HRH Princess Charlotte Augusta of Wales (1796–1817) by Peter Turnerelli.

CHAPTER ELEVEN

from left to right The Sword of Offering, The Sword of State and The Sword of Mercy.

swords for his Coronation from Rundell, Bridge & Rundell. The first was the jewelled Sword of Offering, which cost £5,988 (2022: £559,321); it had a purely ceremonial function in the service and is now in the Jewel House at the Tower of London as part of the Royal Regalia and Crown Jewels. The second sword was a plainer, gold-hilted weapon that he actually wore; today this is held by the Royal Collection Trust. The only other 'State' swords are The Great Sword of State and The Sword of Mercy, both of which are also part of the Royal Regalia and are kept at the Jewel House. Madame Tussaud's 'State sword' was listed in the 1911 insurance catalogue without the 'State' attribution and at the same value as the King's nightshirt and cap, which would seem to confirm that it was not a 'State sword' or even a copy of one of them.

King George IV's successor on the throne of England was the burly figure of Prince William Henry, Duke of Clarence, a former officer in the Royal Navy; he was also a lifelong friend of Nelson, under whose command he had served in the West Indies. This naval service, and his subsequent appointment as an Admiral of the Fleet and Lord High Admiral, earned him the soubriquet of 'the Sailor King'. Madame Tussaud's owned only two relics of this nautical monarch. The first, 'William IV by Simpson' (Item 14: Hall of Kings), was not illustrated, although the 1925 exhibition catalogue recorded that Prince William, when an Admiral of the Fleet, had 'hoisted his flag to escort Louis XVIII to France, in 1814.

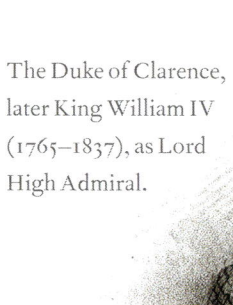

The Duke of Clarence, later King William IV (1765–1837), as Lord High Admiral.

The Tussaud's catalogue also stated that William IV sat for John Simpson, and his pictures now hang in several national collections, here and in the USA. A portrait of William IV attributed to Simpson, now at the Royal Pavilion in Brighton, shows the King in Garter robes and is similar to other portraits of the robed monarch by Sir Martin Archer Shee and Sir David Wilkie. Given that Simpson's portrait of the King hangs in a former royal residence, Madame Tussaud's was probably a studio copy. In any event, in 1911 it was valued at £200 (2022: £18,681) and attributed to Simpson.

CHAPTER ELEVEN

King William IV in Garter robes c.1830 by John Simpson.

'Relics of the Prince Consort, William IV and others (Item 161: Napoléon Ante-Room) listed 'a coat worn by William IV as Lord High Admiral.' The King, whose predecessor in the post was Prince George of Denmark, the husband of Queen Anne, was appointed to this rank in 1827 while still Duke of Clarence. Historically, the office of Lord High Admiral was one of great power and importance, holding overall command of the Royal Navy, and heading-up the naval administration in Whitehall, with a seat in the Cabinet. As Roger Fulford notes in *Royal Dukes*:

CHAPTER ELEVEN

The Government decided that, in the nineteenth century, such powers were too much even for a Royal Duke, and it was arranged that the Duke should not have a seat in the Cabinet, and that the majority of his powers should only be exercised through a Council, drawn from the officials at the Admiralty.

As the Duke was a reformer, and the naval administration in the 1820s was complacent and sclerotic, this led to trouble and the Duke resigned from the job only a year after his appointment in 1827. Exhausted by all the fuss this caused, he took to his bed for a week. The office of Lord High Admiral then lay in abeyance until 1st April 1964 when Queen Elizabeth II appointed herself to the role, only to transfer it to her husband, The Duke of Edinburgh, on 10th June 2011. Since the Duke's death on 9th April 2021 the office is once again in abeyance.

William IV's uniform as Lord High Admiral, valued in 1911 at £20 (2022: £1,868), was displayed at Madame Tussaud's alongside 'embroidery from the uniform of the Duke of Sussex as Constable of the Tower'. The Duke never actually held that appointment, although he was briefly Constable and Governor of Windsor Castle from 1842 to 1843. The 1911 insurance catalogue repeated the error when it stated that this embroidery was 'worn by the Duke of Sussex as Governor of the Tower' and valued it at £50 (2022: £4,670).

Prince Augustus Frederick, Duke of Sussex (1773–1843), by Thomas Phillips.

CHAPTER ELEVEN

The Duke of Sussex suffered from poor health for most of his life. This allowed him to avoid military service, although he was made an honorary Colonel of the Loyal North Britons, formerly known as the Highland Volunteers. Instead, he devoted himself to books and curiosities. In later life, as a protection against chills, the Duke always wore a black velvet cap: on the one occasion he didn't wear it, he temporarily succumbed to a heavy cold. Although not listed in the 1925 catalogue, the 1911 insurance catalogue included a number of items of the Duke's clothing, decorations, accoutrements, and memorabilia with a combined value of £147 (2022: £13,730).

The 'Hanoverian Relics' (Item 152: Napoléon Ante-Room) included 'Coronation robe, with petticoat, of Queen Adelaide, consort of William IV'. In the 1911 insurance catalogue they were described as the 'Embroidered Silk Under-robes of Her Majesty Queen Adelaide' and valued at £10 (2022: £934). This seems more credible, and is confirmed by a coronation portrait by John Simpson which shows the 'Under-robes' quite clearly.

Queen Adelaide, formerly Princess Adelaide of Saxe-Meiningen (1792–1849), in Coronation robes by John Simpson.

The Madame Tussaud's & Sons Exhibition included an eclectic array of relics belonging to, or associated with, some of the notable figures in Queen Victoria's reign between 1837 and 1901, many of whom were also portrayed in wax in the historical tableaux. This bizarre collection included locks of hair from the heads of the Duke of Wellington, Lord Melbourne, Sir Robert Peel and Felix Mendelssohn, the first three of whom were amongst Victoria's Prime Ministers, and the latter was one of the Queen's favourite composers. All these follicles, and the balding Mendelssohn's razor and strop, were acquired by Madame Tussaud's from the sale of the Duke of Sussex's collection. The hair was valued in 1911 at £10 (2022: £934), the razor and strop were not listed, but – somewhat bizarrely – a 'Piece of the Wedding Cake of Duke and Duchess of Albany' was listed with a value of £1 (2022: £93). This last item, from the wedding of Queen Victoria's haemophiliac son, Prince Leopold, to Princess Helen of Waldeck & Pyrmont in 1882, was not in the 1925 catalogue, nor were the autographs of King William IV, Queen Victoria, Pope Pius IX and the King of Sweden, which were collectively valued in 1911 at £30 (2022: £2,802).

The Entrance Hall at Madame Tussaud's displayed busts of Lord Brougham (Item 3), the architect of the Reform Act in 1832 and the 1833 Abolition of Slavery

≈ CHAPTER ELEVEN ≈

Act, and Sir Walter Scott (Item 5), from which the face of a waxwork figure had been modelled. These were listed in the 1911 insurance catalogue with a combined value of £50 (2022: £4,670). In addition, there was a terracotta bust of Léon Gambetta (Item 4), one of the architects of the fall of Emperor Napoléon III. Although not listed in the 1911 insurance catalogue, the sculptor of Gambetta's bust was identified in the 1925 catalogue as the exotically named Émile Coriolan Hippolyte Guillemin, a noted artist of the Belle Époque period, who is now rather out of fashion.

One of Queen Victoria's favourite Prime Ministers was Benjamin Disraeli, 1st Earl of Beaconsfield. He was commemorated at Madame Tussaud's with a number of items, including three of his uniforms: the Full Dress and Levée Dress coats of a Privy Counsellor, and that worn by the Elder Brethren of Trinity House. According to the 1925 catalogue entry for Item 74 in the Napoléon Room, he wore the first 'at the Berlin Congress, from which he returned in triumph in 1878 bringing, as he declared, "Peace with Honour", following the recent Russo-Turkish War'. This phrase would later be appropriated by President Richard Nixon when announcing the end of the Vietnam War in 1973. Together, the coats were valued in 1911 at £125 (2022: £11,675), which is rather less than they would have cost new.

Unlike the disgraced President Nixon of the USA, Beaconsfield kept his reputation intact after leaving office for the last time in 1880. This was epitomised by 'Lord Beaconsfield's Wreath' (Item 18: Grand Saloon), a presentation wreath that was organised by Tracy Turnerelli, son of the sculptor of Princess Charlotte's bust, and given to the retired statesman in 1879. Sometime after Beaconsfield's

right Benjamin Disraeli, 1st Earl of Beaconsfield (1804–1881).

far right The People's Tribute, photograph in the 1925 catalogue.

CHAPTER ELEVEN

death in 1881, the wreath was acquired by Madame Tussaud's, being first described in the 1883 exhibition catalogue and then illustrated in the 1925 edition. The text of the 1883 version read: 'There are forty-six leaves, in which are interwoven the Rose, Shamrock and Thistle. The value represents the Penny Subscriptions of 52,800 persons.' The 1925 catalogue entry stated that each leaf was inscribed with the names of the contributing towns, and the 1911 insurance catalogue gave it a value of £100 (2022: £9,340), which was only half the value of the Penny Subscriptions that had funded it.

Another waxwork study with personal possessions in the exhibition was that of William Turnour Thomas Poulett, Viscount Hinton. He claimed to be the 7th Earl Poulett after the death of his father, the 6th Earl, in 1899. This was challenged by the late Earl's third wife, acting on behalf of her son, on the grounds of paternity: William Turnour Thomas Poulett had been born only six months after his father's first marriage, and there were good reasons to believe that his actual father was Captain William Turnour Granville, with whose first two names he was somewhat tellingly christened. Nonetheless, in 1903 William Turnour Thomas Poulett petitioned the House of Lords for recognition of his claim to the earldom. On 27th July 1903, the House of Lords rejected the claim, and with it the doctrine of *pater est quem nuptiae demonstrant* (a child born within wedlock is lawfully fathered by its mother's husband), and determined the dispute in favour of the 6th Earl's younger son by his third marriage, William John Lydston Poulett. This decision left William Turnour Thomas Poulett destitute, although he continued to call himself Viscount Hinton, the courtesy title of the eldest son of the Earls of Poulett.

William Turnour Thomas Poulett, known as Viscount Hinton (1849–1909).

Most unusually, the 1925 catalogue entry for "Viscount Hinton's Organ" (Item 17: Grand Saloon) included how it was acquired:

> The Claimant to the Poulett estates ... gained his living by means of the instrument here exhibited. The model is dressed in the clothes worn by the claimant when grinding out his melodies for pence. He was very loth to part with the instrument. He himself brought it to the Exhibition, and it seemed, said Mr J. T. Tussaud, "more like parting with a favourite child than a thing of wood and metal, and he positively wept over it."

An expanded, and rather less complimentary version of this story was included in John Theodore Tussaud's book, *The Romance of Madame Tussaud's*:

> ... having modelled his figure and purchased his organ ... we bought the suit of clothes he was wearing, although a friend of his told his "lordship" that he would not

CHAPTER ELEVEN

Wilhelmina Stanhope, Duchess of Cleveland (1819–1901), by Sir Lawrence Alma-Tadema.

below Brigadier (later Major) General Sir Herbert Stewart (1843–1885), in the uniform of an Equerry to Queen Victoria.

below middle General Lord Wolseley (1833–1913) by Francis Montagu Holt.

below right Major General Charles Gordon (1833–1885), in the Ottoman uniform of the Governor-General of Sudan.

have picked them up from the gutter. It appears that "Hinton" went to the Bank of England with the £50 (2022: £4,670) note we gave him and, as is customary, ... he was asked to sign his name. With a flourish he wrote down "Poulett", whereupon the cashier said, "Christian name as well, please." Hinton drew himself up and said, "We Earls always sign our names like that," a remark which, doubtless, duly impressed and abashed the cashier.

Fortunately, two years after Madame Tussaud's bought his organ and clothes in 1899, William Turnour Thomas Poulett's fortunes took a turn for the better when Wilhelmina Stanhope, Dowager Duchess of Cleveland, the widow of a distant kinsman of the 6th Earl and great-great grandmother of this book's editor, left him a bequest of £5,000 (2022: £467,035). This was many times more than the amount he received from Tussaud's or the value of the barrel organ in the 1911 insurance catalogue, which listed it as worth £10 (2022: £937). He used the legacy to buy a tea-plantation in Ceylon, where – safe from the sneers of London Society – he continued to call himself Lord Poulett.

Less fortunate was Brigadier General Sir Herbert Stewart, a battle-hardened heavy cavalryman who led the Desert Column in the 1884-85 campaign known as the Nile Expedition for the Relief of Gordon. Commanded by General Lord Wolseley (later a Field Marshal and a Viscount), the 'very Modern Major General' of Gilbert & Sullivan's *Pirates of Penzance* (1879), the Nile Expeditionary Force's task was to rescue Major General Charles Gordon who was trapped in Khartoum. A former Governor-General of Sudan, Gordon had been sent to the Sudanese capital by the Khedive of Egypt, acting on the orders of the British government, to evacuate the Egyptians and Europeans living there from the advancing forces

CHAPTER ELEVEN

The Desert Column.

of a Muslim fundamentalist known at The Mahdi or 'chosen one'. Gordon defied his orders and quite deliberately allowed himself to become besieged in Khartoum. This was a move designed to get Gladstone's Liberal government, which was averse to 'foreign adventures', to commit more deeply to the region. It eventually worked, hence the Nile Expedition.

Wolseley's unconventional strategy for the rescue mission was to split his forces into two columns, a camel-mounted Desert Column, commanded by Stewart, and a River Column under his own command. The idea was that, should speed become necessary, the Desert Column could dash across the Bayuda Desert from Korti to Metemma and then by boat to Khartoum, which it would seize and then hold until the main force had negotiated the rapids on the much longer eastern loop of the Nile. In mid-November 1884, Wolseley received word that Gordon could survive the siege for only another forty days, and the Desert Column was dispatched.

On 17th January 1885, at the wells of Abu Klea, Stewart and his camel-mounted force of mostly Foot Guards, Household and Line Cavalrymen finally encountered the enemy. In the bloody engagement that followed, Stewart was victorious, but not before the rear quadrant

The Battle of Abu Klea by William Barnes Wollen.

of the Desert Column's defensive square had been broken open. This blot on the British Army's reputation was entirely the fault of a Victorian hero, Colonel Fred Burnaby of The Blues. In a desperate bid to rescue his friend, Captain (later Admiral) Lord Charles Beresford, who was trapped outside the square with his

[209]

CHAPTER ELEVEN

The Death of Colonel Frederick Gustavus Burnaby (1842–1885), at the Battle of Albu Klea.

Gardner machine-gun crew, Burnaby had gallantly but foolishly committed the military sin of pushing his horse through the double line of British rifleman forming the rear of the defensive formation. This action opened a gap through which the spear-wielding Mahdists poured. Although they were swiftly and effectively dealt with inside the square, Burnaby, who was still outside its protective ranks, was accidentally felled from his horse by friendly fire and then hacked to death by the tribesmen.

The event was commemorated by Sir Henry Newbolt in a verse of his 1892 poem of Empire, *Vitai Lampada*:

The sand of the desert is sodden red,
Red with the wreck of a square that broke;
The Gatling's jammed and the Colonel dead,
And the regiment blind with dust and smoke.

Two days later, at a second engagements with the Mahdists at Abu Kru (sometimes known as the Battle of Gubat), Stewart also fell, mortally wounded. He was obliged to hand over command to Brigadier General Sir Charles Wilson, but lingered for a month, which was long enough to learn that he had been promoted to Major General 'for distinguished service in the field', and then died on the way back to Korti. He was buried near the wells of Jakdul and eulogised by Lord Wolseley, who telegraphed the news to London along with the encomium that 'no braver soldier or more brilliant leader of men ever wore the Queen's uniform'.

CHAPTER ELEVEN

How the bloodied 'Helmet and Gloves of Sir Herbert Stewart' (Item 20: Grand Saloon) came to be acquired by Madame Tussaud's was not explained in the 1925 catalogue nor in the 1911 insurance catalogue, which gave them a value of £10 (2022: £934).

'The Relic of General Gordon' (Item 21: Grand Saloon), described as the camel harness used by Gordon in Khartoum, similarly had no provenance. Charles Gordon was a very unusual soldier who, for much of his career, was seconded to foreign governments. A Royal Engineer officer by training, and by conviction a bachelor who was probably a repressed homosexual, he was also an Evangelical Christian with a pronounced death wish. He established his international reputation in the years 1863 to 1864, by ending the fourteen-year-long Taiping Rebellion in China at the head of a mercenary force known as the 'Ever Victorious Army'. Known thereafter as 'Chinese Gordon', in 1872 he was contracted by the Khedive of Egypt to supress a revolt in Sudan. At the time, Sudan was nominally under the control of Egypt, itself nominally a part of the Ottoman Empire, although in reality – because of the strategic importance of the Suez Canal – the Khedive was controlled by the British government through the British Agent in Cairo. Promoted to Governor-General by the Khedive in 1876, Gordon's principal task in his new role was supressing the Arab-run, East African slave trade. By his own reckoning he failed in this task, resigned in 1879 and suffered a nervous breakdown. Nonetheless, offers of work poured in, including one from the King Leopold II of Belgium to run the Belgian Congo, and another from the Emperor Guangxu of China to command the Imperial Army.

Gordon eventually accepted the Belgian offer, but was instead persuaded by the British government to return to Khartoum, once again as Governor-General. This appointment was made despite the advice of the British Agent in Cairo, Lord Cromer, who disliked and distrusted Gordon, saying of him: 'a man who habitually consults the Prophet Isaiah when he is in a difficulty is not apt to obey the orders of anyone'. Nonetheless, the job was offered, and Gordon accepted, arriving in Khartoum on 18th February 1884.

By August of that year his position was perilous, forcing Gladstone, who was under considerable public pressure, to commit to armed intervention and the dispatch of the Nile Expedition. It arrived at Khartoum two days too late, for the city fell on 26th January 1885, and Gordon was killed under circumstances that have never been fully verified. Seeing the city in the hands of The Mahdi's army, Wilson turned his men back without attempting to force an entry into the city.

It was only after the Battle of Omdurman on 2nd September 1898 that British troops entered Khartoum. There, after thirteen years, not a trace of Gordon remained, although his journals had been saved by his secretary, Khalil Orphali, who survived

Statue at Khartoum of General Gordon on a camel.

CHAPTER ELEVEN

above Gordon's Last Stand at Khartoum, tableau at Madame Tussaud's.

above right General Gordon's Last Stand by George W. Joy.

the murder and mayhem that followed the fall of the city. Madame Tussaud's 1925 catalogue entry for Gordon's camel harness did not explain how it was saved from the wreckage, or how it had survived the thirteen-year interval, nor how or when it arrived at the exhibition. It did state, incorrectly, that it was 'used by the hero of the Sudan on his last journey through the desert [to Khartoum]', even though it was well known that Gordon arrived in the city on a Nile steamer.

While the authenticity of Stewart's helmet and gloves were beyond question, there must be considerable doubt about Gordon's camel harness, described rather vaguely in the 1911 insurance catalogue as 'Trappings', with a value of £10 (2022: £934). These items were probably acquired by Madame Tussaud's to enhance the tableau depicting his death, an apocryphal scene based on *General Gordon's Last Stand* by George W. Joy, that was popularly accepted as accurate. It was replicated in the 1966 film, *Khartoum*, in which the American actor, Charlton Heston, was cast as Gordon, and Laurence Olivier played The Mahdi, black-faced and in his most hammed-up role ever.

Although Gordon's camel harness was almost certainly a fake, no such doubt is attached to the 'Oriental Costume of Sir Richard Burton' (Item 43: Hall No 4), which was described in the 1925 catalogue in unequivocal terms:

> The garments with which this model of the late Sir Richard Burton is clothed are those actually worn by the great Orientalist on his return from his pilgrimage to Mecca. They were placed on the model by the late Lady Burton, his devoted wife.

CHAPTER ELEVEN

far left Sir Richard Burton (1821–1885) disguised as Haji Abdullah, 1853.

left Lady Burton (1831–1896).

Sir Richard Burton (1821–1890), whose nickname was 'Ruffian Dick' and whose motto was 'honour not honours', was a famed Victorian explorer, writer, scholar and soldier, who spoke twenty-nine languages. He was also notorious for his very un-Victorian attitude to sex, which embraced a hands-on interest in the subject and its practice (in all its forms) around the world. Burton's most famous achievements included a journey to Mecca (in disguise as Haji Abdullah) in 1853, at a time when Europeans were forbidden access on pain of death, and a journey to the Great Lakes of Africa in search of the source of the Nile. He was also notorious for writing an unexpurgated translation of the *One Thousand and One Nights*, publishing the *Kama Sutra* in English; and translating *The Perfumed Garden* (the 'Arab *Kama Sutra*'). When not involved in either global or carnal exploration, the polysexual Burton was an unlikely friend of the sexually-repressed Gordon, with whom he exchanged many letters from 1876 until the latter's death, albeit they only met twice – in Cairo in 1879 and again in late 1882. For some reason, Burton's clothes were not listed in the 1911 insurance catalogue nor was his figure in wax.

⋖⋅⋗⋅❖⋅⋖⋅⋗

In the midst of these relics of Queen Victoria's reign, there were surprisingly few items at Madame Tussaud's belonging to her or her immediate family, although the 1901 exhibition catalogue opened with a black-bordered statement that read: 'Her Gracious Majesty Queen Victoria, to the grief of all her subjects,

CHAPTER ELEVEN

right Coronation portrait of Queen Victoria by Sir George Hayter.

far right Queen Victoria, photograph in the 1925 catalogue.

Prince Albert of Saxe-Coburg and Gotha (1819–1861) by George Patten.

* Item 1 survived the 1925 fire and was valued by Sotheby's in 1983 at £1,200 – £1,800 (2022: £3,803 – £5,709).

passed away just as the pages of this catalogue were printed.' On the following page, there was an illustration of Item 1 in the Entrance Hall and this entry:

> As visitors pass through the turnstile into the Entrance Hall, they see high on the wall the splendid portrait of Queen Victoria ... in her Coronation robes ... The portrait is from the brush of Sir George Hayter, who ... in 1841 was appointed principal painter to her Majesty.

This portrait, reproduced in the catalogue, was self-evidently a version of the State Portrait of Victoria of 1838, the original of which is owned by the Royal Collection Trust. Several copies were made of this painting with the assistance of the artist's son, Angelo, and used as diplomatic gifts. It is likely that Madame Tussaud's picture was one of those copies, although how it was obtained was not explained. It was valued in 1911 at £300 (2022: £28,022)*.

Item 16 in the Grand Saloon was stated to be a portrait of Queen Victoria's husband, Prince Albert, by George Patten. The artist is known to have travelled to Schloss Rosenau, Albert's home in Saxe-Coburg-Saalfeld, in 1840, to paint the Prince prior to his wedding to the Queen, and was later appointed his Painter in Ordinary. This portrait, engravings of which were sold widely, is in the Royal Collection Trust; the version hanging at Madame Tussaud's must, therefore, have been a copy, probably based on the engraving. It was valued in 1911 at £175 (2022: £16,346), which seems excessive even for a copy.

The exhibition also displayed one of Prince Albert's many uniform coats (Item 161: Napoléon Ante-Room), although which was not specified in the catalogue

CHAPTER ELEVEN

but was described as that of a General in the 1911 insurance catalogue, along with a value of £25 (2022: £2,335); a portrait medallion of him as Prince Consort, by 'the well-known Belgian sculptor, M. Malampré', about whom the authors can discover nothing; and what was claimed to be the playbill from Albert's last visit to the theatre on 14th September 1861 (Item 47: Hall No 4), although which play was not specified. Knowing Albert, it would have been a serious work. The 1911 insurance catalogue, possibly referring to the same item, stated that it was a 'Princess Theatre Programme' worth £2 (2022: £186); in 1860 to 1861 the Princess Theatre in London was showing performances of *Hamlet*, by William Shakespeare.

The last items relating to Victoria and Albert included a pair of busts by an un-named sculptor (Items 32 & 36: Grand Saloon), only one of which – that of Queen Victoria – was listed in the 1911 insurance catalogue with a value of £20 (2022: £1,875). There was also a collection of 'interesting etchings' by the royal couple (Item 34: Grand Saloon). Although not listed in the 1911 insurance catalogue, according to the 1925 exhibition catalogue they were apparently executed in 1840 and 1841, but without any further explanation as to what they depicted or how they were acquired. Finally, there was a facsimile 'Cot containing Model of HRH Prince Edward of York' (Item 15: Grand Saloon) that had cradled Victoria's and Albert's two eldest children, the Princess Royal, who would become Empress of Germany, and the future King Edward VII. It was valued in 1911 at £50 (2022: £4,670), which seems a generous price for a copy.

A royal cot, photograph in the 1925 catalogue.

[215]

CHAPTER TWELVE

A CABINET OF CURIOSITIES

As the Madame Tussaud & Sons' Exhibition was originally presented as a cabinet of curiosities, inevitably that some of the items in the collection fell outside the broad historical themes, and so are considered here. Prior to the 1925 fire, there were no waxwork figures of past Emperors of China. However, the exhibition included several 'Chinese Dresses' and the 'Headdress of a Chinese Lady' (Items 177 & 182: Napoléon Ante-Room). The garments were catalogued in 1925 as 'captured at Pekin [sic] in October, 1860', but without any further explanation, beyond stating that 'three of them distinguishable from the others by their superior richness, formed part of the Emperor's wardrobe'. This minimal information suggests that the robes were spoils of war taken at the sacking of the Old Summer Palace in Peking in 1860, along with an eclectic mix of other items that were not listed in the 1925 catalogue, but were itemised in the 1911 insurance catalogue. They included a pair of spectacles, silver bells, shoes, a doll, four swords and a candle, collectively valued at £300 (2022: £28,022).

The sacking of the Old Summer Palace signalled the end of the Second Opium War (1856–1860) between Britain and China. The disputed and illegal importing of opium first reared its bleary-eyed head as a *causus belli* in 1839, when the Imperial Chinese government rejected a British proposal to legalise the trade from India. Emperor Daoguang appointed one of his Court officials, the scholar Lin Zexu, to solve the problem. He did so by the simple expedient of abolishing imports of the drug, a decision which he backed up by confiscating without compensation 20,000 chests of opium (today worth £340 million) from British warehouses. He then banned all further trade of any sort and confined foreign merchants to their quarters.

opposite Empress Dowager CiXi (1835–1908).

below right Lin Zexu (1785–1850).

below Opium in storage in India before shipment to China, *c*.1850.

CHAPTER TWELVE

Signing and sealing of the Treaty of Nanking, 1842.

The British government, although not officially denying China's right to control imports of the 'blue smoke', as it was known, objected to this unexpected seizure and used its overwhelming naval power to make the point. Negotiations ensued, enforced by British naval cannon, and in 1842 the Chinese reluctantly signed the Treaty of Nanking, bringing the First Opium War to an end. Britain was granted an indemnity and extraterritoriality, the five treaty ports of Shanghai, Canton, Ningpo, Fuchow and Amoy were opened to foreign merchants, and Hong Kong Island was ceded to the British 'in perpetuity'.

However, on other points, including the opium trade and the establishment of diplomatic representation in Peking, China then prevaricated. By 1856 both sides were preparing for another armed confrontation. The spark that ignited this box of firecrackers was struck by the Chinese, who impounded an illegal opium-trading vessel, the *Arrow*, which unfortunately (and quite illegally) happened

right James Bruce, 8th Earl of Elgin (1811–1863)

far right Baron Jean-Baptiste-Louis Gros (1793–1870).

CHAPTER TWELVE

to be flying a British flag. What ensued is probably one of the more curious episodes in the history of British, French and Chinese diplomacy and conflict.

In a nutshell, after bombarding Canton, where the *Arrow's* Chinese crew were being held, the British and the French governments informed the Emperor Xianfeng, fourth son of Emperor Daoguang who had been humiliated in the First Opium War, that they were determined to establish embassies in Peking, as mandated in the terms of the Treaty of Nanking. To that end, the Europeans announced that they were sending a heavily-armed diplomatic mission from the coast, under the leadership of James Bruce, 8th Earl of Elgin, and Baron Jean-Baptiste-Louis Gros.

The Chinese responded with an invitation to the mission to come to Peking, opposed it every step of the way, and then imprisoned, tortured and killed in quite horrific circumstances an Anglo-French negotiating team. On all counts this perfidy, and its barbaric aftermath, was viewed very badly by Lord Elgin and his French counterpart, who ordered a rapid advance on Peking. When the hideously mutilated corpses of the negotiators were uncovered, they ordered the destruction of the Emperor's Summer Palace in retribution .

Prize auction after the sacking of the Old Summer Palace, 1860.

The Yuan Ming Yuan (The Garden of Perfect Brightness), as the Old Summer Palace was known, was the private residence of the Qing Emperors. It covered 350 hectares, and included hundreds of halls, pavilions, temples, galleries, gardens, lakes and bridges. The buildings of this pleasure complex housed tens of thousands of Chinese antiquities and artefacts, some of which were up to 3,600 years old.

CHAPTER TWELVE

Dragon robe of the Emperor Qianlong (1736–1796).

The value of the contents of the Old Summer Palace before its destruction is incalculable, but destroyed it was by English and French troops. Fortunately, wholesale British looting – the French were more intent on wanton wrecking – saved many works of art from the flaming buildings, which burnt for three days. Today, this loot is extremely valuable and highly desirable. In 2018, an Imperial 'twelve symbol' Dragon robe, possibly similar to those at Madame Tussaud's and taken from the Emperor's wardrobe in the Old Summer Palace in 1860, sold at a London auction for £464,750.

The visit to Madame Tussaud's by Naser al-Din Shah Qajar in 1873, covered in Chapter 4, had a coda. Before leaving the exhibition, the Shah commanded one of his suite to give him a copy of the New Testament in Persian, which earlier in the day had been presented to the courtier by Queen Victoria. The King of Kings then presented this volume, listed in the 1911 insurance catalogue as a 'Bible', to Madame Tussaud's, along with an autographed testimonial which read (in translation) in the 1925 catalogue:

> Whilst staying in London I visited Madame Tussaud's Exhibition, and I write these few words in the place itself as a souvenir of my visit.
> NASSERDIN CHAH KADJAR
> 1290 Haegira

New Testament in Persian, photograph in the 1925 catalogue.

'The New Testament in Persian' and the imperial testimonial were displayed in the Hall of Kings as Item 27. They were valued in 1911 at £50 (2022: £4,670) for the book and half that for the signed paper. A wax effigy of the Shah himself was later made to commemorate the visit, although it had been melted down before his son, Mozaffar ad-Din Shah Qajar, visited Madame Tussaud's in 1902. This caused some embarrassment, as John Theodore Tussaud related in *The Romance of Madame Tussaud's*:

> The first model he asked to see was that of his late father, but unfortunately his picturesque parent had disappeared to make room for more up-to-date people. The horrible fact of the remelting to cast a possibly much less distinguished personage could not, of course, be divulged to the royal visitor. A hint to the entourage was sufficient. "*Perished by fire – great accidental fire,*" explained Sir Arthur Hardinge with the aplomb of a true diplomat.

CHAPTER TWELVE

far left Sir Arthur Hardinge (1859–1933).

left Mozaffar ad-Din Shah Qajar (1853–1907).

The situation could have worsened when Mozaffar ad-Din came face to face with his own portrait model, but:

> ...the Shah addressed some presumably humorous remark to it, for sovereign and suite relaxed their facial muscles, and a Persian outburst of mirth succeeded. The stolid monarch actually laughed outright. It was the only recorded laugh of His Majesty during his visit to this country.

If Queen Victoria later heard that her gift of a New Testament to a Persian courtier had been presented to Madame Tussaud's by her imperial visitor, it was not recorded. It is fair to assume that she would not have been amused.

King Alphonso XIII (1886–1941), in the uniform of a British Field Marshal, by Carl Vandyk.

⊰⊱✣⊰⊱

Quite how or why the 'Shoes of the King of Spain' (Item 26: Grand Saloon) ended up at Madame Tussaud's remains a mystery. As with so many other items in the pre-fire exhibition, there was no explanation in the catalogues or the archives. Equally, there was no explanation for the Empress Frederick's slippers and Sir Michael Costa's watch, both in a 'Case of Miscellaneous Relics' (Item 67: Napoléon Room).

King Alphonso XIII of Spain reigned from the date of his birth, 17th May 1886, until he was deposed in 1931. The only monarch ever to have been nominated for a Nobel Peace Prize, he was married to one of Queen Victoria's granddaughters, Princess Victoria Eugenie of Battenberg, who made a fleeting appearance as Queen Ena in Chapter 10. A serial philanderer, Alphonso commissioned and

[221]

CHAPTER TWELVE

The Empress Frederick (1840–1901) with the future Kaiser Wilhelm II (1859–1941).

Sir Michael Costa (1808–1884).

promoted pornographic films, most of which were later destroyed on the orders of Generalissimo Franco.

Her Imperial Majesty Empress Frederick of Prussia was the eldest child of Queen Victoria, Queen Ena of Spain's aunt and the mother of Kaiser Wilhelm II. Before her marriage to the future Emperor, she had been designated The Princess Royal. Other than her disastrous eldest son, the Empress Frederick is today best remembered as the author of a voluminous, and often indiscreet, correspondence with her mother. This cache of letters was smuggled out of Prussia in 1901 shortly before her death by her godson, Sir Frederick Ponsonby (from 1935 1st Baron Sysonby), who was also Private Secretary to her brother, King Edward VII. Sir Frederick later edited and published the correspondence as the *Letters of the Empress Frederick* (1928).

Sir Michael Costa, described in the 1925 catalogue as 'the great conductor', was born in Naples in 1808. He arrived in London in 1830, working at Her Majesty's Theatre, where he exerted real influence for change. He moved to the pit at Covent Garden Theatre in 1847, following unspecified disagreements with the manager of Her Majesty's. His insistence on vocal and orchestral discipline and accuracy, unusual at the time, earned him the admiration both of Giacomo Meyerbeer and Giuseppe Verdi. In addition to conducting, Costa, who was naturalised by the British and knighted in 1869, also wrote several ballet scores, and composed at least two operas and an oratorio. His works are now seldom played, perhaps reflecting a view expressed by Gioachino Rossini who said, on receiving the score of Costa's oratorio, *Eli*: 'The good Costa has sent me an oratorio score and a Stilton cheese. The cheese was very good.'

The royal baby shoes, apparently the first pair the Spanish King ever wore, and the imperial slippers were not in the 1911 insurance catalogue, perhaps because they were acquired after that date, but Costa's watch was – and was valued at a modest £5 (2022: £467). Somewhat surprisingly, the 1925 catalogue failed to include some curiosities listed in the 1911 insurance catalogue, probably because they had been discarded from the collection. These included unspecified items belonging to the ill-fated and executed Emperor Maximilian I of Mexico (1832–1867), the younger brother of Emperor Franz-Josef of Austria-Hungary, worth £25 (2022: £2,335); and the 'air bed, garters, gloves and six plates' of the famous explorer, Dr David Livingstone (1813–1873), valued at £40 (2022: £3,736). A large collection of Zulu artefacts included 'Two Tiger Skins' and an 'Arrowhead Assegai set with Alligator's Teeth, used by the Witch Doctor, each Tooth containing a Drug', and was valued at £50 (2022: £4,670). Alert readers will have spotted that neither alligators nor tigers are indigenous to Zululand, although that may have been an error made by an un-travelled valuer.

CHAPTER TWELVE

above left Shrunken head from the Upper Amazon region, 2006.

above A group of Jivaroans, c.1901.

Of all the treasures, trophies and trivia that were lost in the 1925 fire, the most extraordinary exhibit of all was the 'Head of a South American Chief' (Item 42: Hall No 4). This was the shrunken head, described in the 1925 catalogue in the following rather grisly terms:

> This head is that of a chief of the South American tribe known as the Napos, who dwell near the source of the river of that name, in Ecuador. The Napos are constantly at war with a rival tribe called the Jiberos. It is usual for the women to follow the men into battle, and when an enemy is slain they come forward and cut off the head and carry it back to camp as a trophy. To keep these trophies from decay, they are preserved in a very singular manner, the skin, with the hair intact, being removed and filled with fine sand mixed with tannin, upon which hot water is poured. As the result of this treatment, the head shrinks to about the size of a man's clenched hand, and it is then usually attached to the woman's girdle suspended by a string. The head exhibited is believed to be that of a young chief.

Valued at only £10 (2022: £934) in 1911, the reason for the presence of a shrunken head in the exhibition was not given in the 1925 exhibition catalogue, nor were the circumstances or the date of its acquisition, which must have been after 1883, as it does not appear in the catalogue of that date. As for the catalogue's account of the headhunting Amazonian females, the 'Napos' do not appear to have existed as a tribe, although Napo Province and the Napo River are in Ecuadorian Amazonia. The Jivaroan peoples (*Jíbaro* in Spanish, meaning 'savage' and/or 'rustic') inhabit the area around the headwaters of the Manañon River, also in Ecuadorian Amazonia and contiguous with the Napo River. The various Jivaroan tribes were (and probably still are) in a state of almost perpetual warfare with one another. They were (and still may be) head-hunters who shrank their

CHAPTER TWELVE

George Augustus Sala (1828–1895).

trophies, which were known as *Tzan-Tzas*. The probability is that Madame Tussaud's shrunken head was a casualty of a Jivaroan inter-tribal battle. As it was cremated along with the rest of the items described in this book, the truth will never be known.

It seems appropriate to end this examination of the items in Madame Tussaud & Sons' Exhibition with the 'Bust of George Augustus Sala' (Item 45: Hall No 4). He was a now long-forgotten author and journalist, who wrote extensively for the *Illustrated London News* under the appropriate pen-name of 'GAS', and was most famous for his articles and leaders for *The Daily Telegraph*. In 1879, Sala wrote a bawdy pantomime called *Harlequin Prince Cherrytop*, which was adapted as a monologue known as *The Sod's Opera*. Three years later, he published a pornographic novel of flagellation erotica entitled The Mysteries of Verbena House (under the pseudonym Etonensis). Sculpted by John T. Tussaud, the bust of Sala was exhibited at the Royal Academy and its subject was responsible for penning the often highly inaccurate entries on the portrait models at Madame Tussaud's. Nevertheless, the 1911 valuers thought it was worth £25 (2022: £2,335).

EPILOGUE

It is of course impossible to say how Madame Tussaud's would have developed after 1925, had the devastating fire never taken place. The habit of acquiring props and items associated with the exhibition's waxwork figures and tableaux continued, particularly when celebrities could be persuaded to donate clothes, shoes, and other accessories, or relics of gruesome crimes could be obtained following court cases that usually consigned the convicted criminals to the gallows.

Indeed, in the 1970s, when Madame Tussaud's owned Wookey Hol e Caves in Somerset, they set up a major display for the public, entitled 'Madame Tussaud's Storeroom'. This included 'head moulds' spanning 200 years of the organisation's history, with some dating from the 1770s; several of the earliest surviving 'bodies', dating from the period 1805 to 1835, when Madame Tussaud was travelling throughout Great Britain; countless uniforms, weapons, orders, jewellery, costumes, laces and embroideries, often bought either for historical research purposes or because they had belonged to a person portrayed in past exhibitions; and even two full-length portraits depicting King William III and King George I (Item 196: Hall of Tableaux), the latter attributed in the 1911 insurance catalogue to Sir Godfrey Kneller. Many of these items must have been stored off-site in 1925, which would explain why they were not lost in the fire; a few have recently been rediscovered in storage.

However, it must also be said that in more recent times – and particularly in 2005, following the sale of Madame Tussaud's to Dubai International Capital – many of the oldest and most valuable pieces remaining in the collection were sold at Christie's on 19th October 2005, as already detailed in earlier chapters, along with more recent items that had been acquired long after the 1925 fire. Just a week later, on 27th October 2005, a Music Legends Auction held by Cooper Owen Auctioneers featured 'The Madame Tussauds Collection'. This included a pair of Elton John's boots (£700), Elvis Presley's shirt (£800), original waxwork heads of The Beatles (£4,800); an original set of four suits, tailored for The Beatles and used during the promotion of 'A Hard Day's Night' (£20,000); two signature Beatle suits donated in 1964 directly from the band for their first waxworks (£55,000); and numerous items of rock and pop memorabilia, mostly given by the artists themselves.

≈ EPILOGUE ≈

It seems likely that many other historic items, had they not been consumed in the 1925 fire, would also have been dispersed in similar sales during this period. However, it is only fair to state that these disposals almost certainly owed more to the evolving nature of Madame Tussaud's than to any reckless disregard for the historical importance of the items sold. It is worth remembering that, until the 1960s, the paying public were more interested in often long-dead monarchs, military heroes, and persons of note, than they were in celebrities. So, when the visitors' tastes changed, Madame Tussaud's – which may have been a cabinet of curiosities but was never a museum – was bound to reflect that change.

Fortunately, following further sales of the business in 2007, and with Madame Tussaud's now operated by Merlin Entertainments, a new appreciation of the archives and historic artefacts has recently sprung into life, and significant investment is being committed to cataloguing and conserving anything and everything that has miraculously survived from before the 1925 fire or the sales in the decades since. There are also plans to make these items available for the public to view once again.

In the aftermath of the disastrous night of 19th March 1925, insurance claims were made, the halls were rebuilt, the wax figures recast, the historical tableaux recreated, and Madame Tussaud & Sons' Exhibition once again opened its doors. Since when, and despite further damage as a result of bombing in the Second World War, it has flourished mightily and expanded around the globe. Back in 1925, some of the ashes of the lost collection were placed in a silver urn. This book has only been able to hint at the vast financial loss those remains represent, but it has hopefully made the enormous cultural loss apparent for future generations.

Sic Transit Gloria Mundi

The ashes of Madame Tussaud & Sons' Exhibition, 1925.

INDEX

NB Page numbers in **bold** refer to illustrations and captions

A

Abbott, Lemuel Francis, **90**
Abercorn, John Hamilton, 1st Marquess of, 71
Aboukir Bay, Battle of, 90, 91
Abu Klea, Battle of, **209**, 210
Abu Kru (Gubat), Battle of, 210
Académie de Saint Luc, Paris, 33, 34
Adelaide, Queen, 78–9, **78**
  collection from Windsor Castle, 79
  coronation robe (under-robes), 205, **205**
Albany, Leopold, Duke of, wedding cake, 205
Albert of Saxe-Coburg, Prince, 214, **214**
  portrait medallion, 215
  uniform coat, 214–15
Alexander I, Tsar of Russia, 42
alligator's teeth, 222
Alma-Tadema, Sir Lawrence, **208**
Alphonso XIII, King of Spain 187
  baby shoes of, 221–2
Amazon, shrunken head, 223, **223**
Amelia, Princess, christening robe, 79
Amiens, Treaty of (1802), 41
Anglo-Zulu War (1879), 189, 191–2, **191**
Anne, Queen, 58, **58**
Antommarchi, Dr, 162, **162**, 174

Apotheosis of Napoléon, 104–5, **104**, **105**
  verre églomisé, 126–7
Appiani, Andrea the Elder, **92**, **97**, **146**, **161**
Archambault, Achille, collection, 176, **176**
Archer, Sir Martin, 202
Arcole, Battle of, 89, **89**
Arrow, opium-trading ship, 218–19
Assegai (spear), 222
atlas, Napoléon's, 125, **125**
auctions,
  Bullock's (1819), 118
  Music Legends Auction (2005), 225
  see also Christie's
Aumont, Louise d', Duchesse Mazarin, 53, **53**
Austerlitz, Battle of, 126
Austerlitz (Marshals) Table, 127–8, **127**
autographs,
  King of Sweden, 205
  Napoléon's signature, 125, **125**
  Pope Pius IX, 205
  Queen Victoria, 205
  William IV, 205

B

Bacri, M., 104
Bacton Altar Cloth, 50, **50**
Bailly, J S, mayor of Paris, 81, 82
Bakri, Sheikh Khalil el, 116
Barras, Vicomte Paul de, 89

barrel organ, Viscount Hinton's, 207–8
Barry, Comte Jean-Baptiste du, 68
Barry, Jeanne Bécu, Madame du, 33, **33**, 68, 69
Bastille,
  cell of the Man in the Iron Mask, 82–3
  fall of, 88
  instruments of torture, 83
  keys of, 80–2, **82**
  model, **83**
Bazaine, Marshal, 183
Bazeille, church clock, 184
Béarn, Comte René-Marie-Hector de Galard de Brassac de, 69
Béarn, Comtesse Angélique-Gabrielle de Sufferte-Journard des Achards, 69
The Beatles, wax heads and suits, 225
Beauclerk, Charles, Earl of Burford and Duke of St Albans, 63
Beauharnais, Eugène, Viceroy of Italy, 95, 97, 138–40, **139**
Beauharnais, Hortense, Queen of Holland, 95, 97, 98, 138, 142, **142**
beds,
  curtain from Charles I's, 60–1
  James II's, **60**
  tassel, from Malmaison, 128
  Wellington's camp, 164
  see also death bed
Beechy, Sir William, 78

[227]

INDEX

Béhague, Martine-Marie-Pol de, Comtesse de Béarn, 69
Bellangé, Hippolyte, 161, **161**
Belle, Alexis Simon, 33
Bellerophon, HMS, **166**
Benoist, Marie-Guillemine, **97**
Bentley, Richard, *Bentley's Magazine*, 111
Beresford, Admiral Lord Charles, 209
Berridge, Kate, 32, 36, 40
    Madame Tussaud: A Life in Wax, 31
Berthier, Marshal, 149
Berthon, René, 71, **71**
Berwick, Thomas Henry Noel-Hill, 8th Baron, 138
Biennais, Martin-Guillaume, 118, 121
Bismarck, Prince Otto von, 183, **183**, **185**, 186
Bissen, H.W., **105**
Blofield, John, 169–70
Blücher, Marshal, 155
Blücher von Wahlstatt, Graf, 156
Bonaparte, Caroline, m. Marshal Murat, 95, **97**, 136–8
    portraits by David, **137**
Bonaparte, Elisa, Duchess of Tuscany, 95, **96**
Bonaparte, Jérôme, King of Westphalia, 95, **97**, 101–2, **102**, 110
Bonaparte, Joseph, King of Naples, 95, **96**
    capture of carriage, 162, **162**
    portrait by David, 138, **138**
Bonaparte, Letizia (Madame Mère), 95, **96**, **106**, 113
    bequests to Lucien, 119
    by David, **132**, 133
    by Gérard, **133**
    terracotta bust, 106–8
Bonaparte, Louis, King of Holland, 95, **96**, 110

Bonaparte, Louis Napoléon *see* Napoléon III, Emperor
Bonaparte, Lucien, Prince of Canino, 95, **96**, 109–10, **109**, **119**
    miniature, 108
    Napoléonica from, 119–21, 162, 174
Bonaparte, Matilde-Letizia, Princesse, 147
Bonaparte, Napoléon-Louis-Charles, 142, **142**
Bonaparte, Pauline, Duchess of Guastalla, 95, **97**, 125, **135**
    by David, 134
    as *Venus Victrix* (Canova), 134, **135**
Bone, Henry, **156**
books, Napoléon's, 159
boots, Napoléon's, 126
Bothmann, Georg von, **73**
bottle case, leather, Napoléon's, 126
Boucher, François, painter, 67–9, **67**
    The Birth of Venus, 68–9, **68**
    The Four Seasons, 67
Bourbon, Louis de, Duc de Mercoeur, 54, **54**
Bourbon monarchy, restoration, 179–93, **179**
Bourdon, Sébastien, painter, 66–7, **66**
Bourienne, Louis Antoine Fauvelet de, 174
Bouttats, Gaspar, **52**
Boydell, John, 48
Boze, Joseph, **34**
Braganza, Catherine of, 58
Braganza, Constantine, Duke of, 58
Braganza, Luisa de Guzmán, Duchess of, 57, 58
Brazen, HMS, 171, 172, 173
Breguet, Abraham-Louis, watchmaker, 117
Bristol, Riots (1831), 42
Brougham, Lord, bust, 205–6

Brussels,
    Duchess of Richmond's Ball, 150–1, **150**
    rue de la Blanchisserie, 150
Bucher, Leopold, **97**
Bullock, William, collector, 118–19, **118**
    1819 auction, 118, 126, 151, 158
    and *La Dormeuse*, 151, **154**, 156–8, **157**
Burke, William, 42, **43**
Burnaby, Colonel Frederick, 209–10, **210**
burnous, Mameluke, Napoléon's, 155, **155**
Burton, Lady, **213**
Burton, Richard, 47
Burton, Sir Richard, *Oriental Costume*, 212–13, **213**
busts,
    Gambetta, 206
    Joséphine, 100
    Madame Mère, 106–8
    Napoléon, 102–6, **103**, **104**, **105**, 110, **110**
    Napoléon II, 112, **112**
    Napoléon III and Eugénie, 182
    Sala, 224, **224**
    Sir Walter Scott, 206

C

California, J Paul Getty Museum, 69
Cambacérès, Jacques-Régis de, 91
cameo ring, Napoléon's, 119–20, **120**
Campan, Henriette, *Memoirs of the Private Life of Marie Antoinette*, 36
Candeillé, Amélie-Julie, 150
candelabra, 128
Canizaro, Duchess of, 117, **117**
Canolini, Abbé, 98
Canova, Antonio, 103, 134, **135**
Carey, Lieutenant Jahleel Brenton, 191
Carol II, King of Romania, 69
Caroline (of Brunswick), Queen, marriage to George IV, 200–1, **200**

INDEX

Caroline, Queen, 76, **76**, 77
carriages,
    berline, 149, 153, **153**, 155–6
    La Cuisine Roulante, 149, **149**
    Napoléon III's (at Sedan), 184, **185**
    Napoléon's campaign, *La Dormeuse*, 118, 148–52, **148**, 154–60
    Napoléon's State, 145–6
    St Helena, 169–70, **169**
Carrier, Jean-Baptiste, 38, **39**
catalogues,
    1883 exhibition, 115–16, **115**, 118–19
    1901 (death of Queen Victoria), 213–14
    1925 exhibition, 99, 100, **100**, 132
    insurance (1911), 20, 27–8
Catherine of Württemberg, Queen of Westphalia, 102, **102**
ceiling panels, Sir James Thornhill, 66, 77
chairs,
    from St Helena, 171
    Voltaire's library, 70–3, **70**
chandeliers, 117
Channon, Sir Henry 'Chips', 25, **25**
Charles I, King, 55, 57, 58–62, **59**
    curtain from State bed, 60–1, **60**
    execution, 58–61, **59**, **61**
    handkerchief, 60
    piece of cravat, 60
    vertebra, 61–2, **61**
    waistcoat, 60, **60**
Charles II, King, 57, 58, **58**, 62–3, **62**
    baby clothing, 62
    horn book, 62
Charles X, King of France, 54, **54**, 179, 180–1, **180**, **181**
Charlotte, Princess, lock of hair, 79
Charlotte, Princess of Wales, 42, 201, **201**
Charlotte, Queen, 78
Chaudet, Antoine, 103

Chauveau, François, 70
Chelmsford, Lieutenant General Lord, 189, 191
Chevallier, Napoléon's tailor, 122
China, imperial robes, 217, 220, **220**
Chinnock & Galsworthy, auctioneers, 80–2, **81**, 83
Chislehurst, Kent, Prince Imperial Memorial, 192, **192**
Christie & Manson, auctions (1843), 49, 50, 63
Christie's,
    1849 auctions, 172
    1998 auction, 105
    2005 auction, 99–100, **99**, 117, 124, 225
Christina, Queen of Sweden, 66, **67**
CiXi, Dowager Empress of China, **216**
Cleopatra VII Philopator, wax statuette, 46–7, **46**
Cleveland, Wilhelmina Stanhope, Duchess of, 208, **208**
cloak, Napoléon's, 122, 124
clocks,
    Bazeille church, 184
    Napoléonica, 121
    two Empire, 128
'Cloth of Gold', Piece of, 49–50
clothing, Napoléon's, 175–7
    Madras scarf, 176, **176**
    nightshirt, 175–6, **176**
    shirt, **175**
    stockings, 119, 122, 176, **176**, 177
Clouet, François, **51**
coffin, Napoléon's, 174
Conti, Louis François de Bourbon, Prince de, 33, **33**
Cooper Owen Auctioneers (2005), 225
Copley, John Singleton, **79**
Corday, Charlotte, 38

Cossia, Francesco, **88**
Costa, Sir Michael, conductor, watch, 79, 222, **222**
The Court for the Trial of Queen Katherine, 50, **50**
Crépin, Louis-Philippe, **179**
Crippen, Dr, waxwork of, 26, 28
Critz, John de, **57**
Crocker Art Museum, Sacramento, 68, **69**
Cromer, Lord, 211
Cromwell, Oliver, 57–8, **57**
'Cross and Shoes', worn by Kemble, 50
crowns,
    Empress Eugénie's, **186**, 187
    George IV's, 198–9, **198**
Cumberland, Duke of, 61
Cumberland, William Augustus, Duke of, 76–7, **76**
    wax model, 77
Curtius, Dr Philippe (uncle), 20, 32, **32**
    cabinet de cire, 34–5, 36–7
    Caverne des Grans Voleurs, 35, 41
    death (1794), 40
    early career, 32–3
    and French Revolution, 38
    gun, 87–8, **87**
    Mazarin collection, 53
    sale of residual collection, 40
    Salon Cire in Palais Royal, 35
    studio in Paris, 33–6
    Théatre Curtius, 37, 41–2
    and Voltaire, 71
    wax models, 34, **34**, **35**, **37**, 47
Curtius's Grand Cabinet of Curiosities, London, 42, **42**
Curzon, George Nathaniel, 1st Marquess, death, 23, 25
cutlery, Napoléonic, 118, 119, 174

[229]

INDEX

D

Dabos, Laurent, 101
The Daily Telegraph, on the fire, 25
Damiens, Robert-François, 52
Danton, Georges, 38
Daoguang, Emperor of China, 217
David, Jacques-Louis, painter, 94, 95, 131–43
    Cardinal Fesch, 134, **134**
    Coronation of Napoléon, 132, **134**, 137, **138**, **142**
    Festival of the Supreme Being (1794), 39
    Marshal Macdonald, **141**
    Napoléon Crossing the Alps, **114**, 116
    Napoléon's Entry into Vienna, 133–4, **133**
    Pauline Bonaparte, 134, **135**
    Princess Caroline Murat, 137–8, **137**
    Queen Hortense, **142**
    self-portrait, **130**
Davie, Howard, 48, **48**
death bed, Napoléon's, 122–5, **123**, 175
    counterpane, 124–5, **124**
death mask,
    of Napoléon, 162, **162**
    of Wellington, 165
Delaroche, Paul, **98**
Demidov, Count Anatoli Nikolaievich, 147
Denis, Madame Marie-Louise, 72, **72**
Denon, Dominique Vivant, Baron, 101
Derbais, François, 69
Desaix, General, **92**
Detroit Institute of Arts, 68–9
diamonds,
    Napoléon's, 156, 158
    tiara, 156
Dickens, Charles, *A Plated Article*, 78
dinner services,
    Grand Maréchal, 173–4
    Napoléon's (St Helena), 171–4
    Quartiers Généraux, 172–3, **172**

Disraeli, Benjamin, Earl of Beaconsfield, 206–7, **206**
La Dormeuse, Napoléon's campaign carriage, 118, 121, 148–52, **148**, 154–5
    Bullock and, 151, **154**, 156–8, **157**
    captured at Genappe, 153–5, **154**
    contents, 121, 156, 157–8, 159–61
    description, 151–2, **151**
    at Madame Tussaud's, 158–9, **159**
dressing cases, Napoléon's, 121
Dubai International Capital, 225
Dulaure, Jacques-Antoine, 37
Dumas, Alexandre, *The Man in the Iron Mask*, 82
Dumonstier, Daniel, 54
Duroc, Grand Marshal Gérard Christophe Michel, 135
Dyer, A.R., London Fire Brigade, 24, 25

E

Eagles, Napoléonic, taken at Waterloo, 126, 147–8, **147**, 161
Eau de Cologne, Napoléon's, 121, 122
Edict of Nantes, 52
Edinburgh, Curtius's Grand Cabinet of Curiosities tour, 42
Edinburgh, Philip, Duke of, 204
Edward V, King, 47–8, **47**
Edward VII, King, 86–7
    facsimile cot, 215, **215**
Egmont, Justus van, 62
Egypt, Napoléon's campaign in, 89–90, 91
El Naseri Stud, 116
Elba, island of, 145
    flag, 146–7, **146**
Elbourne, Gertrude, 24
Elgin, James Bruce, 8th Earl of, **218**, 219
Élizabeth de France, 35–6, **35**
Elizabeth I, Queen, 57

chemise, 50
dress fragment, 50, **50**
Elizabeth II, Queen, 204
Elle, Louis Ferdinand, the elder, 54
Elsholtz, Ludwig, **128**
Emanuel, Emanuel, 172
Ena (Victoria Eugenie), Queen of Spain, 187, **187**, 221
Epernon, Duc d', 52
Eugénie, Empress, **182**, 192
    crown and jewels, **186**, 187
    emerald tiara, 187, **187**
    facsimile necklace, 182
    riding habit, 182
Evans of Pall Mall, Messrs, 49

F

Fabre, Xavier, **96**
fakes, 21, 46
    see also provenance
Farnborough, Imperial Crypt at St Michael's Abbey, 192, **192**
Fatum, Prince Imperial's horse, **190**, 191, 193
Ferdinand IV, King of Naples, 137
Ferri, Gaetano, **144**, 145
Féry, Charles-André, 85
Fesch, Cardinal, by David, 134, **134**
Field of the Cloth of Gold, 49–50, **49**
fire,
    Madame Tussaud's (1925), 22, 23–9, **26**, **27**, **159**, **169**
    as threat to heritage, 19–20
    Windsor Castle (1992), 19, **19**
Fischer, Paul, 43
FitzClarence, Lord Augustus, 78–9, **79**
Flahaut, Charles, Comte de, 113
Fotheringay Castle, 51
Foulon de Doué, Joseph-François, 34–5, **34**

[230]

INDEX

Fouquier-Tinville, Antoine Quentin, 38
Fox, Lt Col Charles James, London Salvage Corps, 24, **24**
France,
　1830 Revolution, 180
　Imperial Family, 95, **96–7**
　see also French Revolution
Francis I, King of France, 49, **49**
Francis II, King of France, 51
Franco-Prussian War (1870), 107, 183–6, **184**, **185**
Franklin, Dr Benjamin, 34, **34**, 35
Franque, Joseph, **96**
Franz-Josef, Emperor of Austria-Hungary, 222
Franzoni, Francesco Antonio, 103
Fraysse et Associés, auctioneers, 172
Frederick Augustus, Prince, Duke of Sussex, 48–9, **48**
Frederick William III, King of Prussia, 155
French Revolution, 34–5, 37–40, **37**, 79–80
　Reign of Terror, 38
　royalist insurrection (1795), **89**
　Storming of the Bastille, 38, **38**
　Thermidorian Reaction, 38–9, 40
French Royal Family, Curtius's waxwork groups, 36, 37, **37**
Fryman, Dr Olivia, 60
Fulford, Roger, 203–4

G

Gambetta, Léon, bust, 206
Gardner, Isabella Stewart, collector, 147–8
Genappe, Napoléon's carriage taken at, 153–5, **154**
George I, King, 74, **75**
　portrait, 225
George II, King, 75, 76
　wax statuette, 75

George III, King, 42, 76, 78
　painting of daughters, **79**
　relics, 75–6
　wax statuette, 75
George IV, King,
　coronation, 196–9, **196**, **197**, **198**
　coronation robes, 196–8, **197**, **198**
　crown (facsimile), 198–9, **198**
　diamond diadem, 199, **199**
　marriage, 200–1, **200**
　night shirt and night cap, 201
　portraits by Lawrence, 27, **156**, **195**, **196**
　shirt, 199
　sword, 201–2, **202**
　tableau at Madame Tussaud's, 196–7, **196**
George IV, King, as Prince Regent, 61, 155, 156, **156**, 157, **194**
George, Prince of Denmark, 203
Gérard, François, 102, **102**, 106, 110, **141**
　Charles X, **54**, 181, **181**
　Empress Marie Louise, **111**, **112**
　Imperial family portraits, **96**, **97**
　Louis XVIII, **179**
　Madame Mère, **133**
Getting, coachmaker, 153
Gheeraerts, Marcus, the younger, **50**
Gillingham Case, Napoléon Room, 159, 160, 161, 162
girandoles (chandeliers), 117
Glassenbury Park, Kent, 129
Goff, Miss Moyra, 78, **79**
Gordon, Major General Charles, 208–12, **208**, **211**
　camel harness, 211–12
　Last Stand, **212**
　tableau, **212**
Gordon, Miss, and Lucien Bonaparte's Napoléonica, 120–1, 133, 160
Gramont, Comte Philibert de, *Mémoires*, 63

Grassi, Josef, **135**
Great Fire of London, 19
Greenshields, J.B., 104
Greville, Charles, 117
Gros, Baron Antoine-Jean, 40, **116**, **141**
Gros, Baron Jean-Baptiste-Louis, **218**, 219
Grosholtz, Joseph (father of Marie Tussaud), 31
Grosholtz, Marie (mother), 31–2, 39
　and Curtius, 32
Guangxu, Emperor of China, 211
Guillemin, Émile Coriolan Hippolyte, 206
Guillon-Lethière, Guillaume, 109, **109**
guillotine, 34, 38, 53
　blade, lunette and axe from, 38, 68, 84–7, **84**
　tableau in Chamber of Horrors, 84, 86–7, **86**
guns,
　Curtius's, 87–8, **87**
　Napoléonic, 125
Gwynne, Nell, 62–3
　as Venus, **64–5**
　wax statuettes, 62

H

hair,
　King of Rome's, 108, 112, **113**
　locks from Victorian notables, 205
　Marie Antoinette's, 87
　Napoléon's, 112–13
　Princess Charlotte's, 79
Halford, Sir Henry, and vertebra of Charles I, 61–2
Hamilton, Alexander Hamilton, 10th Duke of, 104
Hamilton, William, 200
handkerchiefs, Napoléon's, 119, 122, 125–6, 177
Hardinge, Sir Arthur, 220, **221**

INDEX

Hare, William, 42, **43**
Harlow, George Henry, 50, **50**
Hart, Charles, 62
Hartley, Winchcombe, 128, **129**
hats, Napoléon's, 155, **161**
Haydon, Benjamin Robert, 163, **163**
Hayter, Angelo, 214
Hayter, Sir George, 122, **123**, 124, 163, 195, **214**
Head, Guy, **48**
Hébert, Jacques René, 38
Helen, Princess of Waldeck & Pyrmont, Duchess of Albany, 205
Henri IV, King of France, 51–2, **51**, **52**
  assassination, 52, **52**
  shirt of, 52–5
Henry VIII, King, 49–50, **49**
Herbert, Mr, Charles I's valet, 60
Herbois, Jean-Marie Collot d', 40
Herodotus, 45
Hesse, Captain Charles, 107
Hillingford, Robert Alexander, painter, 147, **150**
Hobbs, Dr, 59
Holt, Francis Montagu, 208
Hoppner, John, painter, 77, **77**, 79
Hornn, Jean, coachman, 151, 154–5, 156
horses, *Fatum* (Prince Imperial's), **190**, 191, 193
horses, Napoléon's,
  Jaffa, 128–9, **128**
  Marengo, 116–17, **116**, **117**, 129
  Sara, 116, **116**
Houël, Jean-Pierre, 38
Hudson, Thomas, 75, 76
Hull, Fort Paull Museum, **61**, 62
hunting crop, Napoléon's, 125
Hurt, William E., preface to *The Romance of Madame Tussaud's*, 31–2

I

Ibbetson, Denzil, **167**
Imperial Family, 95, **96–7**
Ingres, Jean Auguste Dominique, **91**
insurance catalogue, and valuation (1911), 20, 27–8
insurance claim, 27–8
inventories, 132
  (1856), 132
Ireland, John, Dean of Westminster, **198**
Isabey, Jean-Baptiste, 127
Italian Campaign, Napoléon's, 89, 93

J

Jacob, Georges, 112
Jacob-Desmalter, François-Honoré-Georges, 112
Jaffa (Napoléon's horse), 128–9, **128**
James I, King, 55, **56**, 57
James II, King, 57, 63, **63**, 66
  snuff box, 63
Jamin, Paul Joseph, **191**
Jeaurat, Edmé, 69, 70
Jeaurat, Étienne, painter, 69–70, **69**
  The Mountain in Labour, 69, 70
Jeffreys, Robert, 158
Jervas, Charles, 76
Jivaroan peoples, Upper Amazon, 223–4, **223**
John, Elton, boots, 225
Johnstone, Sophia, Duchess of Canizaro, 117, **117**
Jonsen, William, coachman, 156
Jordan, Dorothea, 78, **79**
Joséphine de Beauharnais, Vicomtess (later Empress), 39, 40, 89, 95, **96**, **100**
  bust, 100
  commission for model of Napoléon, 40–1

coronation (1804), **94**, 100
coronation robes, 100, **100**
Joy, George W., 212, **212**
Junot, Marshal Jean-Andoche, Duke of Abrantes, 161, **161**
Juxon, William, Bishop of London, 59–60

K

Keller, Major Freiherr Heinrich Eugen von, 118, 159
  capture of *La Dormeuse*, 154–8
Kemble, John Philip, actor, 50, **50**
Kérouaille, Louise de, Duchesse of Portsmouth, 63
keys,
  Bastille, 80–2, **82**
  Fortress of Metz, 184, **184**
Khartoum (1966 film), 212
Khartoum, Relief of (1884-85), 208–12
Kléber, General Jean-Baptiste, 40
Kneller, Sir Godfrey, 66, **74**, 75, **75**, 225
knife, table, Napoléon's, 118
Knole, Kent, James II's State bed, 60
Krutz, Marie *see* Grosholtz, Marie
KwaZulu Natal, Prince Imperial's Memorial, **191**

L

La Belle Assemblé or Bell's Court & Fashionable Magazine, 40–1
La Fontaine, Jean de, *Fables*, 69–70
La Plaigne, Eléonore Denuelle de, 107
Lagrenée, Jean Jacques, 126, 127–8
Lally-Tollendal, Thomas Arthur, 106–7
Lally-Tollendal, Trophime-Gérard de, 107
Lamballe, Marie Thérèse Louise de Savoie, Princess de, 38
Lampsonius, Eugène, **38**
Landseer, Sir Edwin, 117

[232]

Largillière, Nicolas de, 70
Las Casas, Count Emmanuel de, 169, **169**, 170
Lawrence, Sir Thomas, **180**
    portraits of George IV, 27, **156**, **195**, **196**
Le Brun, Charles, 66, 67
Le Brun, Élizabeth Louise Vigée, 80
Lebrun, Charles-François, 91, 101, **101**
Leclerc, Major General Charles Victoire Emmanuel, 125
Lefèvre, Robert, 96, 101–2, **101**, **102**, **135**, 180, **180**
Legion of Honour, Grand Cross of the, star and riband, 181, 182
Legras, August, Auguste and François-Théodore, 102
Lejeune, Napoléon's tailor, 122
Lely, Sir Peter, 57–8, **57**, **58**, 63, 64–5
Léon, Charles, 108, 109
Léon, Count Charles Denuelle de la Plaigne, 106–8, **107**, 113
Leopold I, King of the Belgians, 42
Leopold II, King of the Belgians, 211
Leslie, Anita, and Pauline Chapman, *Madame Tussaud, Waxworker Extraordinary*, 39
library chair, Voltaire's, 70–3, **70**
Lin Zexu, Chinese scholar, 217, **217**
Linwood, Mary, 77–8, **77**
    Salvator Mundi (needlework), 77–8
Livingstone, Dr David, 222
Livre du Sacre, 98, 99, **99**
L'Olive and de Beuvry, Mlles, 122
London,
    Assembly Rooms, Gray's Inn Road, 43
    Baker Street Bazaar, 43
    Egyptian Hall, Piccadilly, 81, 118, **118**
    English Opera House, Covent Garden (now Lyceum Theatre), 41, 42

    Eturia Lodge, St John's Wood, 119
    Marylebone Road, 24, **24**, 43
    Princess Theatre programme, 215
London Salvage Corps, 25, 28
Longford, Elizabeth, 151
Louis Joseph, Dauphin of France, 37
Louis Philippe I, King, 168, 180, 181–2, **181**
Louis XIV, King of France, 33, 66–7, **66**
Louis XV, King of France, 33, 67
Louis XVI, King of France, 35, **35**, 37, **37**
    hair and shirt, 87
    memorial ring, 87, **87**
    portrait, 80
Louis XVIII, King of France, 98, 120, 127, 178, 179
Louis-Napoléon, Prince Imperial, 188–92, **189**, **193**
    death in South Africa, 189–92, **190**, **191**
    painting of, 193
    relics of, 192–3
    statuette, 193
L'Ouverture, Toussaint, 125
Lowe, Sir Hudson, Governor of St Helena, 168
Lowe, Lady, 172

M

Macdonald, Marshal Etienne Jacques-Joseph-Alexandre, Duke of Taranto, 138, 141–2, **141**
Machiavelli, Niccolò, *The Prince* (Napoléon's copy), 156
Madame Tussaud & Sons' Exhibition, 24, 36, 42–3
    1883 exhibition catalogue, 115–16, **115**
    1901 catalogue, 213–14
    advertising poster, **18**
    ashes of lost collection, 226
    Cabinet of Curiosities, 217–24

    Chamber of Horrors, 26, **26**, 28–9, **28**, 38, 42
    disposals, 226
    fire (1925), 22, 23–9, **26**, **27**, **159**, **169**
    Hall of Kings, 23, 180
    insurance claims after 1925 fire, 226
    insurance plan, **16–17**
    Merlin Entertainments and, 226
    Minutes (1926), 170
    Minutes (1937), 198
    Napoléon group (1900), 142–3, **143**
    Napoléon Room, 47
    Napoléonic exhibition (1843), 158–9
    sale to Dubai International Capital (2005), 225
    Second Empire tableau, 100
    Second World War bombing, 226
    Shakespeare Gallery, 48
Maitland, Captain Frederick, 167
Malampré, M., 215
Malmaison, Château de, 167
    berline, 153, **153**
    Napoléonic National Museum, 93, 100, 127, 128, **128**
The Man in the Iron Mask, 82, **83**
Manchester Guardian, on the fire, 28, 29
Mancini, Hortense, Duchesse Mazarin, 53
Mancini, Laura, Duchesse de Mercoeur, 54, **54**
Mankiewicz, Joseph L., 47
Mapledurham, 78–9
Marat, Jean-Paul, 38, **38**, 88
March, Charles Lennox, Earl of, 150
Marchand, Count Louis-Joseph-Narcisse, Napoléon's valet, 113, **113**, 122
Marengo, Battle of, **92**, 93
Marengo (Napoléon's horse), 116–17, **116**, **117**, 129, 153

INDEX

Marie Antoinette, Queen of France, 36, 37, 37, 39
 execution, 84, 85
 hair, 87
 portraits, 80, 80
 wallpaper, 87
Marie Leszczyńska, Queen of France, 33
Marie Louise, Empress, 97, 98, 110–11, 111, 112
 La Dormeuse commissioned by, 121, 150
 marriage to Napoléon, 110, 111
Marie-Thérèse-Charlotte de France (Madame Royale), 37
Mark Antony, 46
Marlet, Jean-Henri, 118
Marshals Table (Austerlitz Table), 127–8, 127
Mary, Queen of Scots, 57
 embroidery, 51
 execution, 50–1, 51
 rosary, 51
Mauzaisse, Jean-Baptiste, 113
Mawe, John, 119, 158
Maximilian I, Emperor of Mexico, 222
Mazarin diamonds, 53
Mazarin, Jules, Cardinal, collection, 53, 53
Measures, Harry Bell, 192
Melbourne, Lord, lock of hair, 205
Mendelssohn, Felix, lock of hair, and razor, 205
Merlin Entertainments, 226
Metz, Siege of, 183, 184
 Keys of the Fortress, 184, 184
Michael I, King of Romania, 69
Mirabeau, Comte Honoré Gabriel Riqueti de, 34, 34
Moltke, General von, 186
Monaco Collection, auction (2014), 176

Montholon, General Count Charles Tristan de, 169, 169, 170, 173
Montrose, Duke of, 157
Moreau St Méry, A.M., 81
Morgan, Sydney, Lady, 71–2, 71, 73
 France, 71
 The Wild Irish Girl, 71
Morgan, Sir Thomas, 71, 71, 72
Morret, Jean Baptiste, 36
Mould, Philip, 132
Mozaffar al-Din, Shah of Persia, 87, 221
 visit to Madame Tussaud's, 220–1
mummy, Egyptian, and sarcophagus, 45–6, 45
Murat, Joachim, King of Naples, 95, 97, 110, 137
Murray, Alexander, 104
Museum of London, George IV's coronation robes, 198

N

Nanking, Treaty of (1842), 218, 218, 219
napkin, Napoléon's, 155
Napo region, Amazonia, 223
Napoléon Bonaparte, 88–91, 89, 93
 Apotheosis of Napoléon, 104–5, 104, 105
 battles, 88–91
 busts of, 102–6, 103, 104, 105, 110, 110
 capture of *La Dormeuse* at Genappe, 153–5
 clothing, 175–7, 175, 176
 commission for model, 40–1
 coronation (1804), 94, 95, 98–9, 145
 coronation robes, 98–9, 99
 Crossing the Alps, 114, 117
 death bed, 122–5, 123, 124, 175
 death mask, 162, 162
 equestrian statuette (bronze), 116–17, 117
 exhumation (and State Funeral), 168, 175, 175
 exile in Elba, 145–6
 exile in St Helena, 166, 167–77, 167, 168, 169, 171, 175, 176
 farewell to the Imperial Guard, 145
 first abdication, 144, 145
 as First Consul, 40, 41, 91, 91, 92, 93
 and Imperial Family, 95, 96–7
 as King of Italy, 145–6, 146
 last will, 173, 173
 Lefèvre portraits of, 101
 locks of hair, 112–13
 and *Marengo*, 116–17, 117
 memoirs, 168, 169
 pencil drawing of, 106
 portraits of, 88, 98, 100–1, 101
 second abdication, 167
 signature, 125, 125
 snuff box, 108
 toilette, 121
 uniforms, 121–2, 121
Napoléon II, Duke of Reichstadt, King of Rome, 97, 98, 111–13, 112, 113
 bust, 112, 112
 cot, 111–12, 112
 lock of hair, 108, 112, 113
Napoléon III, Emperor, 126, 171, 182–8, 182
 Chemical Case, 186–7
 death, 188, 188
 in England, 186–8
 and Franco-Prussian War, 183–6, 185
 'Napoléon Ladder', 102
Napoléonica collection, 20, 98–9, 115–29
 lost in fire, 27, 28
 Prince Frederick Augustus's collection, 49
Naser al-Din, Shah of Persia, 86

[234]

donation of New Testament in Persian, 220, **220**, 221
State Visit (1873), 86–7, 220–1
wax effigy, 220
nécessaires de voyage, Napoléon's, 118, 159, **160**
Necker, Jacques, 37
needlework, Georgian, 77–8
Nelson, Admiral Viscount, 90–1, **90**
uniforms, 90–1
New York, Frick Museum, 67
Newbolt, Sir Henry, *Vitai Lampada*, 210
Newman, C.E., *The Fourth Cervical Vertebra of Charles I*, 61
Nicholas I, Tsar of Russia, 73, **73**
Nicholay, General Sir William, 196
Nicolay, Lt Gen Sir William, 27
Nile, Battle of the (Aboukir Bay), 90, 91
Nile Expeditionary Force, 208–10
Desert Column, **209**
Nixon, Richard, US President, 206
Northcote, James, 47–8, **47**
Northumberland, HMS, 167–8, **167**

O

Oliver, Isaac, 50
Omdurman, Battle of (1898), 211–12
O'Meara, Dr Barry, 174, **174**
Napoléon in Exile (1822), 174
Opium Wars (with China), First, 217–18, **217**
Orchardson, William Quiller, 166, **169**
Orleans, Louis Philippe II, Duc d', 37, **37**
Orphali, Khalil, 211–12
Osenat, French auctioneer, 175
Napoléon Bicentennial sale (2021), 176, 177

P

Palace of Westminster, fire (1834), 19
Palace of Whitehall, fire (1698), 19
Palloy, M., 81, 82
Paris,
Bastille fortress, 80–2, 83, **83**
Boulevard du Temple, 34–5, **35**, 37
Champs de Mars, 146–7, **146**
Hôtel d'Aligre, 33
Hôtel de Béhague, 69
La Force prison, 38
Les Carmes prison, 39
Les Neuf Soeurs Masonic Lodge, 72
Notre-Dame Cathedral, 67, **94**
Palais Royal, 35, 37
Place de Grève, 52–3, **52**
Tuileries Palace, 38, 89
Paris Commune (1871), 126
parrot, 24
rescued from fire, 26, **26**
Passe, Crispin de, 52
Patten, George, 214, **214**
Patterson, Elizabeth, wife of Jérôme Bonaparte, 102
Peace, Charlie, waxwork of execution of, 28, **28**
Peel, Sir Robert, lock of hair, 205
Peel, Superintendent, Metropolitan Police, 24, 25
Peking (Beijing), sacking of Old Imperial Palace, 217, 219–20, **219**
pen, Napoléon's, 174
The People's Wreath, given to Disraeli, 206–7, **206**
Pepys, Samuel, 62
Percier, Charles, 112
phantasmagoria shows, 41, **41**
Philipstahl, Paul de, phantasmagoria shows, 41, **41**, 42

Phillips, Thomas, **204**
Pichat, Oliver, 193, **193**
Pilartz, Jacques, **183**
Pingret, Édouard, **169**
Pius IX, Pope, autograph, 205
Pompadour, Madame de, 33, 67
Poniatowski, Prince Józef, 135–6, **135**, **136**
Poulett, William Turnour Thomas, Viscount Hinton, barrel organ, 207–8, **207**
Pourbus, Frans, the younger, **51**
Presley, Elvis, shirt, 225
Princes in the Tower,
Burial of, 47–8
Murder of, 47–8, **47**, **48**
provenance, 48–9
Apotheosis of Napoléon, 104–6
bust of Madame Mère, 106–8
contents of *La Dormeuse*, 159–61
Napoléon's coronation robes, 98–9
St Helena relics, 168–9
shirt of Henri IV, 52–5
Voltaire's library chair, 70–3
provision box, silver, 159, **160**
Prud'hon, Pierre-Paul, 111, **112**

Q

Qianlong, Emperor of China, Dragon robe, 220, **220**

R

Ravaillac, François, 52–3, **52**
Redford, Thomas, 129
Revolutions of 1848, 181–2
Reynolds, Sir Joshua, 78, **78**
Richard, Duke of York, 47–8, **47**
Richard III, King, 47
Richmond, Duchess of, Ball, 150–1, **150**
Riesener, Henri-François, 100, **100**

INDEX

rings,
  memorial (Louis XVI), 87, **87**
  Napoléon's cameo, 119–20, **120**
  onyx (Napoléon's), 174
  worn by Kemble, 50
Roberts, Andrew, 107
Robespierre, Augustin, 88
Robespierre, Maximilien, 38, **39**, 90
  and Mme Tussaud, 83–4, 88
  relics, 88
Robins, George Henry, 119, 174
Rocchi, Guiseppe, 110, **110**
Romania, 69
Ross, Captain Charles Bayne Hodgson, 167
Rouget, Georges, 94, 110, **111**
Royal Horse Guards (The Blues), 76
Rubens, Peter Paul,
  A Storm, 55–6, **55**
  The Coming Storm, 54
Rundell, Bridge & Rundell, 198, 199
Russell, Mr, 117
Russia, Napoléon's invasion of, 98
Rutxhiel, Henri Joseph, **112**

S

Sackville, Charles, Lord Buckhurst, 62
Sade, Marquis de, 106–7
Sainsbury, John Davis, 80–1, **80**, 103
  1845 sale of collection, 127
St Helena, island of,
  Longwood House, 168, **168**, 171, **173**, 174
  Napoléon in exile on, 167–77
  Napoléon's grave, **171**
  relics, 168–77
Sala, George Augustus, bust, 224, **224**
Sales, Carl von, 113, **113**
salt cellar, vertebra, 61–2, **61**
Sandhurst, RMA, Prince Imperial's statue, **192**

Sandman, Franz Josef, **168**
Sanson, Charles-Henri, executioner, 38, **38**, 40, 84–5, 86
Sanson, Gabriel, 85
Sanson, Henri, 84–5, **85**
Sanson, Henri-Clément, 85–6
Sara (Napoléon's horse), 116, **116**
Sauerweid, Alexander, **116**
scarf pin (diamond), Napoléon's, 118, 119
scent bottle, Napoléon's, 160
Scots Group tableau, 51, **51**
Scott, Sir Walter, 158
  bust, 206
Sedan, Battle of, 184–5, **185**
Senusret II, Pharaoh, 44, 45–6
Sesostris, King of Egypt, 45–6
Shakespeare, William,
  Henry VIII, 50
  Richard III, 47–8
Shepheard, Captain William, 171, 172, **173**
Simons, Jean, coachmaker, 150
Simpson, John, 202, **203**
Sithathor, Egyptian Princess, 45
snuff boxes,
  made from Napoléon's outer coffin, 174
  Napoléon's, 119–20, **120**, 156
Soane, Sir John, 80
Sobieski, John III, King of Poland, 161
Sokolov, Oleg, *L'Armée de Napoléon*, 141
Sotheby's, 1916 auction, 104
Soult, Marshal Jean-de-Dieu, 138, 140, **140**
Spring Rice, Sir Cecil, *Balliol Masque* (1880), 23
Stafford, Gee & Stafford, solicitors, 119, 120
Stephanoff, James, **198**
Steuben, Charles de, **123**, 146
Stewart, Brigadier General Sir Herbert, 208–10, **208**, 211
  helmet and gloves, 211, 212

Stieler, Joseph Karl, **139**, 140
Stockholm, Nationalmuseum, 68
stockings,, Napoléon's, 119, 122, 176, **176**, 177
Stroehling, Peter Edward, **76**
Suchodolski, January, **136**
Sussex, Duke of, 204
  auction of collection (1843), 127, 199, 205
  uniform as Constable of the Tower, 204
Sutherland, Duke of, 87
Swiss Guard, massacred at Tuileries, 38
swords,
  George IV's, 201–2, **202**
  Sobieski's, 161–2
  and sword belt, King of Rome's, 119, 122
  Sword of Honour, 161

T

Tattersall's, sale of Napoléon's horses, 158
Taube, Jacques, violinist, 26
Taylor, Elizabeth, wax model as Cleopatra, 46, 47
teeth, Napoléon's, 174
telescope, Napoléon's, 159, **160**
Thomire, Pierre-Philippe, *bronzier*, 117
Thornhill, Sir James,
  Allegorical Picture of the Duke of Cumberland, 76–7
  ceiling panels, 66, **77**
Thorvaldsen, Bertel, 104, **104**, 105
tiara, diamond, 156
tiger skins, 222
The Times, 158, 159
  reports on the fire, 25, 26–7
Tipoo Sultan of Mysore, ambassadors at Versailles, 36, **36**
Tokyo, Japan, fire (1925), 23
toothbrushes, Napoléon's, 119, 121, **121**, 174
Toulon, Siege of, 88

Town, Charles, 172
Trentanove, Raimondo, 103, **103**, 109
Turnerelli, Peter, 201, **201**
Turnerelli, Tracy, 206
Tussaud, Bernard, death (1967), 43
Tussaud, François, marriage to Marie, 40
Tussaud, François (son), 40, 42
Tussaud, John Theodore, 32
   bust of Sala, 224
   on Curtius, 32, 34
   and David paintings, 143
   on the fire, 26, 27
   on guillotine knife, 85–6
   on Lord Hinton's barrel organ, 207–8
   models by, **35**, **39**
   and Napoléon's deathbed tableau, 122–4
   on Robespierre, 83–4
   The Romance of Madame Tussaud's
   (1921), 31, 40, 71, 73, 107–8
   visit of Mozaffar ad-Din Shah Qajar,
     220–1
Tussaud, Joseph Randall (1830–92), grandson, diary, 20–1, 107–8
Tussaud, Joseph (son), 40, 42, 77
   and *La Dormeuse*, 158
   and Voltaire's library chair, 72
Tussaud, Marie, Madame, 30, 31–2, 43
   and David, 132
   death (1850), 43
   and French Revolution, 38–9
   imprisonment in Paris, 39–40
   inaccuracy of *Memoirs*, 32, 34, 35–6, 39–41
   interview with *La Belle Assemblé* magazine, 40–1
   marriage, 40
   Memoirs & Reminiscences of France, 31, 35, 88
   moves to London, 40–2

   in Paris, 33, 34, 38–40, 79–80
   relations with Curtius, 33–4
   and Robespierre, 83–4, 88
   tours of United Kingdom, 42
   at Versailles, 36
   wax-modelling, 34, 36, 38

U

uniforms, Duke of Sussex 204
   Napoléon 121–2, **121**
   Nelson 90–1
   Prince Albert 214–15

V

Valentinois, Duc de, 53
valuations (1911), 20, 46, 47, 50, 54–5
Van Dyck, Sir Anthony, **59**
Vendôme Column, model of, 126, **126**
Vernet, Carl, 116
Vernet, Claude Joseph, 116
Vernet, Horace, **89**, 105
verre églomisé (reverse painting on glass), 126–7
Versailles, 36
Vestier, Antoine, **53**
Victoria, Princess Royal,
   as Empress Frederick of Prussia, 222, **222**
   facsimile cot, 215, **215**
   slippers, 79
Victoria, Queen, 79, 86, 192
   coronation portrait, **214**
   death, 213–14
   diamond diadem, **199**
   and Napoléon III, 188
Vien, Joseph-Marie, 101
Vien, Marie-Joseph, 101
Villette, Marquise de (*Belle et Bonne*), 71–2
Vitoria, Battle of, capture of Joseph Bonaparte's carriage, 162, **162**

Voltaire (François-Marie Arouet), 34, **34**
   library chair, 70–3, **70**
   portrait, **70**
   wax statuettes, 47, **70**
Vouet, Simon, **53**
Vredenburgh, Captain Edric, *The Palace of Enchantment* (guidebook), 48, **48**

W

Wallace Collection, 68
wallpaper,
   from Longwood House, 174
   Marie Antoinette's, 87
Walmer Castle, Kent, 164–5, **165**
wash-stand and towel horse, from HMS *Northumberland*, 167–8
Washington, George, 82
watches, gold repeater (Napoléon's), 117–18
   Sir Michael Costa's, 79, 222, **222**
Waterloo, Battle of, 98, 145, 149–50, 153–5, **154**
wax modelling, as French fashion, 35–6
Wellington, Arthur Wellesley, 1st Duke of, 77, **163**
   camp bedstead, 164
   coat and waistcoat, 163
   death of, 164–5, **165**
   duelling pistols, 164, **164**
   lock of hair, 205
   memorabilia (facsimiles), 162–5
   and Napoléon's deathbed tableau, 122–4, **123**
   and Napoléon's memorabilia, 155
   'Orders, Stars and Bâtons', 163
Wheeler, W., *Catalogue of Pictures and Historical Relics* (1901), 31
whip, riding, 170
   hunting crop, 125

INDEX

Wilkie, Sir David, 202
William III, King, portrait, 225
William IV, King, 78, 202–3, **202**, **203**, 204
   coat as Lord High Admiral, 203, **204**
   portrait (copy), 202
Williams, Charles, **194**
Wilson, Brigadier General Sir Charles, 210
Winchilsea, Earl of, 164, **164**
Windsor Castle,
   fire (1992), 19, **19**
   Queen Adelaide's collection, 79
   St George's Chapel, 61, **61**
Winkes, Benjamin Foulkes, 31
Winterhalter, Franz Xaver, **181**, **182**, **199**
Wolseley, General Lord, 208, **208**, 210
Wolsey, Thomas, Cardinal, 49, 50
Woods, Mr, London Water Board, 24, 25
Wookey Hole, Madame Tussaud's stores at, **45**, 46, 75, 225
Wurmser, General Dogobert Sigmund von, 31
Wyndham, Samantha, 20

X
Xianfeng, Emperor of China, 219

Z
Zeughaus Museum, Berlin, 155, **155**
Zulu artefacts, 222

ABOUT THE AUTHORS

CHRISTOPHER JOLL MA is the regimental historian of the Household Cavalry, an advisor on militaria to auctioneers Cheffins and Sworders, a lecturer for several cruise lines, and the author of a number of books of 'faction' and fact. As an historian, he is fascinated by the coincidences, quirks and trivia of history. See Christopher's entry in Wikipedia or visit *www.christopherjoll.com*.

PENELOPE, VISCOUNTESS COBHAM CBE is a Trustee of the British Napoléonic Bicentenary Trust and the Shakespeare Birthplace Trust. For eight years she was Chairman of VisitEngland, the national tourist board, and recently stood down as Director General of The 5% Club. Inter alia, she has been a Director/Trustee of Historic Royal Palaces, English Heritage, and the V&A. See Penny's entry in Wikipedia.